DATE DUE			

The Mysteries of Social Encounters

The Anthropsophical Social Impulse

by

Dieter Brüll

Translated
by
Thomas Forman and Trauger Groh

Introduction
by
Christopher Schaefer, Ph.D.

Published by:
   AWSNA Publications
   The Association of Waldorf Schools of North America
   3911 Bannister Road
   Fair Oaks, CA 95628

Title: The Mysteries of Social Encounters:
   The Anthropsophical Social Impulse
ISBN # 1-888365-41-2
© 2002 AWSNA Publications
Translated from the German: Der anthroposophische
   Sozialimpuls—ein Versuch seiner Erfassung
First published by: Novalis Verlag
   ISBN #3-7214-0521-8
Author: Dieter Brüll
Translators: Thomas Forman and Trauger Groh
Published in conjunction with the Cadmus Corporation
Editors: Ann Erwin, David Mitchell
Layout: David Mitchell
Proofreaders: Alice Groh, Nancy Jane
Cover: Hallie Wootan
Cover painting: "The Archetypal Social Phenomenon" by Einar
   Eising, Copenhagen, Denmark: 1982, with kind
   permission of his wife Ulla Strand

Spirit of Love
Open our Eyes
To see the Heavens

Spirit of Love
Open our Arms
To help each other

Spirit of Love
Open our Hearts
Justly to judge

— Thomas Forman

Table of Contents

Translator's Introduction 9

Introduction 11

Foreword 27

Chapter I
Social and Antisocial 33

Chapter II
Basic Elements of Social Activity 81

Chapter III
The Basic Sociological Law 95

Chapter IV
The Principal Social Law 135

Chapter V
The Archetypal Social Phenomenon 159

Chapter VI
The Threefold Social Order 181

Chapter VII
An Image of the Four Elements Working Together 209

Chapter VIII
Anomalies of Social Life 237

Chapter IX
Aphorisms to the Pathology
of the Anthroposophical Movement 255

Chapter X
The Social Impulse in Rudolf Steiner's Life 285

Chapter XI
Questions in Lieu of a Conclusion 293

Translator's Introduction

We live in a world dominated by hugely escalating material progress. The technical advances of the last century tend to blind us to two important facts. First, all we create as products originates from the earth, and the earth's resources are obviously limited. Secondly, the neglect of moral issues, due to the prevalent hedonistic materialism, is increasing along with the increase of "national product," crime and brutality in the world. The development of the human spirit has brought about this situation as a natural consequence of the realities of evolution.

The ability to concentrate on a narrow field is responsible for our colossal material "technological" progress as well as for the facility, evident in modern minds, to totally exclude matters that are not the focus of the microscope or technical research.

This book provides a basic text, introducing all-important realities that have been overlooked in this way. These realities have been defined by Rudolf Steiner and can be recognized by anybody willing to read Dieter Brüll's book. This is not to say that there is a lack of other literature on the subject, including Rudolf Steiner's works. His lectures and writings on pertinent subjects are amply documented in numerous foot notes.

It is, sadly, remarkable how relatively ignored the social implications of anthroposophy are among Anthroposophists. Dieter Brüll has devoted much of his life to defining these implications and to elaborating them with living thinking. *The Mysteries of Social Encounters* is Dieter Brüll's principal work. This impulse has not, as yet, been taken up with the seriousness it deserves. This book may, with some justification, be compared to that of Steiner's *Philosophy of Freedom*. Both books do not merely help us to think clearly and logically; their study provides an important exercise toward spiritual insights

A realistic, and much overdue, image is here before our eyes. It shows how we humans actually live together in history and how we have arrived at this point. It also gives us the tools to work creatively on social, economic and rights issues. In so many ways here is the map out of the modern chaos.

Although the elements of social life are described in detail here, the reader must bear in mind that Dieter Brüll was Dutch and involved in the development of Waldorf schools in Europe in a very important way. Many examples and expressions fit conditions in Holland and Europe in general and may be hard to understand for English speaking readers. Additionally, Brüll writes prior to the time of the collapse of the Soviet Union and takes many examples from the communist "mother and father state." Had he written from the point of view of today's English speaking world, he could have used examples of ignoring the realities of social life, taken from capitalistic practice.

This work is a fundamental text and should be studied by all serious Anthroposophists who wish to be active in the public arena. It can only be hoped that the knowledge here presented will be used with increasing intensity by a world so near to chaotic catastrophe!

— Thomas Forman
Translator
Peterborough, NH
2002

Introduction

by

Christopher Schaefer, Ph.D.

In 1984, Dieter Brüll, a sociologist and professor of tax law in Holland, published *The Mysteries of Social Encounters : The Anthroposophical Social Impulse*. This very thorough and detailed study of Rudolf Steiner's social ideas and intentions is to my mind the best single introduction to a spiritually based sociology available today. It is with great pleasure that I recommend this new translation by Thomas Forman and Trauger Groh to the English reading public.

Brüll's exposition begins with an examination of social and anti-social forces in the human being and in society, linking it to the evolution of consciousness. He then moves to exploring the main social laws or social principles which Rudolf Steiner formulated, giving interesting examples and interpretations. These laws or principles include the basic sociological law, the fundamental social law and the archetypal social phenomenon. Each of these laws or principles is then connected to one domain of social life: cultural, rights and economic life.

It is the description of the threefold social order, Steiner's response to both capitalism and communism, which constitutes the heart of the book. As this formulation of an alternative way of organizing society offends both liberal and conservative sensibilities, the threefold social order forces us to come to grips with our own political and social prejudices. This struggle is worthwhile, because it leads the reader to envisage new possibilities for recreating our society. The original presentations in English of Rudolf Steiner's social thoughts are contained in *Towards Social Renewal, The Social Future,* and the *Inner Aspect of the Social Question* (available from Anthroposophic Press).

In order to provide the reader with both a historical and biographical context for understanding this book, I have added a sketch of the evolution of Steiner's social thought.

The breadth and time spread of Rudolf Steiner's contributions to social and economic questions create a particular challenge in finding the right organizing principle. I have chosen to follow a biographical approach because I believe that in so doing the basic pattern of his biography as a spiritual teacher and a thoroughly modern human being stands revealed.[1]

A particular characteristic of Rudolf Steiner's work on social and economic renewal is that, along with his detailed work on karmic relationships, it did not arise in response to the questions of his pupils or of the general public. Rather, he put forward these concerns and ideas on his own and, as with his karmic studies, met with limited response and understanding among theosophists and the later members of the Anthroposophical Society.[2] The fact that he was for much of his life concerned with these issues and repeatedly put forth ideas and suggestions without the stimulus of external interest, suggests that social renewal was a particularly intimate part of his biographical task.

The earliest known work by Rudolf Steiner on social questions was an essay he wrote as a 23-year-old student in Vienna called "A Free Perspective on the Present."[3] A little later, in 1886, when he was already involved in editing Goethe's scientific writings, he published *A Theory of Knowledge Based on Goethe's World Conception*.[4] This slim volume provided a philosophical foundation for all of Rudolf Steiner's later work by addressing the relation between the inner world of the human being, of thinking, to the outer world. It also contained in it a number of very significant thoughts about the nature of social inquiry. In the section on the spiritual or cultural sciences, he stated that the cultural sciences have as their object of study the human being: "It is human actions, creations, ideas with which we have to be involved," and that the task or mission of these sciences is to "interpret the human being to himself and to humanity." With these seemingly simple phrase, Rudolf Steiner sciences and that their task is understanding human consciousness as expressed in social creation. Laws, organizational structures and political, social, and economic forms reveal the contours of consciousness: they are an external manifestation of the ideas and values of individuals and groups. Since social and economic life is a human creation, reflecting consciousness, and social science has the task of interpreting the human being to him- or herself, the social or cultural sciences "are in the highest degree sciences of freedom." (p. 103) Rather than causal explanation it is understanding which the cultural sciences must strive for, and it is in the particular event, act, or personality, that a general principle or law of the cultural sciences is revealed. (p. 103)

With this view of the cultural sciences or "Geisteswissenschaften" Rudolf Steiner directly aligned himself with social thinkers such as Max Weber and historians such as Dilthey and Rickert, who argued for a separation in purpose and method between the natural and cultural science. However, in positing the necessity of direct, spiritual perception into spiritual and psychological realities, Steiner clearly went beyond the views of these contemporaries.

The next major step in the unfolding of Rudolf Steiner's social ideas came when he was in Berlin, editing the *Magazin für Literatur*. Here he was in contact with a wide arena of people—artists, poets, writers, scientists, theosophists, and workers. He frequently commented on the social and political issues of the day, defended Haeckel and Darwinian concepts against the attacks of dogmatic church groups, and was a member of the Giordano Bruno Association. In two issues of the *Magazin für Literatur* in 1898 he formulated his "basic sociological law:"

> At the beginning of culture humanity strives to create social arrangements in which the interests of the individual are sacrificed for the interest of the whole. Later developments lead to a gradual freeing of the individual from the interests of the community and to an unfolding of individual needs and capacities.[5]

This law or principle exists in time, in all likelihood covering the whole Post-Atlantean period. Certainly when one ponders the sweep of history and the gradual emergence of individual rights from Greco-Roman times to the present, it appears justified and points to one of the central aspects of historical evolution, the emergence of individual consciousness. Based on my observation of institutional development, I would also say that it applies to the life cycle of institutions, which require the energy and sacrifice of individual interests in order to be established and are then more able to respond to the needs of individual members.

In 1905, while active within the Theosophical Society, Rudolf Steiner formulated what he called the "fundamental social law."

> The well-being of a community of cooperatively working human beings is the greater the less individuals demand the proceeds of their work for themselves or, in other words, the more they make over these proceeds to their co-workers and the more their needs are met not by their own work but from that of others.[6]

This law was formulated in the periodical *Lucifer-Gnosis*, which Rudolf Steiner was editing at the time. It represented an effort to make the principle of brotherhood and sisterhood practical within theosophical circles and also to separate wages and work. It is not coincidental that in the same year in which he formulated the "fundamental social law," he was asked to resign from the Workers' Education Institute, where he was a popular teacher. The German Labor Movement was to concern itself more with increasing the wages of its members than in seeking to abolish the commodity character of work, or wage slavery, a lifelong concern of Rudolf Steiner's.

If we survey these three basic steps in the development of Rudolf Steiner's social thought, we see that he begins by describing the aim and method of a spiritually-based social science, and then proceeds to formulate two laws or principles resulting from this research. The first law is concerned with time, connected to the evolution of consciousness and its impact on the relation between the individual and the community. The second is a vital principle concerning motives that seek to institutionalize a form of cooperation and thereby combats the antisocial egotism of the age. "He who works for himself, must eventually become egotistical. Only when one works totally for others, can one become unegotistical." Therefore, work and wages must be separated so that the human being has the opportunity to develop new social faculties. The reverse of this law is that "suffering, poverty, and want in society are nothing other than a consequence of egotism."[7] The truth of this insight has been brought home to me in observing the suffering and want evident in cities like Detroit or even in villages like Spring Valley, NY. Without denying the enormous productivity of the American economic system, it is difficult to escape the conclusion that, despite great wealth, it does not produce "well-being" for all or even for the great majority of its citizens.[8] The explicit pursuit of self-interest within this economic system can be seen as responsible for great disparities in wealth and well-being.

There are few significant contributions on social issues by Rudolf Steiner between 1905-6 and 1917. This was a period in which he fully devoted himself to the development of anthroposophy, the arts, and the elaboration of a new Christology. However, in December 1912, he gave a lecture in Zürich on "Love and its Meaning in the World."[9] While there are limited direct references to social life in this address, it is important to note a few significant thoughts, since they later form the center of his lecture on *The Inner Aspect of the Social Question* given in 1919.

> Our egotism gains nothing from deeds of love, but the world all the more. . . . Love streamed into the world through the Mystery of Golgotha . . . hence the beginning of the era of love coincided with the era of egoism . . . yet with time the Christ Impulse, the impulse of love, will overcome the element of separation that has crept into the world. . . . In the monumental words of Christ we feel love pouring into the hearts of men. "Where two or three are gathered together in my name, there I am with them." (pp. 13-25)

The struggle between the forces of egoism and love, of antisocial and social tendencies within human consciousness, became Rudolf Steiner's fundamental concern as he experienced a Europe ravaged by World War I, a war which marked the end of an era and brought untold suffering to a generation. The Threefold Social Order, and the threefold image of the human being to which it is so intimately connected, arose out of the suffering of this war and was meant as a structuring principle that could bring healing to social life. But the inner aspect of this new approach to social questions was a listening to the revelation of Christ in our time: "In this epoch the Christ declares to us—Make new your ways of thinking (as his forerunner John the Baptist said 'Change your thinking'), so that they may reveal to you man's threefold nature which demands also that your social environment on earth shall have a threefold membering."[10]

With these statements and the many lectures, activities, and initiatives for social renewal in which Rudolf Steiner engaged between 1917 and 1921, Christ's mission found an advocate and a form of social expression. At the same time the truth that all social reality is Christian reality, and that a spiritually-based social science must concern itself with the gradual unfolding of the Christ mystery in social life, was revealed.

The period 1917-22 was the high point of Rudolf Steiner's engagement with the social questions of his time. Three interrelated areas of activity can be discerned. Externally, he sought to influence the ending of the war through contacts with leaders in Germany and Austria, issued an appeal to the German nation, and founded the League for the Threefold Social Order. In order to lend reality to his appeals for reform in society, he also encouraged the creation of *Der Kommende Tag* (The Coming Day)—a stock company "for the Advancement of Economic and Spiritual Values," and its sister organization in Switzerland, Futurum. (p. 13) The source of this outpouring of activity was Rudolf Steiner's deepening insight into the threefold nature of the human being and its connecting to the threefold restructuring of society. Behind this new image of the human being and of society Rudolf Steiner unfolded an esoteric perspective on social issues for the members of the Anthroposophical Society in relation to the Christ impulse (*The Inner Aspect of the Social Ques-*

tion), the work of the angels in the subconscious of the human being (*The Work of the Angels in Man's Astral Body*), the working of social and antisocial forces in the human soul, and the role of reincarnation and destiny in social life. As part of this deepening of spiritual and social understanding for the membership of the Anthroposophical Society, he pointed to a conversation, to an encounter between two people, as the archetypal social phenomenon.

The year 1917 can be seen as a turning point in modern history. It was the year of the Russian Revolution in which Lenin and the Bolsheviks came to power, and it was also the year in which the United States overcame its isolationist tendencies and entered the World War. In hindsight one can see how from this point onward the United States and the Soviet Union were to play major roles in the evolution of Europe and the world. Europe was engaged in a World War which brought about its decline and marked the end of the nineteenth- century social and political order. Out of this war experience Rudolf Steiner gave birth to the threefold imagination of the human being and showed how this imagination could lead to healing social forms.

He indicated that he had worked over 30 years to be able to give the right form to this imagination of the threefold nature of the human being and of society. Although the outlines of the threefold social order were already contained in two communications to the German and Austrian governments in July, it was in November 1917 that these ideas were first publicly presented in a series of lectures entitled "Anthroposophy and the Academic Sciences."[11]

The threefold image of the human being—relating to psychological faculties of thinking, feeling, and willing to the physiological functions of the nerve-sense system, the working of heart and lung, and the metabolic limb system—may appear to be quite commonplace to someone who has lived with these ideas for some time. Yet in relating psychological processes to physiological functions and later to the active working of spiritual forces, I believe that Rudolf Steiner was giving expression to the archetypal spiritual form of the human being—the archetype out of which we are created. To be able to think, and through the Foundation Stone mantram, to meditate on our own nature was a priceless gift of freedom given by Rudolf Steiner to humanity.

It also had, and still has, far-reaching implications for social life. If we accept that social life in its myriad aspects is a human creation, more or less reflecting our consciousness and self-understanding, then the healing social consequences of ever greater numbers of human beings carrying a true picture of humanity are profound.

In the same way that the three physiological systems of the human being are semi-independent, yet serve the totality of the human organism, so, too, should the three realms of cultural, political, and economic life have a certain independence, while serving the whole of society. For Rudolf Steiner, the dominant value of cultural life is freedom, that of political-legal life is equality, and that of economic life is cooperation and brotherhood (sisterhood). This implies a structural principle separating cultural life from that the state and also of creating a separate administrative form for economic life based on associations. While there is not the space to present these ideas in their many-sided and practical aspects, it should be noted that Rudolf Steiner's approach to the threefold ordering of society provided an alternative to both capitalism and communism or socialism.[12] It is one of the great tragedies of the twentieth century that the threefold social order was ignored, for it provided a healing alternative to a crippled Europe, which in a few years was to experience the rise of fascism.

The threefold image of the human being and of society provided the foundation upon which Rudolf Steiner and his co-workers sought to influence the restructuring of European society and the peace negotiations in Versailles. These efforts not only involved many lectures, multiple conversations with individuals, private letters to people of political influence, and a public appeal to the German nation, but also led to an attempt to send copies of General von Moltke's private diaries to the Versailles Peace Conference in order to show the inaccuracy and one-sidedness of the "war guilt clause."[13]

While the attempts to help end the war in 1917 and to influence the peace negotiations in Versailles failed, Rudolf Steiner proceeded to elaborate his ideas for a new social structure in his book *Toward Social Renewal* (1919), which received wide distribution. He also founded the League for the Threefold Social Order in Germany and Switzerland in order to carry these ideas into practical life. A weekly paper, *The Threefold Social Or-*

der, was started, for which he wrote many of the lead articles, and he gave many lectures on a variety of social and political themes throughout Germany and Switzerland. Some of these lectures and articles are available in English in the recently published volumes *The Renewal of the Social Organism* (1985) and *Spiritual Science as a Foundation for Social Forms* (1986).

As part of the activity of the League for the Threefold Social Order, Rudolf Steiner and co-workers such as Carl Unger, Emil Molt, Emil Leinhas, Ernst Uehli, and Hans Kuhn met in late 1919 to discuss the possibilities of creating a variety of working associative forms such as a bank or a stock company. The first Waldorf School in Stuttgart had already grown out of the activity of Rudolf Steiner and the League, and it was hoped that other successful models would follow. So on New Year's evening 1919 it was decided to create "The Coming Day—A Stock Company to further Economic and Spiritual Values." In time it was to embrace some 20 organizations, including farms, the Waldorf School, research institutes, chemical factories, two printing companies, and the Waldorf Astoria Cigarette Factory. This practical experiment in the application of threefold ideas is not well known in the English-speaking world, yet it is worth studying despite its eventual closing in 1924.[14]

In late 1922, attacked by a rising tide of nationalistic and fascist elements, Rudolf Steiner withdrew from his extensive public efforts to influence social, economic, and political events. He remarked, "I knew that people had not yet achieved sufficient maturity and insight, yet the attempt had to be made, for I might well have been wrong."[15] His social ideas were radical, egalitarian, and anti-nationalistic. The people of Central Europe were not ready to receive them.

It was previously indicated that while Rudolf Steiner was unfolding his public work for a threefolding of society and elaborating a threefold image of the human, he was also sharing a more esoteric perspective on social questions with the membership of the Anthroposophical Society. In Bern on December 12, 1918, he gave lectures on the "Social and Anti-Social Force in the Human Being."[16] In this lecture he described a process of meeting, of conversation between two people, which he later called the archetypal social phenomenon:

> If we have any kind of relation to other people, or any communication with them, then a force flows between us creating a bond. It is this fact which lies at the basis of social life. . . The impression which one person makes on the other has the effect of lulling the other to sleep. . . . On the other hand something else is also working. A perpetual struggle and opposition to falling asleep in social relationships is also present.
>
> . . . This always happens in the meeting between two people—a tendency to fall asleep—a tendency to keep awake. "The tendency to fall asleep represents a social force in the human being, analogous to our sleeping state when our soul and spirit freely intermingle with the soul and spirit being of others, unencumbered by the physical body. The waking-up force is antisocial in nature as we become aware of our identity, our thoughts, feelings, and intentions as earthly beings.[17]

As ego meets ego we are in the supersensible realm, subconsciously experiencing pictures of both past and future destiny, but our ordinary consciousness is still unable to deal with this, so we withdraw into our own soul. Rudolf Steiner suggested that the growing self-consciousness of the modern individuality necessarily is antisocial. As a force of evolution this self aware, antisocial tendency will continue throughout the consciousness soul age. All social instincts will be lost, and more and more the human being will be like "a hermit wandering through the world."[18] This natural tendency brings with it the possibility of self-knowledge and self-development, but it has the social consequence of separating individuals and groups so that we are as strangers to each other. The resulting misunderstandings, conflicts, and forces of social fragmentation are visible in every sphere of life, blinding us to our connections of destiny.

Understanding the antisocial nature of modern consciousness, so visible in our every conversation, is the beginning of a healing process for ourselves and society. The balancing forces pointed to by Rudolf Steiner are a new form of social understanding and society, and a process of individual inner development through spiritual science. A new, spiritually-based social understanding can enkindle interest and warmth of heart—for in the study of temperaments, life phases, and soul orientations, we can begin to learn to see the other. Collegial institutions and the threefold social order are social arrangements through which we need to meet, struggle with each other, and develop understanding. All of Rudolf Steiner's work on the threefold social order and in economics can, I believe, be seen as providing a necessary outer balance to the antisocial forces working within the human soul. "The antisocial forces must work inwardly so that human beings may reach the height of their development. Outwardly, in social life structures must work so that people do not totally lose their connection to life."[19]

Yet it is not only the human being who is active in the struggle for a social future. Through a battle in the spiritual world and the technological nature of the age, human beings increasingly inhabit a demonic world which works against the proper course of human evolution. These demonic forces work subconsciously, attempting to bring about the mechanization of the spirit, the vegetablization of the soul, and the animalization of the body. From the realm of the angels a potentially healing counterforce is also present, as described in *The Work of the Angels in Man's Astral Body*. Yet awakening to these images woven into our soul life requires self-development and a new level of inner consciousness.

Also working into this human and spiritual struggle for a social future is the Christ Being.

> At this critical moment humanity is faced with a momentous decision. On the one hand stands the Christ Being, calling us of our own free will to do what we have been speaking about today, to receive consciously and freely the social impulses which can heal and help humanity . . . opposed to this will stands the adversary who is called in the *Bible* "the unrighteous Prince of this World.[20]

The free path to the healing power of the Christ is portrayed by Rudolf Steiner in *The Inner Aspect of the Social Question*. It is a path of thinking through developing an intense interest in the words and deeds of others and a path of willing by achieving inner transformation through a vigorous process of inner development. Social interest and meditative work together form the doorway through which the healing power of Christ can be experienced.[21]

While Rudolf Steiner withdrew from his intense engagement with the external political and social issues of the time after 1922, I do not believe that his work for social renewal stopped at this time; rather, his focus shifted. On New Year's Eve 1922, the first Goetheanum was burned to the ground. Ten years of work disintegrated into flames. Despite his own grief and that of his students and co-workers, he went on with his activities. Then over the Christmas season 1923-24, he re-founded the Anthroposophical Society as a totally free world society, founding it on a mantram—the Foundation Stone Meditation. Over the following year and a half, until his death, he was to give this society an esoteric center in the School for Spiritual Science and in its Sections. In addition, his many lectures on karmic relationships gave hundreds of detailed examples of the formative forces in social life, the working of karma, and reincarnation

It was as if his efforts had shifted to another, still deeper, plane. Politicians, academicians, factory owners, and workers had not taken up his ideas, so he created a new, open, yet deeply esoteric human society for the future, founding it on a mantram which consciously connected the human being to the earth and the macrocosm. This mantram he laid into the hearts of those present, into the hearts of the members of the new Anthroposophical Society, and into the hearts of all humanity. With this social and spiritual process of education he began the task of building the new mysteries for our time, a task he did not live to complete.

If we now step back from this very condensed review and commentary on Rudolf Steiner's work for social renewal, I believe we can discern a pattern of development, a gradual intensification of thought and activity:

1. 1886— *A Theory of Knowledge Based on Goethe's World Conception*, which outlined the nature, purpose, and method of a spiritually-based social science, a "science of freedom."

2. 1899—*The Basic Sociological Law,* a law focusing on the evolution of consciousness and the changing relation of the individual to the community in history.

3. 1905—*The Fundamental Social Law* describing the interaction of approaches to remuneration with the soul forces of egoism and altruism and their impact on the illness or health of a community.

4. 1912—*Love and its Meaning in the World,* a lecture indicating the spiritual source of healing social forces in the individual and society.

5. 1917—*The Threefold Image of the Human Being.* The human archetype is for the first time presented, relating physiological processes to psychological qualities and spiritual forces. With a consciousness of this archetype a new structuring of social life is possible.

   —*The Threefold Social Order,* a principle of structuring society in such a way that the antisocial forces of modern individual consciousness can be balanced. I believe that the threefold social order could be seen as a law of societal structure for our time: the more a society manifests the principles of a threefold ordering, the greater will be its creativity and well-being.

6. 1917-1922—*Public Work for a New Society,* which are the efforts to influence the peace process and political thinking, Rudolf Steiner's work for the League of the Threefold Social Order, the creation of new social forms through the Waldorf School in Stuttgart, and the creation of the Coming Day and Futurum in Switzerland.

   —*The Archetypal Social Phenomenon.* The social creation process revealed through human encounter. The working of social and antisocial forces in the individual and in society.

—*Esoteric Perspectives on the Inner Aspect of the Social Question*. The ever-deepening insights which Rudolf Steiner shared with the members of the Anthroposophical Society about the working of spiritual forces in human evolution.

— *The Founding of the New Anthroposophical Society* as an open society requiring its members to sign no oaths or pledges, and the development of an esoteric school at its center. Entry to this school was largely a matter of individual decision, whether one had the desire to represent anthroposophy in the world and was judged to be a person of serious intent and mental health. Around this school the sections were created in order to further professional life on an esoteric basis. Rudolf Steiner had thereby responded to Ita Wegman's question: was it possible to create new mysteries for our time?

—*The Foundation Stone Meditation*, given every morning between December 24th, 1923 and January 1st, 1924 by Rudolf Steiner. This meditation or mantram deepens the threefold conception of the human being first presented in 1917, connecting it both to the working of the spiritual hierarchies and to the forces of the trinity.[22]

—*Karmic Relationships*, the multiple lectures and studies on karma and reincarnation showing the inner dynamic and content of all social life. [23]

Rudolf Steiner's work on questions of social renewal spans 40 years. It moves from a methodological and philosophical grounding in *The Theory of Knowledge Based on Goethe's World Conception* through the formulation of two laws to a connection with the Christ mystery and ultimately to the realm of deed, first in the external work for a threefold society from 1917-1922 and later to the re-founding of the Anthroposophical Society. The movement is from thought through feeling to will. While there is a pattern of intensification in this work, there is also a balance. The work for the League for the Threefold Social Order was balanced by the archetypal threefold image of the human being and the more esoteric studies of social and antisocial forces. The re-founding of the Anthroposophical Society was balanced by the Foundation Stone Meditation and the founding of the School for Spiritual Science. Outer and inner activity were kept in harmony. Through each step of this unfolding there is a thread: social life both reflects and shapes individual human consciousness; the task of social renewal requires a path of individual spiritual development. That is why the "Motto of the Social Ethic," which Rudolf Steiner gave to the English sculptress Edith Maryon in 1920, captures the essence of his work for social renewal.

> The healing social life is only found when in the mirror of each human soul the whole community finds its reflection and when in the community the virtue of each one is living.[24]

This does not just happen; it must be achieved through inner and outer work.

I hope this biographical overview will give the reader a better understanding and appreciation of Dieter Brüll's book.

Endnotes:

[1] In this essay I am deeply indebted to Dieter Brüll. *Der Anthroposophische Sozialimpulse.* Novalis Verlag, 1984. In particular, see Chapter 8.
[2] See the excellent biography of Rudolf Steiner by Rudi Lissau, *Rudolf Steiner. Life, Work, Inner Path and Social Initiatives,* Hawthorn Press. 1987, p. 125.
[3] Not available in English, published in GA 31, 1966, p. 32 ff.
[4] R. Steiner, A *Theory of Knowledge Based on Goethe's World Conception.* Anthroposophic Press, 1968.
[5] Contained in GA 31, 1966, p. 147. Translation by the author.
[6] Translated by the author. Contained in R. Steiner, *Geisteswissenschaft und soziale Frage, GA 34, 1960.*
[7] Cited in Brüll, pp. 119-20. In GA 34, 1960, pp. 190-92.
[8] Camphill Communities, the many income-sharing communities in Europe, as well as some Waldorf schools and adult education centers are actively working with the fundamental social law.
[9] R. Steiner, *Love and its Meaning in the World.* Rudolf Steiner

Press, London, 1972.
[10] R. Steiner, *The Inner Aspect of the Social Question*. Rudolf Steiner Press. London, 1974, p. 34.
[11] R. Steiner, *Anthroposophie und akademische Wissenschaften*, Europa Verlag, Zürich. 1950 (also GA 73, 1950).
[12] For Rudolf Steiner, threefoldness in social life was not a theory but a reality which people would in time be able to see and experience.
[13] For an excellent review of the manifold political and social activities in which Rudolf Steiner was engaged between 1917-22, see Hans Kuhn, *Dreigilederungs-Zeit: Rudolf Steiner's Kampf für die Gesellschaft*. Philosophisch-Anthroposophischer Verlag. Dornach, 1978.
[14] See Hans Kuhn. *Dreigliederungs-Zeit* for a full description of these activities, esp. pp. 101-38.
[15] Cited in Brüll, *Der Anthroposophische Sozialimpulse*. pp.273-4.
[16] See R. Steiner. *Social and Antisocial Forces in the Human Being* [GA 186], Mercury Press, Spring Valley. 1963, lectures IV and VII.
[17] For a deeper analysis of the "archetypal social phenomenon," see Brüll, pp. 141-62.
[18] R. Steiner, "How Can the Soul Needs of the Time Be Met?," Zürich, Oct. 10, 1918. The only published English version I know is in *Results of Spiritual Investigation*, Rudolf Steiner Publications, Blauvelt, N.J., 1971.
[19] R. Steiner. *Social and Antisocial Forces in the Human Being*, Mercury Press.
[20] Ibid.
[21] R. Steiner, *The Inner Aspect of the Social Question*, pp. 41-43.
[22] See *The Foundation Stone*. Anthroposophical Publishing, 1957, and its many newer versions. Also, Zeylmans van Emmichoven, *The Foundation Stone*, Rudolf Steiner Press, London, 1983.
[23] R. Steiner. *Karmic Relationships, Vols. I-VIII*, Rudolf Steiner Press, London.
[24] R. Steiner's own translation from *Verses and Meditations*, Rudolf Steiner Press, London, 1985, pp. 11617.

Foreword

It is customary to think of the threefold order as soon as the anthroposophical social impulse is being mentioned. This is quite justified because the threefold order is the fruit that grew out of the anthroposophical social impulse, perhaps the only fruit available in Rudolf Steiner's time. There is, however, more to the social impulse itself. It is the object of this work to illuminate it.

At first glance the social impulse does not clearly show up in the work of Rudolf Steiner, the founder of Anthroposophy. It is spread throughout his work and, therefore, does not clearly surface. We shall discuss this in chapter ten. As a result two opinions have arisen. One is that Steiner's ideas on the social impulse were incomplete, lacking certain building blocks. The other is that the threefold order had to be put on hold because the preconditions for its "introduction" were lacking. Those who wanted to support their work based on Steiner's *Threefold Commonwealth*, his principal work on the subject, lacked a general theory and thus often worked in a vacuum. Even Stefan Leber's book "Selbstverwirklichung— Mündigkeit—Sozialität" (*Self Realization—Maturity—Social Attitude*) deals with only half of the anthroposophical social impulse, even though it mirrors the concept of threefoldness in the sociological lore of the time in a very knowledgeable way. Without the missing half, the threefold order becomes a mere program.

Four elements work together within this social impulse. Two may be called laws in the sense of natural science, one is a principle controlled by time, and the last is the essential element which gives shape to the whole. Before we deal with these elements, the following has to be noted:

Although these four elements have a common root, they affect the three spheres of life—macro, meso, and micro spheres

—in different ways. I therefore have to start by defining these spheres. The macro sphere encompasses all of humanity. In real life, this means groups in which people do not know each other, such as workers in Detroit who manufacture ice boxes for China, or the greengrocer who knows his customers merely as buyers - merely one aspect of a person. The Meso sphere deals with institutional life, for example, people who belong to a school or are employees of a factory. Whether one knows the other person intimately is of little importance in the meso sphere. Here one has to reach the essence of one's fellow humans on the institutional level. Finally, the micro sphere describes the way a person relates to fellow human beings. I have dealt in some detail with the latter area in my essay "Sozial und Unsozial." It appeared as special issue No. 28 of the "Contributions to the Threefold Order of the Social Organism." This essay also explains why my concept of what is social differs from what is understood in constitutional law and/or everyday language. Unless otherwise stated, in this book social means: to make another person's need the motive of one's own action. (See GA13/1925/174f). According to this definition "social" can mean neither a law that relieves us from responsibility for our fellow humans, nor does it have to mean the habit of working for little money, so epidemic in anthroposophical circles. Least of all is it any inter-human connection, the approximate meaning of the word in conventional science. The social impulse, then, is accurately defined as a moral force, a moral force to be found only in individual human beings. Therefore, our social macro- and meso- worlds are moral insofar as morality enters from the micro sphere.

Because the above article is long out of print and because the micro concept of what is social introduces the thoughts presented here, I have included the article as an introductory chapter.

The three levels of social life are not separate categories with differing ground rules; they merely are spheres with their own specific social problems. Although we can discuss each one separately, let us not forget that in reality these three ideal types never appear in pure form. Thus, meso elements are always present in the micro sphere. Whatever its specific coloring, social behavior can usually be understood according to the values found in the particular group. These are active in the macro sphere as well. Group-specific qualities sneak into anonymous relationships. One tends to use stereotypes because the macro sphere really does not deal with personal relationships. We shall encounter this phenomenon of inter-penetration again.

One can always discover the sphere one is in according to the social problems that surface. For example, when the borders of institutional life are being overstepped, problems of order may surface. In the social life, it is always the human being who creates his relationships, be they personal, institutional or anonymous; thus, it is impossible to separate the three social planes in a radical manner.

This work is written primarily for anthroposophists who want to come to terms with the anthroposophical social impulse. I therefore chose documentation and language with the assumption that the reader will be acquainted with basic anthroposophical knowledge and, in particular, with Steiner's social-scientific starting point. An economist has no need to support his or her mathematical equations with lessons in mathematics. Yet because my intention is to present Steiner's social impulse as central to anthroposophy, I looked for the basis of this impulse in the general anthroposophical works. "... social knowledge in particular had to be extracted from this anthroposophical knowledge"(GA 211/1963/61).

If one reads Steiner's work from this point of view, one is surprised at how many comments, directly or indirectly significant for the social question, one finds. Due to this oversupply, the choice of quotations is somewhat arbitrary. Many of them could be replaced by ten others. To be sure, a thorough research of sources would be of great significance to the understanding of the social impulse, yet it would not enhance the purpose of this book. The following thoughts are intended to help one feel one's way, as it were, toward the anthroposophical social impulse. If they cannot stand by themselves, quoting Steiner will not support them. They point to the fact that the social impulse is an integral building block of anthroposophy—they are not intended to show how it lives within all its ramifications. Should one attempt to examine all Steiner's—often very diverse and even seemingly contradictory—comments, one would risk that the reader could not see the forest for the trees.

I regret that I could not adequately acknowledge the many pioneers of this line of thought. Publication of the following thoughts, however, seemed to me more important at the moment than documentation of their history. I hope to make up for this sometime in the future. At that time I could examine the question of where and, as far as possible, why other authors come to other conclusions. It is my secret hope that Heinz Kloss, whose comparative studies are beyond compare, will beat me to it.

Even if they remain unnamed, I owe a great debt of gratitude to the many thinkers and pioneers on the social field, even and especially if I could not agree with them. Yet I wish to make two exceptions. Karl König provided the first impulse to these thoughts. Although not responsible for the quality of the fruit, it is he who planted the seed for what can now be presented. I discovered, to my own surprise, how strongly his influence had subconsciously continued to work within me, when after having concluded the manuscript, I accidentally came upon his Brachenreuth and Fröhrenbühl lectures on the threefold order, which I had misplaced. I found that my premises are the same as his, not so much as concerns my results as in the consistent Christ-centered orientation. I am further infinitely indebted to my wife. Her unerring feeling for what is social again and again brought my mental leaps back to the level of social reality.

Without examples taken from real life, a study like this one is not only unthinkable but also unreadable. Such examples are, of course, difficult to give. Should we allow ourselves to cover our anthroposophical doings with the cloak of love, as we are only too inclined to do? Certainly, up to a point, one can handle things in this way. But if we really wish to make progress, we must not shy away from bringing into our consciousness what is incomplete and backward. Such comments should not be taken as criticism and even less as accusations. They should point to tendencies that need to be overcome (understandable due to the difficult wrestling with resistances).

Since Leber explicitly excludes the interaction between human beings, I would do an injustice to his significant work if I were to (critically) discuss his more or less casual comments to my theme.

I quote Steiner by indicating the volume of the complete edition [GA]. This contains the source. This is followed by the year of the edition I quoted from. (This can be a date prior to the date of the complete edition). After this either the page (in arabic numerals) or the lecture (in roman numerals). In the above example: this can be found starting on page 174 of volume 13 of the complete edition as it appeared in the edition of 1925. From time to time other sources are quoted and accurately identified

— Dieter Brüll

Chapter 1

Social and Antisocial: An Attempt to Define the Basic Phenomena of a Jurisprudence

The ability to be open to seeing man in connection with the entire universe evokes thoughts within us that lead into the ethical, juridical concept of the world, in reality the most elevated one. . . .

— *Rudolf Steiner (GA 181/1967/33)*

What is social?

Nowadays it is almost old hat to talk about the social question. In our modern welfare state, social laws ensure that life's emergencies (sickness, unemployment, invalidism) do not deprive the citizen of his daily bread. For the borderline cases, for people who are in danger of going under or have little or no ability to adapt (the so-called asocial ones), we have special institutions. The social question, which once engaged the consciousness of mankind like a threatening cloud, today is relevant only for the so-called developing nations. The mass media daily drum into us that misery is a distant thing, that here, at home, all is in perfect order. If, indeed, disturbances sometimes surface they have to do with imported workers, individual criminals or a few yokels paid by foreign agents, who should be dealt with quite severely.

Experts, however, whose voices at times surface, take a different view. Of course, these "intellectuals," who claim to know more than regular citizens with common sense, are being foul-mouthed in the press. In the United States the name "egghead" became popular for FDR's experts and later for all scientists, albeit only if they did not represent the optimistic and patriotic point of view. The leading tabloid in the Netherlands, "De Telegraaf," popularized the term "Doktorand" as a swear-word. This sort of thing is probably not too different in other countries.

One speaks of a social market economy, of a social education system, and so forth. Yet calling things "social" does not make them so, quite the contrary. Fostering dreams about a social paradise only makes one feel more dissatisfied and ostracized because one has no part in the common happiness. One then looks for the promised bliss within oneself by squeezing out of one's body as much gratification as possible via sex, sensationalism and power. It is tragic—as every psychologist knows and as many people must experience again and again—that the resulting emptiness becomes ever more oppressive. According to one's disposition, one becomes an aggressive philistine, a regular visitor to the psychiatrist, or an addict who finally flees society and himself in his intoxication.

Could it be possible that the social question is not yet fully resolved? Could it be that the very visible capitalist, who exploits the working man, has been replaced with an invisible exploiter? One who continually offends our sense of smell, deafens our ears, robs us of the water we need, only to replace it with an undefinable liquid in the water mains? One who poisons the air and the soil, who removes the taste from our food and the joy from our pleasures? In the face of this who can really still maintain contact with his fellow man? The business acumen of an American real estate agent who offers "homes with fitting friends attached" appears to us as bland derision. The writer of romantic belle lettres, who concentrates on every nuance of feeling of the other person, may well seem ridiculous to us today. And how can one judge "sensitivity training" sociologically? Have you ever experienced the boredom of young people who sit around together—in silence? Now and then somebody drops a word, unconnected to anything, often without any content. It is akin to the way that birds modulate their voices depending on whether they've found food, or feel the desire to mate or have seen the cat prowl around. Is it not significant that the always desired "discussion" is really a process of tearing people apart, that it is a time when each utters his or her opinion without considering the opinion of the other person? Does not every teacher know that it gets harder every year to convey a concept? The capacity to take in what a fellow human being has to say has dropped close to zero. Could one not almost get nostalgic for the proletarian feeling of solidarity? Although it is not really social (because it is an offshoot of the class war), it has at least a consoling effect in misery.

This brings us to the core of the social question. What is really social? We all know her, the slightly aging lady who is ever ready to look after the children, to help in the kitchen, to water the flowers. Perhaps she really does it because her helpful soul discovers a human need. But perhaps, too, because she herself has a need for warmth and recognition. I have an acquaintance who is known to be very social-minded and who possesses the unusual virtue of being fairly honest. He once told me: "I want everyone to consider me a nice person and behave accordingly." Of course, this is in no way indecent, on the contrary. But one should not take it as being social.

Then, too, we know that other old codger. He has good advice to give in every situation and does so without expecting anything in return. He invariably does this without being asked and without asking the one in need for specifics. Should we call such a person who scatters his inner gifts so lavishly social? Certainly not.

What, then, is really "social"? In theory, one can define it rather simply: Social is to make the need of one's neighbor the motive of one's actions. And it makes no difference whether the need is physical or spiritual. Does anything like this still exist? Does not social Darwinism teach us that man's only motive (whether personal or in groups) is egoism? And does not government base its thoughts about the state on this very idea? And is not the state charged with keeping our egoism within bounds?

This scientific point of view is only too easy to understand. After all, psychology promotes hardly anything else other than egoism and striving for power. And in no way does daily life contradict all this. Rudolf Steiner explains in the fundamental social scientific lecture "Soziale und Antisoziale Triebe im Menschen" ["*Social and Antisocial Drives in Man*"] (GA 186/1963/VII) that in the age of the development of the self-conscious ego, "insofar as man does not rise to clairvoyance he is imbued with social drives only when asleep. And only what continues from sleep into wakefulness acts when awake as social drive." In light of this fact, it would be an illusion to expect much that is social in the life of society. To be sure, Steiner continues: "The love for the fellow man is mostly a terribly egotistical love. Many a person patronizingly supports his fellow man with that which he has first, so to say, captured for himself. He does this only in order to create for himself an object for his self love. Now he can cozily warm his inner being by thinking: " you are doing this." One fails to recognize how a great part of so called benevolent love is only masked self love.[1]"

One comes closer to answering the question "How can one be social?" if one starts by looking for the basic requirements. On one hand, I must give the other person the opportunity to express himself within me. In the same lecture, Steiner describes this as a process where the other puts me to sleep, thus totally filling me for a moment. On the other hand, I must have the ability to bring to my consciousness what he really wants; that is, I need to hear the developing question of the other's self behind his wish-nature.

The full extent of these questions belong to a future cultural period (GA 159-160/1970/XIII). For this very reason, working with the social question must remain theoretical and speculative. This increases the need for us to come to terms with the only too familiar concepts of what is antisocial. Perhaps addressing these will awaken an inkling of what being social can mean. The only way to address the social question in a responsible way is to look at it in this light.

The Antisocial

As hard as it is to characterize the reality of social experience, it is easy to do so with the antisocial one. Simply because we are all human, we are forced to be antisocial several times each day. Out of the plethora bestowed upon us by the earth and available for all living beings to share, we pick out and use up something for ourselves whenever we eat, dress ourselves or find shelter. Our existence was bought at the expense of others. What it might possibly mean for them in the future is a different matter. Consequently, it is antisocial.

Not even a decade ago this sentence would have exposed anybody to ridicule. Today it is common knowledge, or at least it should be. We have learned from environmental pollution that, what used to be called "goods that are for free," namely air, water, space, really come at a cost. Everything is in short supply. Speaking globally, everything is merchandise. In fact, a strange reversal seems to have taken place. The greater the surplus of traditional merchandise appears to be—at least in the industrial countries—the greater is the shortage of things formerly considered freely available. Today it is literally true that human beings take something away from their fellow beings by merely living and breathing. Even the borderline cases, such as a Robinson Crusoe (the science of economy so loves to takes its departure from him—as one deceives oneself for didactic reasons) or the recluse living in the desert have become socially relevant. That one has at last become conscious of this is one of the most important social phenomena of our time.

If we conclude that simply by being a human on this earth, man must be antisocial, then "antisocial" implies no trace of moral judgment. Antisocial behavior is a universal phenomenon of inter-human behavior, because the natural urge to stay alive always happens at the cost of another fellow human. Antisocial actions beyond this are another story.

The above characterization has allowed us to feel our way to the core question of the economy. People, each with specific needs, are faced with limited means to satisfy these. If one's starting point is taken exclusively from human antisocial drives, the logical result is the liberal economic philosophy that openly, or in a masked form, provides the basis of Western economic science. It says that the human being is antisocial and, therefore, tries to grasp the largest possible piece out of the (economic) pie.[2] Every realistic economic theory must proceed from this basic fact if it does not want to wind up with unrealistic constructions. This leads to a war, where the individual looks after his needs and in so doing sees himself opposing all other humans collectively. The global marketplace becomes the ideal, where the individual has no way of influencing supply and demand. Let us note here that one's fellow human being does not exist in this economic theory.

Now the ethical philosophers have joined the rank of the liberal economists. The father of economic science, Adam Smith, was one of the first leaders in this direction. He spoke of an invisible hand that directed the ruthless striving of all individuals toward the well-being of the community. This is expressed in the friendly saying of Manville: "private vices are public virtue" (quoted in English). Today such a thought may sound abstruse or even perverse, but one has to consider that every economic system needs a myth to assuage its bad conscience. It is not difficult to discover "God's invisible hand" in our times as well because the Western economical system is still based on the antisocial behavior of the consumers, albeit in a masked manner (healthy self-interest as the driving engine to affluence). This attitude is still very much alive today in the conventional concepts of the power of the state, which bases the economy on antisocial motives without causing the losers in the battle for existence to revolt. Smith's invisible hand has been replaced by the hand of the sugar daddy state, now burdened with the task of transforming the unsocial behavior of the individual into collective well-being. True to form this modern variation of Smith's theory is called "social market economy."

In reality something like the global marketplace exists only as a borderline case.[3] Yet the existence of the antisocial drive is a real fact. This results in two phenomena. First, production is concentrated increasingly in the hands of gigantic international corporations, whose number gets smaller and smaller and whose power greater and greater (it is estimated that 80% of production is in the hands of 300 to 400 corporations). Their push for profits, their drive for self-preservation, their effort to make their investments pay off, their overall self-centeredness, force the small corporations into dependency. They dominate the consumers either directly or through psychological persuasion. They have become so powerful that they topple governments, start revolutions, incite wars and are able to pay every imaginable bribe. They force the governments to create an infrastructure friendly to their purposes. Often the threat of pulling out of a given country, a move that dooms this country's economy, is sufficient to result in special legislation or well disguised special dispensations.

This spreading of power does not stop at the doors of the spirit. By subduing the people who have creative ideas, the creative power of the human spirit is placed into the service of the giants of industry. The military-industrial complex, with all its personal and business interconnections, is really a monolithic complex involving all society, built up of impenetrable fellowships of common interest.[4]

The hypertrophy of production would be unthinkable without its counterpart of consumption. At this point we do not want to go into the cause of this. We know, however, that the human drive to consume can be incited to grow to infinite proportions. Sociologists have determined that spending money can, in itself, give satisfaction, and that human cravings can be extended to new and even unreachable objects. We also know that the insatiable consumer has found his high priest in the capitalist. Ruthless production was favored during the early days of capitalism, as long as it did not lead to excessive consumption (more clearly: as long as overproduction served to build capital). Today, when the economy itself generates capital beyond its worth, people are encouraged to consume "so as to prevent psychological complexes."

This image of an economic system is far removed from our starting point. We have said that antisocial behavior is necessary for human existence. It most certainly does not necessarily follow that this behavior evolves in the described manner. But it is one possibility of how a real human drive can find expression within society— perhaps the most prevalent possibility in our society. Man's drive to make everything "his own" is a drive that need not always have negative consequences. Yet when consumables are scarce, the drive becomes antisocial.

Let us add the following to prevent misunderstandings. It is true that man must act antisocially in the economic life—not because the economic life is inherently antisocial, but because man is, among other things, a biological being. It is wrong to attribute human characteristics to the economic life. The economy has its own laws, which one cannot violate with impunity. It is, however, a human creation, an expression of how man deals with nature. One could arrange the economy so that the individual has the opportunity to cut the biggest possible piece from the pie. On the other hand, both scientifically and practically, one could start from the premise that, because resources are in short supply, the economy should be designed to ensure that the earth nourishes all . An example of this idea is Koch's sentence: "The common applicability and elemental nature of consumption makes it possible to make it the principle of economic self-determination and self-administration."[5]

Biological constraints, then, make participation in economic life inescapably antisocial. Yet they need not lead to the escalation of antisocial behavior in production as well as consumption. It is easy to recognize this escalation as a hallmark of our times. Nature's forces of regeneration, paired with human science are easily capable of nourishing all mankind. The tendencies to dominate, the reaching of the economy into the life of rights and spirit, and the destruction of the environment to satisfy ever increasing consumption, all this has absolutely nothing to do with our biological needs. Consequently, these anomalies cannot be justified as part of the battle for existence. These excesses always arise when biological needs transform themselves into psychological cravings.

When this happen, man starts to subjugate not only nature but his fellow humans as well. The call of the suppressed, the victimized, the disenfranchised has always been heard whenever history has reached this stage. They demand that the life of rights limit these antisocial possibilities and that the treatment of both nature and human beings as objects be prevented.

In ancient times the observation of limits was imposed from above. The "taboo," for example, is a last remnant of measures to keep antisocial tendencies within bounds. We know today that governments develop other measures to impose limits, such as the use of high taxes to return ill-gotten gains to the victims. Such measures are mere quackery, however. The antisocial threatens the whole of humanity. Counteracting this threatening force involves two tasks. One is preventing the suppression of fellow humans. The other is curing the flight into addiction.

The Asocial

We have sketched the basic features of what is antisocial. Before we can attempt to approach the social sphere, we need to become familiar with another human drives: the polar opposite of what is antisocial. We must live with it as inescapably as with the antisocial. I call it the asocial.

This is not to be understood as the negative concept usually associated with the colloquial expression. It does not mean those people who, from the bourgeois point of view, live on the edge of society and, at its cost, ever close to criminality. Here the word "asocial" is meant in its linguistic intent, namely, out of contact with human society. As irrational means beyond rational judgment and therefore is not rational, so, too, is the amoral person not constrained by moral principles and is therefore not immoral. In the same way, the asocial person withdraws within himself, or herself without having to be antisocial. In fact, in this condition a person cannot possibly be antisocial because he or she has cut the connection with fellow humans. The concept used here then is similar to the psychiatric expression. The difference is that the person suffering from psychiatric asociality, the autistic person, cannot entertain human contact, whereas the person who is asocial in the sense of his societal attitude does not want to take up such contact.

Social science hardly comprehends the asocial as a separate drive. Certainly one is acquainted with people estranged from the world. One also knows of the loneliness of modern men and women. One attributes these conditions to such circumstances as overpopulation, urbanization, etc., but not to the basic needs of human beings.

Asocial behavior, like antisocial behavior, is an indispensable condition for humans on earth. In fact, the person striving for knowledge must be asocial. He must separate himself and devote his whole being to the search for the unknown.

We have made the acquaintance of the antisocial person in the consumer. In the same way, we can see the extreme example of the asocial person in the meditant. He could never arrive at meditation were he not to disassociate himself from his fellow men—indeed, from all of nature. But in more everyday ways, this attitude applies to us all. We are familiar with the defensive feeling that arises when we are in the middle of trying to formulate a train of thought and someone disturbs us. The interruption breaks our concentration, and we are no longer able to remain alone with ourselves, to be asocial. If social contact is established, we are unable to comprehend the unfamiliar, the unknown—the objective of the concentrated thinking. We know this phenomenon in many guises. We laugh at the absent-minded professor. He is engrossed with his own problems, asocial to the extent that he quite forgets what is going on around him. A classic example is Archimedes who, engrossed in his geometric designs, staved off foes with the words: "Do not disturb my circles!"

The antisocial drive has its origin in the human instinct for self-preservation, the asocial one in the will to develop and unfold a life of the soul. There can be no economic development unless man first feeds himself by engaging in antisocial behavior. In the same way, there can be no social progress unless man ascends in his development through asocial behavior. We need not have the inventor in mind in this connection. "The outer world can never tell us that three times three is nine. We need to let our inner being reveal this to us." (GA 136/1960/53) Indeed, each person's development consists of gaining for himself in an asocial process that which has already been won for all mankind and is now common knowledge. Reading, writing, arithmetic, the simplest geometrical theorems, all require a repetition of asocial concentration and of the asocial striving for knowledge of which they have at one time been won by their founding genius. No man can feel himself as human on earth unless he lives this drive for knowledge to some extent. That which transpires from this urge to develop and gain in knowledge we call the spiritual life.

If we now observe this process more closely, we find that the Pythagorean theorem was not created for the child and the law of gravitation for the youth. Whoever believes he had a thought for the first time or made a simple or key invention will find that it had already existed. Indeed, the Pythagorean theorem was true long before Pythagoras formulated it. It is usually the case that the idea existed long before it was realized. The mathematician Pointcare said: "I already have the result, if only I knew the road to it!" In this respect the striving for knowledge is not a creative act but a fetching down of already given truth, an act of making it accessible to human thinking. The "freedom" entailed in this process is merely the freedom to grasp the truth in more or less understandable form. Indeed, I am not "free" to allow the sum of the angles of a triangle to be 150 degrees, or to insist a "deer" seen at a distance is a deer after I discover that it is really a bush.

In regard to our inner wrestling, we cannot speak of freedom in its true sense. Humans may be free in the degree to which they engage in the striving for knowledge. There is a parallel here with the degree to which one follows one's antisocial instincts. Yet the essence of the striving for knowledge finds us driven, haunted, if not even addicted. Don't we all know the preoccupation with an idea that hardly lets us sleep, wakes us up and has us under its spell to such a degree that we can no longer function socially, makes us start up when asked a question? Only with an unwilling effort can we allow ourselves to be called back, as though from a long distance away. This is when we experience the condition of being asocial.

This brief description of the asocial phenomenon may show more clearly that it—exactly like the antisocial—is morally neutral. Both are part of being human, one of a biological and the other of a psychological nature. Only the question of how we can deal with them leads us into the moral field. Just as I can place the force gained from antisocial consumption at the service of others, so, too, can I make the results of my asocial striving for knowledge available to all humanity. Is there an analogy in the asocial sphere to making consumption a goal in itself—to grab the largest possible piece of the economic pie for myself? What is the right analogy to this greed?

In contrast to grasping consumption, one takes nothing away from anybody else by striving for knowledge. The Pythagorean theorem does not diminish if others "consume" it. Something else replaces this. It is rare that a person who has found a truth (or at least thinks that he has found it) will be content to keep this for himself. Usually he is not satisfied simply to make it available to the public. He wants to spread it around. His truth makes the ideas of other people be untruths or at least half-truths. Now the missionary in man awakens. He wants to bestow his truth on all mankind. He does not merely want to create, he wants to convince.

Let us not think exclusively about religious fanatics. Everyone is closer to this phenomenon than we think. We all know the couple where the wife wants to relate whom they had met one day. "We had just walked around the corner of Main Street..." Her husband interrupts her: "Excuse me, we were already on Schiller Square!" A stubborn fight ensues, which can even result in pushing and shoving because only one of them can be right: either they were on Main Street or on Schiller Square. This quarrel, of course, bores the listeners because they wanted to learn something about their encounter, but the opponents fail to see this.

Although this behavior makes social intercourse impossible, one can, given enough time and sense of humor, see the funny side of this all too human event. Yet on the world stage, the same event can become bloody reality. We see scientists broadcast their truths into the wide world—of course, for the salvation of humanity. They create clans to outlaw different interpretations of research or educational results. They form lobbies to urge the state to allow only their point of view and to permit only their solution to be practiced. There is no more dogged fight than the one between two specialists of the same discipline. It can rage all the way to personal defamation. The worst fights take place in politics. There, one tries to at least silence those of different opinion, if not imprison or liquidate them.

Thus, the asocial nature of all earthly spiritual life carries intolerance within itself. At first glance this is peculiar. Experience shows that the asocial, something with no social relevance, leads to something of immense social significance, namely, to intolerance. How can one explain this?

We have come to know the asocial as a learning process that leads to the unfolding of the whole personality. Yet it is more than that. Inner enrichment not only confirms one's own being, it also, in the form of knowledge, strengthens my place in society. I no longer need the specialist, I can judge the situation by myself. If I have learned to read, I can open the law books myself, can control the milkman's bill, etc. My store of knowledge is accepted because I share it with others. However, today's oversupply of laws has a very threatening effect. One is no longer able to know all the regulations.

The learning process provides more than societal confirmation; it also reassures the individual. If my striving for knowledge is successful, I can trust my ability to learn. This makes the soul feel that it exists. Biological self confirmation is a visible result of eating and drinking. In contrast, psychic existence is no visible fact; hence, it ever demands confirmation from outside.

This is why it shakes the personality to the core if its own truths are not recognized by the surrounding world. The mere fact that others possess a different truth makes us unsure, which can lead to feeling existentially threatened. Every teacher knows that he or she can destroy the confidence of 95% of his or her students by reacting to the correct answer with a simple: "Do you really believe that?"

Another reason exists why we feel the need to have our truth confirmed by our environment. In most cases we know, even if subconsciously, that we do not possess the whole truth. A "different" truth, then, grows into the accusation that we have failed to bring our own knowledge cleanly enough down from the spiritual world.

Thus, we can state that intolerance is a result of a threat to soul existence, just as the antisocial trait of the human being is based on fear and worry about biological existence. The weaker the individual's soul life, the more it will seek recognition of its own truths. Such a being basically feels assured of its own psychic existence only if its truth comes to meet it from all fellow humans. Primitive man believes that he lives on in his children. Modern man considers his soul life assured if other people's world of ideas is shaped according to his own truths. His being must be resurrected in every other human being.

We find that the asocial gesture is the opposite of the antisocial one. An antisocial act is to grasp something and take it from another person; in asocial behavior a person spreads his soul out within others. He wishes, as it were, to become resurrected in his fellow men.

The concept of the antisocial has made us understand certain aspects of Western economic liberalism. That of the asocial can reveal to us certain aspects of Eastern socialism.

Marxism preaches that man is by nature a social being—Rousseau's good savage. He has become antisocial merely through the economic conditions of his time. Thus, in theory, the East knows only the asocial and the West only the antisocial person. Since the theory is gained by scientific methods and therefore infallible, and since practical experience has shown that the new Soviet person, in spite of Communist education and without capitalism, remains antisocial, it follows that man has to be changed. When theory and facts don't agree, so much the worse for the facts.[6] The confirmation of the sacrosanct theory then requires that man be robbed of his human rights, if need be even brainwashed. To the degree that this effort is successful, it results not in the social person but in what we have characterized as the final aim of intolerance: the subject who mirrors in every detail the ideas of the leading elite, the robot man who now lacks not only the social drive but the antisocial as well. The termite state has been created. We shall come back to this subject.

In Soviet days one spoke of Moscow as the red Vatican. Indeed, there are many similarities, yet one needs to consider that the emancipation of the life of rights has not been without consequences. Therefore, the measures taken today assume different forms than at the time when the Holy Sea enjoyed absolute power. The differences between now and then are but minor, and one should be able to see through them. Therefore, let me add another parallel. Marxist theory proclaimed that the human being is social, and that the unsocial is imposed from outside. Similarly, Augustinus pronounced that human beings are good, and that evil is merely the absence of good. Evil per se does not exist. If, then, evil is a nothing, nothing exists to limit the spread of the divine gospel. In their mission, church and state have the license to destroy those who do not accept the divine truth. After all, they destroy a nothing. In exactly the same way, the Red church habitually destroys both types of the unsocial, if they cannot be transformed by brainwashing. Its destruction proves its nonexistence. It simply no longer exists.

What has just been said shows that Marxism does not understand either the antisocial or the asocial, at least not as indigenous human traits. True, one knows asocial behavior very well. Certainly the lack of social engagement of scientists and artists has not been ignored, but it is written off as bourgeois perversion.

However, if one understands that the antisocial and asocial represent primary forces, one knows also that they can not be eradicated. Either a rebel or a robot will be created if one prevents a human being with the elemental need for self development from unfolding his soul forces.

This second tendency to suppress others occurs in the sphere of the spiritual life, when one person rapes the soul of another and makes use of the power of the state to implant his own ideas in another human. In the end the attempt is made to force compliance with economic methods by withdrawing the means for existence from those who resist. The twentieth century is full of horrible deeds brought about by ideology. Now we understand Steiner's saying that the worst dictatorship is created when the sphere of the spirit assumes power. (GA339/1971/72).

These problems are nearly as old as mankind. Homo sapiens has always been dogmatic even to the point of tyranny. It may be that we should view this tendency as a price for his Promethian strivings. The cry for protection against rape of the soul has sounded since the Renaissance and the Reformation and has never been silenced. Again one turns to the state, but this time to get certain guaranteed rights of development and freedom: freedom of religion, freedom of the press, freedom to gather, freedom of speech. These are rights designed to protect the individual against having the other person force his truth on him. This cry was first and foremost a demand of conscience. Obey God, before man! At the same time it arose out of the growing consciousness that every human being has the right to unfold according to his own inner character. It may be that the recognition of this right dawned slowly to some. Since time immemorial wise men have pronounced that truth has many facets, and that the knowledge of the greatest genius remains partial and in need of being supplemented by others. Even today—or perhaps particularly today?—one finds it very hard to accept this wisdom, although experience should have taught us that what we accept as truth today is unmasked tomorrow by today's heretics.

Let us emphasize that the freedoms referred to here have nothing to do with man's real freedom. They are mere political freedoms. This sort of freedom allows us to be free to undertake something or not, even if public opinion considers the action insane. Within the spiritual life on earth, man is not really free within himself. Here we experience him as one driven, obsessed, who snatches what he can of spiritual reality according to his disposition. Nor is he free when, as researcher, he makes use of prescribed methods of research, or holds routine lectures as a professor. At best he can attain freedom if he rises above what we call spiritual life on earth. This shows that freedom of the spiritual life is never a matter of one's own freedom, but always of the freedom of those with different opinions.

We face a peculiar paradox. We find that freedom is being claimed for the very areas where man cannot be free at all. One calls for freedom of spiritual life, for possibilities for human development, in spite of the fact that here we are tied by the very nature of our soul. And we demand freedom of consumption although we are biologically constrained. The paradox disappears if we consider that the possibilities for human development are most restricted if one intervenes in areas where inner constraints are already severe. One cripples or kills a fir tree by cutting it back to the shape of a cypress. In the same way one cripples man's soul, or one may even kill his body, if one forces him to eat food inappropriate for his soul or biological being. Freedom of the spiritual life is needed for man to unfold the talents he brought with him.

The desire to support freedom of inner development is based on the feeling that every man has a right to his own opinion, to his own truth. Yet within the last decades we have seen the increasing deterioration of the concept of truth. Statistics replace truth. What happens with a high degree of probability is "true." As a result, the degree to which probability can be manipulated becomes the degree to which truth can be manipulated as well. A way of thinking that sees the human being as a mere statistical grain of sand must consider the right to individual truth outright ridiculous. Thus, we see the concern for the rights of freedom gradually turned into a humanistic tradition that is undermined by interpretations whenever it gets to be a nuisance. Driven by either asocial or antisocial forces, the state becomes the suppresser of powers instead of the preserver of human rights. With this statement, we have, however, gone beyond the limits of the life of rights.

What really is social?

We have approached justice from two angles. We saw how the victims of man's antisocial behavior turn to the state for protection against exploitation. And we saw the people who had been violated by asocial behavior call on the state to be the defender of the rights to freedom. This presents us with the following question: Is justice merely the negative component of both these primary drives? Is it a power that has to protect us against something?

We have seen earlier that social behavior is constantly being denied, that it is not accepted as a reality. Strangely, the same is now the case with justice. Many Marxists and capitalists nowadays are conscious of the independent existence of both economic and spiritual life. It is even surprising (and often leads to unjustified optimism) to what a large degree the need for a free spiritual life and a socialistic economy is recognized. Yet the significance of an independent life of rights is rejected across the board. For the disappointed ones from East to West, justice is merely an expression of what is economically or spiritually desirable. Up to this point, this view agrees with our first encounter with justice—a claim for legal protection—sounding out of the economic and spiritual life.

Laws that express this protection originate in the experience of inhumanity. This understanding permits us to lay hold of the origin of the laws but not of the inhumanity. How does man get to discover inhumanity and the rape of human dignity within society? The prevention of such injustice will not be found in man's involvement with the economy because there he has to be antisocial. The life of the spirit necessitates asocial behavior, so it is also out of the question as the source for the prevention of injustice. Where, then, is the source of human indignation?

There is no need to doubt that it exists. Every newspaper presents wrongs that are being inflicted on some group of people. This stimulates emotions in the reader into which he can rather easily smuggle his own views and interests. One knows very well from experience that man's indignation is aroused not only when he himself experiences injustice but also when this happens to somebody else.

We cannot get around the fact that man has feelings for right and wrong. Of course, these feelings depend on economic conditions, on the cultural milieu and, above all, on the traditions surrounding each person. Feelings for right and wrong differ from group to group, from nation to nation. A murder driven by passion is twice as great a crime for the Calvinist, while a Frenchman gets lyrical over a "crime passionnel." Different laws, regulations and rules are created from different emotional backgrounds. Here we find the facade of the constitutional state. Ideally, this will see to it that we live in peace with each other within the realms of the economy and the spirit.

Yet the human being as an individual is absent in all this. Of course, we can state, after the fact, that the state keeps the war of all against all and the domination of the strongest within bounds. This makes it sound quite logical that in order to survive we have delegated the power to the state. All these theories have only one flaw—this is not what really happens.

Let us set aside where law and justice originated historically. We can start from the fact that in spite of all his greed, in spite of all his dogmatic tendencies, man at times feels himself to be his brother's guardian (more or less consciously) . This means that next to our unsocial drives, we also have the impulse to ask ourselves what is appropriate in relation to our fellow human beings. This and no other is the question of justice.

At the same time, it must be conceded that this impulse is in no way a dominating force within the individual. As a natural being, man must follow the antisocial drive. As a being with a soul, he must follow the asocial drive. There is no necessity for him to follow his social drive, to live within rights and obligations in relation to his fellow human beings. In this realm, he is free.

We get closer to the nature of justice if we expand on the basic problem, namely, what is appropriate for me in relation to my fellow human beings? We have already touched on the inter-human relationship, the life of rights. It is presupposed by the antisocial that human beings will act in an antisocial manner. Likewise the asocial presupposes that there will be people I shun. From the purely economic point of view, the power-grabbing person does not see the human being as human but as an object to be exploited. From the purely spiritual point of view, the unfolding human being sees his fellow human simply as a creature to be re-created after his own model. The experience of the other person does not come from either of these areas. It stems solely from the direct encounter with other human beings (see GA 271/1975/95 and 112). This experience creates each individual's specific consciousness of rights and duties. We do not refer here to legal and societal rights and duties but rather to purely human ones.

It is necessary to talk about the direct encounter to differentiate it from the indirect one provided by a novel, a film or the above mentioned newspapers. These encounters, too, try to provide us with a feeling for what is appropriate with another person. Yet the desired effect would not be achieved if we could not connect what is seen or read with a real-life encounter, which allows us to feel in a living way what is right and wrong, as well as experience the hero or the victim as though we were them.

If we focus our attention on what sense of justice we feel toward our fellow humans in the realm of the economy, we can make the following observations: In our work-sharing society, everything I consume for myself is produced by others. They have produced what I need. Therefore, I am indebted to them. My sense of justice tells me that I have to work for them by producing what they need. For justice there are no rights (no issues of justice), only obligations. From this point of view, the objective of my economic participation must be to produce what they need. For the first time we find the connection to our original concept of what is social, namely, to make the other's need the motive of one's action.

The objections to this economic exchange are obvious. Just as the other person works for you, so you work for others. This evens out. It may well be that at times some underhanded business takes place, but in principle, rights and obligations are in balance. Our reservations indicate how strongly our thinking is tied to economic considerations. The concept of this sort of exchange takes us out of the domain of justice. To be sure, the other person has probably worked for me simply to make money. Perhaps he never asked what my needs are but simply talked me into whatever he wanted to unload. In reality, he has made life possible for me and works for me. If he does this from impure motives, it is he who has to come to terms with that. I have no reason to deny his objective performance. In the realm of justice it is true that my stealing does not become a right simply because it is a common activity. At best the fact that stealing is habitually done can become an alleviating factor under the law, but never the reason for a "not guilty."

If I am honest about my relationship to my contemporaries in the economic sphere, I must admit again and again that, even with the best of intentions, I am insufficiently motivated to fill their needs. Indeed, I can ask what their needs are, disregarding that under the existing societal conditions even asking this question is hardly possible. My attempt will usually be inadequate because my ability to put myself in their position and gain an in-depth and accurate idea of their needs is inadequately developed. A debt is always left over, however diligently I might try to pay it.

Let us make a similar attempt to encounter our fellow men in the realm of spirit. Here I have to admit that, whatever I have achieved in this area, including my own development, was possible only because others paved the road for me and gave me answers to my developmental questions at the right time. They may have been contemporaries, parents, teachers, artists, doctors, priests or simply a friend who found the right word at the right time. It can also be people long dead. Indeed, what more can we do than to add a small stone to the edifice built by our forebears? I no longer need to discover the Pythagorean theorem, to invent the steam engine, create an art nouveau.

The feeling for justice and of deep indebtedness can reawaken anew in me. I have no prerogatives, only obligations. But to whom should I repay this debt? Those who helped me very rarely need my help, and many windows were opened anonymously. The only way for me to fulfill my obligations is to render the same help that I experienced to those whose paths have crossed my own.

Here again we find a connection to the concept of "social." We make our fellow human beings need for development the motive of our actions. This I can do only if I abstain from overwhelming them with what I have gleaned from the life of the spirit, namely with my own truths. I can succeed only if I invite them to unburden themselves in my own soul. "Self-surrender does not imply imprinting oneself on the other person. One gains access to the other person by allowing him to enter into one's soul."[7] If the other fills my soul completely in this sense, then I am able to give an answer to his life's problems based on his own path of development.

We have discovered a peculiar reversal. The antisocial person takes something from his fellows in the economic realm. If he is permeated with social forces, he then gives them what they need. In the realm of the spirit the asocial person overwhelms his fellows with his own accomplishments. If he permeates himself with social forces, he takes the fellow human being upon himself; he takes on the other's soul troubles.

Taking our point of departure from the two great realms of social life—the economic and spiritual, it is justice that makes us take the need of the other as the motive of our actions. What is appropriate for all of us in relation to our fellow men? This question generates the criterion for all justice. Now we can conclude that, taken in its total context, what is right coincides with what is social. This idea explodes the conventional concept of justice but encompasses a much larger meaning.

This meaning differentiates between justice and law. This differentiation is indispensable if one wishes to recognize justice, that is, the social force, as a primary human drive.[8] The cries for protection against such things as rape and exploitation stem from the life of the spirit, and economics turn them into laws. But such laws can never direct me to make the misery of my fellow human beings the motive of my actions. I discover this possibility within myself as an independent quality. The rampant injustice within society "only" serves to awaken this response in me.

If we add up our indebtedness in the economic and spiritual realms, a deep sense of gratitude dawns. I sense myself as the recipient of many gifts from my fellow human beings. My situation then assumes the image of self-renunciation. The human being deems all "possessions" unjust, and he experiences his poverty. Now the words of the old Latin song become the truth in his life:

Ego sum pauper	I am a beggar
nihil habeo	I own nothing
et nihil dabo	and I can give nothing

Once I feel myself to be only a debtor, a person who has to thank others for all he possesses, then the core of my personality is no longer weighed down by anything. Now I am only entelechy—a spirit being. As such, I resemble all other human beings. At this point I am able to grasp equality as a principle of justice in its primal source.

It is surprising that this inter-human concept of equality coincides with the concept of personal freedom. Even commonplace daily experiences give us examples of this. It can be a deeply felt liberation to rid oneself of possessions, because henceforth one needs no longer live for them.[9] Only when one loses the possibility to provide for one's own existence does one get to be truly free to apply one's creative power. Anonymity removes the pressure of dragging along one's own views, and so forth. He who succeeds in this to the furthest degree passes, according to the biblical word, through the eye of the needle and has thus mastered real freedom.[10] The freedom of spiritual life on earth is always the freedom of others who think differently, not my freedom. I experience my own freedom in the relationship to my fellow beings in the life of rights.

Understanding these thoughts does not make social behavior a reality. An abyss yawns between the thought and the deed. Not only does this abyss explain the empirical lack of social behavior, but it also brings us to the essence of the law.

Two facts are noticeable wherever formal rules are created in a real striving for justice. The first is that an attempt is made to set the standards higher than existing practices, to bring our behavior up to the law. The other is that these standards must never exceed the capabilities of the majority. Otherwise, the law would be overwhelmingly violated. Thus, laws can tell us a lot about the level of justice in a given society.

Even in their imperfections the laws reveal the principle of freedom on which they are based. We must, however, make a sharp distinction between the way the individual and society are affected.

If a group of people attempts to codify a real question of justice (this can take place within a parliament, a municipal council, a society meeting), the result is no foregone conclusion. What is right or wrong (or the sense of right or wrong) is different for different groups. This discrepancy has, for example, given us our party system. It is possible to use more or less police to guard citizens against gangsters, or to increase or decrease safeguards against noisy neighbors. One can set the old-age pension at a higher or lower level. From an absolute point of view of what is social, one can certainly find one solution more just than the other, but this does not make the other solution an injustice. "Within jurisprudence a particular answer to a specific question can never be deemed unequivocally "right" or "wrong." At best it can be "tenable."[11] This qualification belongs to the aspect of justice we already discussed, namely, that it must be tolerable for the majority of those affected. Here, too, a certain latitude prevails.

Such latitude is not unimportant because it enables jurisprudence to develop. It also provides a benchmark to determine whether one is dealing with a question of justice or with other concerns. It is a fact that one does not have the freedom to decide that two times two make five! This would simply not be true. We can generalize by saying that laws that regulate questions of knowledge are lies. In the same way, one cannot legislate that cane sugar is better than beet sugar, and that the latter is no longer to be produced. Whether this is in fact the case really depends on the constitution of the consumer. A government authority giving preference to one product at the expense of another inflicts an injustice on the individual. But, to pick a very controversial question, one can increase the defense budget at the cost of old-age pensions. This need not necessarily be an injustice.

When a law or regulation is agreed upon, the individual is free to recognize it or not. Each individual can claim the rights bestowed on him on the basis of his own sense of justice. Nobody can force him to behave less socially toward his fellow men than he deems proper. Conversely, he can exceed the limits, disregard the legal obligations and bring on the punishment himself. It would be wrong to condemn such an attitude on principle. After all, the law might set too high a standard and ask too much of people. Yet the standard may also be too low. History teaches that in such a case a purposeful violation of the law may give justice a sudden push forward.

Let us once more return to the duality of right and law. What we recognize as right in no way forces us to act accordingly. Koch mentions a number of values (justice, brotherliness, love, human dignity) and notes that: "To find a level of human behavior which as such is performed in freedom, cannot be demanded and yet forms the basis of the liabilities that surface of demand and justice. We shall have a closer look at this polarity of right and law as a process. It surfaces as the contrast between freedom and coercion. Freedom is based on the individual. The body applying coercion is the state. Its emblem is power. A state with no power is no state.[12]

The following results from this polarity: Freedom can stretch in all directions. Human values as they emerge from the sphere of rights cannot be limited. One can realize ever more justice and human dignity. The state, in contrast, is able to usurp all values and dictate them by virtue of its power. The following three behaviors, however different, are an expression of the will: antisocial greed, which wants to use the law as its tool; asocial proselytizing zeal, which tries to coerce where persuasion has failed; and thirdly, the social striving to protect men against these two.[13] We shall get to know the state as the pit that can be filled with justice as well as with injustice.

Justice between Economic and Spiritual Life

Let us examine what it means to participate in the economic and spiritual life from the point of view of justice. Let us first look at the life of the economy. This examination will yield a few guidelines for those who feel themselves a debtor.

1. To work for the needs of one's contemporaries. We have already pointed to this impulse. It expresses a different aspect of what Steiner described as "The Main Social Law."[14] It is the realization that I work without demanding compensation, i.e., that I have confidence that others will work for me as I work for them. Work and income become separated. The creation of income, then, appears as a question of justice rather than of economy.[15] Yet an individual has no need to use all of what the law assigns for one's own use. This creates the area of freedom referred to in the previous section.

2. To be as thrifty as possible with the resources needed for production. Note that this idea does not agree with the principle of economy as conventionally formulated in the science of economics. This is not a matter of private thrift or thrift within the national economy in the name of profit maximization. We already know that waste can be an economical demand. In contrast justice tells us that every waste of natural resources in production is perpetrated at the expense of my fellow men, however much it may benefit my own process of production.

3. The needs of our fellow men are a given fact for production. Nobody has the right to patronize the consumer, let alone to preach to him of morality. The fact that I allow only myself to judge my own requirements gives me no right to judge those of my fellow men. When decisions about production are being made, "there must be no trace of an opinion as to whether a requirement is justified or not . . . the decision must merely involve the objective identification of a need" (GA 338/1969/148). By the way, this does not imply in any way that from now on I am obligated to participate in every type of production. If, as a publisher, I refuse to print sensational matter despite an existing demand, this means no more than I limit myself to a particular market niche. From a societal point of view, however, it is necessary that every kind of production can and may be performed, given existing demand—unless the product is a danger to others (for instance, weapons).

4. As a citizen I will work toward changing the economic life so that it is legally impossible to work in any way that is not based on the needs of fellow humans. This attitude toward justice demands that I stand for legal regulation that separates work and income just as much as for elimination of means of laws that enable the economic exploitation of individuals.

5. My feeling of indebtedness will lead me to constrain my own needs to my specific biological requirements. "The best way to help one's fellow men is to have no wants" (GA 97/1981/196).

6. And finally, it is up to me, as a participant in spiritual life, to spread these thoughts about justice and business.

These changes would create a situation in which I no longer work for myself (as would fit the spiritual life), no longer allow the immediate encounter to motivate me (as would fit the life of rights), but where I work for my unknown brother. When business is permeated with the social idea, I follow the needs of others and my own biological needs, ahead of the laws of technology, organization and profitability.

Let me point out again that these guidelines are a mere outline, and that they have the character of an ideal—each point would need a detailed discussion. Here are questions arising from the rights sphere and directed to the life of business. Hardly anyone, let alone a community of people, will be able to do full justice to these questions.

Yet these are not utopian requirements. If one wished for an appeal to asceticism or self-flagellation, one would miss the gist of what is meant here. The real world is found in the interplay of social and unsocial forces, using "unsocial" as the collective term for anti- and asocial. If one wishes to understand the processes taking place within society and perhaps even to intervene to create some order, it is mandatory to know the forces at work in their pure forms. So far we have concentrated only on the social component. We still need to address what happens when this component is more or less absent.

Let us now enter the life of the spirit with the debtor's feeling for justice. What does it mean to be social in this realm? It cannot mean that I simply place at the disposal of others what I have worked for. If being social in business means producing only what my contemporaries need, the situation is profoundly different in the life of the spirit. In the realm of spiritual life on earth, my feeling for justice tells me to help my contemporaries on their path of development. In the economic life, I can help him—actually work to satisfy his needs—if I put myself in his place. Our common biological nature makes this possible. In the spiritual life, this does not work because I would bring myself along, which always results in something like: If I were Mr. Meyer, I would administer a beating to this lout. If I were you, I would take Müller to court. "To put oneself in somebody else's place" (and all too often in real life as well) stands for the very tendency of the person active in the spiritual life to experience himself in the other person, to impose on him his own views.

The social aspect of the spiritual life demands that I open myself to the other person, invite him to express himself in me. In this way I am able to experience his questions of inner development as my own. One should speak only after having really heard these questions. "Not even a truth should be produced based on human predilections." (GA 190/1971/217)

This waiting until invited in to express himself in the other person, this waiting with the answer until the question is heard, may be compared to what used to be called the virtue of chastity.

Freedom of (earthly) life is thus illuminated from a new angle. True, I am not free to acknowledge anything else than what I have recognized as the truth. This part is a matter of freedom of the one who thinks differently. Yet, along with the social aspect, a piece of freedom enters into the life of the spirit. To be sure, I cannot take over an opinion differing from my own and living within the other person. But I am free to accompany him in his thoughts with my own. I can even help him to grow, based on his specific view of the world, even if it in no way matches my own.

To be social is the exact opposite of the asocial and antisocial drives. The grasping gesture in economic life changes to a giving one, and the overwhelming gesture in the life of the spirit changes to an accepting one. Man as a biological being is indeed condemned to be antisocial in the economic life. Yet the social drive within us can confine this fate to our role as consumers. As producers we can be social. In the same way, man is condemned to be asocial in the spiritual life, but the social drive within him can confine this fate to his role as "producer," as one who brings down and acquires truths. He can be social as consumer in this realm, as recipient of other people's ideas.

To the extent that the essence of what is social has been recognized, it has condensed itself in laws. These, of course, show all-too-human frailties. It is Thomas Aquinas's *Lex Humana*. Nobody will deny that much has been done to protect man from exploitation by his contemporaries, and that a number of rights have been granted to protect him against outrage. However, it would be unreasonable to consider all this inadequate. One feels increasingly that legislation creates the very opposite of a social situation. Is this a fact? If so, how are we to understand this?

Justice and Law

Justice is as old as mankind. As a community-forming being man had to find some way to order the way of living together. Custom and habit are the oldest known forms. They have often been more powerful than the more recent laws, taboos and people's courts. In what American sociology calls "social control" customs and habits exist to the present day, and become conduct dominated by the prevailing ideas of the region. The modern "upper-class lady" is a good example when she finds that she cannot wear the same dress two days in a row, because "someone" (i.e., people of her class) may think that she cannot afford a second dress. It is, in essence, the same thing when her daughter refuses to wear a dress because anyone who does not come to school in jeans is ridiculed.

A law is necessary only when customs and habits dissolve, or when a powerful group decides that the existing legal order needs to be changed. In the long run the latter succeeds only when the first has already taken place to some degree.[16]

In Western civilization with its urbanization, the power of custom and habit has increasingly disappeared. This means that much that had been a matter of course now has to be legally prescribed. Both the old conventions and new demands for justice called for legal regulation.

Humanity has for millennia fought for liberation from exploitation. This development—constantly backsliding—has allowed the total slave to gradually become a serf, later a bondsman and finally a "wage slave." In the process owners lost more and more of their rights. It is a fallacy to think that the increasing volume of social legislation presents a "justice versus welfare" dilemma, because it threatens to strangle our economy. In reality it is the sense of justice that powerfully strives to surface. That sense grants every human being the right to a dignified human existence, whether the person is diligent or lazy, honest or a criminal, clever or stupid, black or white. Slowly this new sense of justice displaces the remnant from the nineteenth century, which looked upon work as a commodity that was assigned a price on the open market, the seller having a right to the proceeds. The consequence of this view is that he who has no salable merchandise to offer belongs on the rubbish heap along with merchandise that cannot be sold. Today this is no longer acceptable. Deep down we all know that we depend on work performed by all of us. This realization in turn would demand that we also work for all human beings. The fear of getting rid of the old capitalistic dogma, on the one hand, and on the other, the attempt to eliminate the worst consequences of the labor market, create hundreds of laws, needing hundreds of thousands of officials. All this happens instead of the one law that makes income an issue of justice.

Right and justice collide again when it comes to using the earth's riches and the disposition of capital. Is it not true that the former are a gift for all of mankind and the latter an achievement of humanity as a whole? Yet when property is totally private, both the riches of the earth as well as capital become tools for exploitation. Again we are faced with a dogma, in fact, with several, namely, that every object must be private property, that only the capital market can prevent failing investments, that personal gain is the only possible driving force of the economy. Again our sense of justice opposes these dogmas as it rejects exploitation stemming from the private ownership of land and capital. Hundreds of laws are being generated, and hundreds of thousands of officials are employed to reduce the worst consequences of exploitation—all instead of the one law that socializes capital, land and natural resources. The protection of the individual demands a separation of work and income. In this sphere a separation between administration and disposition of the earth's riches is overdue.

One reason explains why the social struggles aimed at protecting man against the antisocial tendencies of his contemporaries are inadequately expressed in legislation, and that reason is that the sense of justice prevailing today is permeated with ghosts from the spiritual life of the past which have settled in the economic life as ideologies.

If the above dogmas were the only reasons for the contrast between justice and law, one could expect that gradual enlightenment would eventually bring about justice in legislation. In the long run the law would remove the rights from the economic life, which the latter had illegitimately acquired. Thus, the economy would be able to function based on its own economic laws. This would optimize its functionality without damaging the social life.

Unfortunately, a power very different than the law of inertia comes into play here. This power makes use of the above named dogmas as welcome tools. The origin of the dogma is no doubt based on honest search for truth in the spiritual sphere. This power is the antisocial striving itself. Blocking social legislation, it tries to seize the legislative process.

We have seen that the need for laws arose when routinely established behavior began to be questioned, when custom and habit were no longer imperatives. The law that took their place no longer rests on solid emotional foundations because it lost its authority. Superficially, the law is in force, but it no longer evokes the feeling that it must be this way and no other. This disintegration allows laws that support the greed of interest groups. It then becomes vital to gain influence over the legislative machinery. We all know the concept "lobby," the art of influencing, convincing and even bribing representatives of the people. Watergate and its sequels opened the eyes of anyone who believed our laws were democratically derived. Millions of dollars influence legislators. Millions were used to convince the commissions and experts that the fighter planes —of a democratically elected government—had to be replaced with an American model. The pressure of the automobile industry has cost thousands of lives as it blocked the introduction of a speed limit on the super-highways in Europe.

Business has long ago ceased to believe in the state as a mystical entity; its orientation is far too international for this.

The nationalistic noises merely promote orders for the armament industry. The state has become a vacuum that is simply left to be filled with the right people. Thus, legislation is no longer an expression of a social sentiment that curbs exploitation but, on the contrary, a means to satisfy antisocial desires.

In the long run this can be achieved only by corrupting the social feelings of the population. One can no longer stop at the legislative process but must penetrate the spiritual life. Advertising (hidden persuaders) and propaganda ("repete et impere" ["keep repeating and rule"]), persuade the average person that the legislation produced by the striving for antisocial power is an unavoidable measure, even if it is not the epitome of justice. Orwell's ingenious power of observation named the ministry of torture the "ministry of love." Social phenomena everywhere receive names that express the exact opposite of what they stand for. One of the newest is the "sanitary fill" for an atomic junk yard. Abusing the state and abuse to the life of the spirit result in the business empire where each individual is degraded, exploited and brainwashed. This empire, this Western centralized state, is commonly called the welfare state.

A similar history can be found regarding the spiritual life. Here, too, we can see a long development. Only as late as the end of the Middle Ages claims for legal protection of personal development arose. Freedom of conscience toward the church, autonomy in teaching and research at the first universities, and the demand for political freedoms originated—mostly in the Western world. All these merged into constitutions in most of Europe and the U.S. wherein the state guarantees the basic rights of its citizens. If only the thoughts expressed after World War II in the declaration of human rights were common practice today! In that case the sense for social justice would have created a bulwark against unsocial tendencies of individuals and groups. And then we could only talk about historical remnants of a barbaric past.

Here, too, laws designed to defend against asocial tendencies brought about their realization as well. It was shown that it is possible to force one's own views of the world, one's own truths, upon the underlings. The history of the Soviet Union demonstrates this so vividly that further description can be dispensed with. The life of the spirit has, along with the life of the economy, discovered the state to be a vacuum to be filled with the "correct" people.

But just as in the economic life, here, too, the state usurping all the power by itself is not enough. Man does not live from bread alone, nor solely from propaganda. The economy must be brought into the service of ideology, if not, as in Russia, it becomes the expression of that ideology. The state's taking over is of necessity followed by the take-over of the economy. In no way does the imperialism of the spirit rank second behind that of the economy. The goal to demean the human being to a brainwashed object can be reached only if he is robbed of all rights and economically atomized as well. The Eastern totalitarian (unified) state and the western (welfare) state resemble each other like identical twins, not in all methods but in structure.

The spread of anti- and asocial conduct provides an explanation for much, but by no means all, of our present social struggles. We need to acquaint ourselves with a third factor.

Observation of the inner structure of our mammoth corporations shows that those higher on the ladder always fire those below them as soon as the latter fail to strive first and foremost for maximum profit. Efforts are totally directed toward reaching established performance standards. The latest technical innovations are brought into play to accomplish this. The human or inhuman conditions created and the measures needed to cope with them are judged exclusively by how they affect the path toward the goal. The computer dictates the next step. The whole enterprise is held together by naked fear for survival—fear of being fired on the part of the laborers and fear of losing out in the competitive battle with the other dinosaurs on the part of the managers. The principle of economic efficiency, fully justified when it comes to merchandise, is thus applied not alone to merchandise but to human relationships as well.

We are still within the realm of antisocial conduct, and what begins to emerge from this phenomenon is the bureaucrat. To him his contemporaries are as unimportant as the merchandise that streams in and out of the establishment. Faithfulness, love, being human, solidarity are for him only words like treason, hate, egoism, etc. It is as if the entire range of emotional life were extinguished within him. For him the surrounding world is only a means to an end, which is not the corporation or the office where he works. For him his own job is being elevated to an end in itself. The outer kindness is a mask.

Business life is not the only place where bureaucrats are created. In a certain sense capitalism is a sort of "backward oasis" in this area, because it still allows its functionaries a modest measure of private life. If this private life is used to develop human qualities, strangely split personalities result. This could best be observed within the primitive games in totalitarian states. Here, for example, we can see an Ilse Koch, whose harmonious family life is illuminated by a lamp whose lampshade is made from the skin of a tattooed erstwhile prisoner, who was killed for this purpose. (By the way, this horrible scene could well serve as a symbol for our affluence within today's world economy.)

In areas where the life of the spirit reigns, this type of person appears in even more pronounced form. We like to call him by his Russian name: Aparatchik. Compared to him, Ilse Koch seems human. It is common knowledge that under the Russian system only those who follow all the twists and turns of the elite with a minimum of friction can survive in their positions. Anybody who cannot do this loses at least his position, and under Stalin, even his head. As a result he will not commit himself totally to his goal. Otherwise he would expose himself and risk being liquidated next time the direction is changed. Nobody who has read Wolfgang Leonhard's "Die Revolution entlässt ihre Kinder" (*The Revolution Dismisses Its Children*) will ever forget Ulbricht's first appearance in 1945 in Berlin.

Attempts have been made to understand this phenomenon from many sides, yet it remains somehow elusive. One talked of "desk murderers" (Eichmann). Yet the term itself distracts one from the fact that it is quite unimportant that he was a murderer. Under different circumstances, he may have sent a Christmas parcel to all invalids. This, too, he would not have done from social motivation but because it was part of his function. This makes it an extremely delicate matter when it comes to judging functionaries.

Here we approach the distorted picture of a state official. In fact, this type is part of the caricature of the state machine. It is no more than the dreadful truth that more and more often, this is no longer a caricature but living reality. To the degree that business or ideology dominates the state—or, like our corporations, forms a state power in itself—the bureaucrat assumes power, both superficially and within us. All human beings are subconsciously attracted by the image of the bureaucrat. Why is this so?

In the case of state activities limited to the judicial system, the official is still able to gain an overview of his activities. He knows when these actions have just consequences or when they contain an unintended severity. The true public servant has always been able to temper unneeded severity, to suggest different ways to approach the citizen, or to refer him to the official channel for exceptional cases. He felt himself to be a servant to the population, and this gave him his mission in life. The traveler to England or Ireland can still encounter this type of policeman.

An official today cannot possibly gain an overview of the mesh of legislation spread over humanity as well as its consequences. The laws have lost their originally intended significance. They are "off the cuff" regulations. This means that they are devoid of inner moral life. Therefore, they lack a driving force that could be considered a restraint. In practical life one is satisfied if 70% to 80% of those affected obey. Therefore, prosecution of offenses is largely neglected and left to chance or used to put an undesirable person out of action. It needs to be added that regulations of the life of the spirit or of the economy basically have no value on their own. They are not expression of moral judgments—unless they protect people in specific areas. In reality they result from cold factual or expert-generated points of view.

The confusion of legislative problems with problems pertaining to spiritual or economic spheres gets in the way of an understanding of what is really intended with laws. Should an official presume to judge whether an aspiring medical student should be admitted to the university, if he felt called to the medical profession since childhood, but if his grade average was below the limit? How can he know whether the closed quota system has made the grade the deciding factor because this would eliminate those who have a deep therapeutic feeling right from the start and who could later become rebels? Should a colleague of this official show a small farmer how he can avoid regulations that drive him into bankruptcy? Does he know whether the regulations are the way they are because government wants to drive out the small farmers?

The hour of the bureaucrat has struck in this world of semblance and facade. He is not interested in the results of his actions. For him, the law is an end in itself. Something like Gresham's law (bad money drives out good money) starts to apply to officialdom. The bureaucrat finds a perfect spot for himself in the state, while the "old-fashioned" official no longer feels at home there. But what interests us most is that the result of asocial and antisocial attitudes is a new quality. If we have called the two primary forces drives, we here have to talk about a drive block.

Eastern society produces the official who, for the sake of self-preservation, cannot connect himself to the goals that underlie his tasks. Western society produces a type of official who is no longer able to judge the aims of his activities. His drive for self-preservation makes him carry out his instructions to the letter. Both are estranged from ideological and economical goals. The social impulse, a force alive in every human being, cannot be brought to bear in the workplace. Eventually, the more or less natural and human drive for self-preservation disappears. It is transformed into automatic execution of every command. The climax is logical: self-destruction when one accuses oneself of a misdeed that carries the death penalty. The reversal of values is complete. The newly generated bureaucratic type knows only a world of objects within which he functions. Nature, thoughts, fellow humans, he himself, all have become objects that have to be dealt with in the prescribed manner. He has become the human being without a heart.

Here again we encounter a paradox. In the sphere of rights, of all places, where human beings encounter each other, there should be no functionaries. After all, the person who acts out of a sense of justice does so based on the immediate encounter with his fellow man, out of the moment of becoming one with him, out of social intuition. He who works out of his sense of justice is really an artist. This has an echo in an old tradition where justice was still called "ars aequi," the art of what is equal.

This very area of justice is the domain of the state to its core. However, the state as we know it demands impersonal bureaucratic pettiness from its servants. In the exact measure to which the state fails its social task,[17] i.e., acts impersonally, the resulting vacuum creates the opposite of a socially active person, namely, the bureaucrat.

Here, too, the revolution devours its offspring. The bureaucrat, transformed to a willing tool, becomes immune to the methods used toward their asocial and antisocial ends by the two usurpers; bribery and deification of individuals. The bureaucrat lacks the human drive for status and power. He no longer looks at the law in regard to its significance for the life of the spirit and the economy. For him the law is meaningful only from the criterion of convenience of its enactment. Gas chambers are thus better than shootings.

The question of easy enactment brings up the other side of the coin, namely, the institutional one. Laws attempting to have an effect on cultural or economical matters cannot be carried out, because the areas to be controlled are too diverse to be controllable by a general regulation. The solution is the generic law, which empowers the executive to carry out the intent of legislation. The factual legislation is then placed into the hands of the functionaries.

Regulations are created that can be changed at any time without input from parliament and, if desirable, with retroactive force. Rubber rules arise. Against these there is often no possible appeal or only a useless one, because no postponement is possible. Nevertheless, legal or regulatory matters remain a nuisance, which at times places great demands on the officials. It would be ideal if a computer could deal with the entire matter. In some areas of taxation, this has already happened (the judge's decisions have a way of adjusting with remarkable speed to the fact that personal conditions must not be taken into account).

Before one can switch on the computer, a further step is needed. The area to be reformed must first be standardized. One can carry out every law and reign with the computer once every farm has the same circumference and every medical practice the same composition of patients. This enforcement of common denominators is already being practiced on a large scale, albeit under the guise of different motives.

This predicts a society resembling a colony of termites, where everyone has become a bureaucrat, where human tendencies are totally excluded. The ultimate consequence is the uniform state, whether ideological or economical. Such a society destroys the economic and spiritual life and finally the individual.

Regardless of whether antisocial or asocial attitudes reign, the human being is needed either as work- or consumer-slave or as yes-sayer.[18] This is why we rediscover, however corrupted, the human being in both embodiments. Along with the human being's threefold being the threefold social structure is then somehow revealed, of course not as a structure but as three streams of force recognizable even in this extreme caricature.

This is not the case in a state of functionaries. There the computer-driven digital thinking and action are fully entrenched. We can discover rudiments of this everywhere around us. Every phenomenon is considered exclusively from the point of view of usefulness and execution. Therefore, whatever comes up is either black or white, good or bad, right or wrong. The human middle is missing—a society without heart.

In this section we have tried to depict a way of dealing with the social question, different from the one presented by the state. We could use the state to free man from exploitation and violence. If we do this, a threefold society is created in which the spiritual life can be free, because the state guarantees freedom to every person, and in which the economic life is allowed to operate autonomously because the venomous tooth of exploitation has been pulled.

We can also use the state for our asocial and antisocial ends. This creates an unholy alliance. It consists of a technocracy that increases human desires to their greatest extent, a theocracy that blocks every personal development, and an almighty bureaucracy that, in the long run, will shelter these hostile brothers under its wings where all differences will be extinguished. This is Koch's gray totalitarianism.

This is how I understand Steiner's statement that the future will be either threefoldness or Bolshevism.[19] The freedom that belongs to the human being within the life of rights is expressed here in its ultimate consequence. It is humanity's free decision whether the social structure is based on a sense of social justice or whether humanity sinks to the subhuman level.

The final theme of these considerations is the question how the human individual can fit in the threefold stream.

Man and Society

We have attempted to develop the concept of threefoldness from its basis in the life of justice. Man's asocial and antisocial drives stimulate social activity, which results in the creation of laws to protect man against his contemporaries. Looking up at it from below, as it were, threefoldness appears as a question of order. From this point of view, problems of society appear as legislative questions. It is certainly legitimate to treat them as such.

This is why, when politicians speak about freedom of the spiritual life, they speak about legislation designed to guarantee this freedom. It appears that this development has reached a crucial stage. Does free information still exist at all? Do the authorities have the right to block free choice of doctors and medicines? Is it free to put fluoride into drinking water? Is it allowed to establish preconditions for training and education? In many countries, movements are working to fight the tyrannical alliance between certain philosophical "scientific" schools of thought and the state.

Politicians also like to talk about legislation that aims to remove power from the economy by legislative action. This approach, too, is legitimate. But where the state has provided protection against antisocial tendencies, it has only applied band aids to the symptoms, if it did not itself become an exploiter by nationalizing enterprises.[20] It starts to look as though Marxism has defamed certain demands to such a degree that they have become abhorrent to the non-Marxist society. These demands are: to cease (expropriate) the possession of land and capital, to withdraw human labor from the circulation of goods, and to depreciate money as a function of time.

Finally, the question must arise whence justice takes its standards. It is desirable to seek the standards for the economy (business) and spiritual life from their own phenomena. In these spheres, one can wait to find out how a free spiritual life and an economic life, free of exploitation, will fill with meaningful content. When it comes to justice, form and content coincide. Justice can be nothing but what the majority finds to be just.

In this respect, mankind faces a fateful watershed. If we pursue the question how social behavior was born, we find that it arose from being immersed in the economic life, in the profession. When that life was not as devoid of spirit as it is today, it fashioned man into a social being. He was baker or shoemaker, peasant or carpenter, assessor or merchant. He learned demeanor by practicing his trade. He became one with it and could not depart from it through social control. Social demeanor became a habit. Only with age came contemplation and the wisdom of the profession. The social mood lived deep down in the soul and determined the content of knowledge. Maturity brought insights about the profession and later insights about man's rights in relation to his contemporaries. New justice was born as content of consciousness. From the master it was handed down to the craftsman. It became standard procedure. If it stood up to the test of the spiritual life, it may have found its way into regulations and laws. It traveled from the economic life via the life of the spirit to the source of justice—and back again to new legislation via the economic life and the spiritual life. Law approached justice.

In our time a social sense, born out of professional ethic, can be found only in remote "backward" areas and within a few isolated professions (military officers, diplomats). In the latter areas, this ethic is a frozen status symbol more than a real way of thinking. Without addressing the reasons, today's business life is unfit to evoke social initiatives, and young people are unwilling to have a work ethos forced on them on the job. Their attitude is formed by the social Darwinism underlying the labor market, namely, to do as little as possible for a given wage. In a certain sense we can see a sort of social justice in this. It is the reversal of getting minimal reward for a given job. This philosophy can no longer lead to justice.

If the present generation is to find a way to attain a social attitude, it must start at the life of the spirit. One can be socially creative within the life of the economy only after one has gained insight into the forces working within society and after one has recognized one's own social and unsocial drives. Only when we know what work really means can we work in a responsible manner. This implies the need to work for others. Only when we stand within the life of the economy in this manner can we start the hard fight against our own asocial and antisocial drives as they constantly oppose that which we have consciously understood. Unfortunately modern social practices allow free reign to antisocial tendencies. All this forces one personally and in freedom to stand up for social reality again and again.

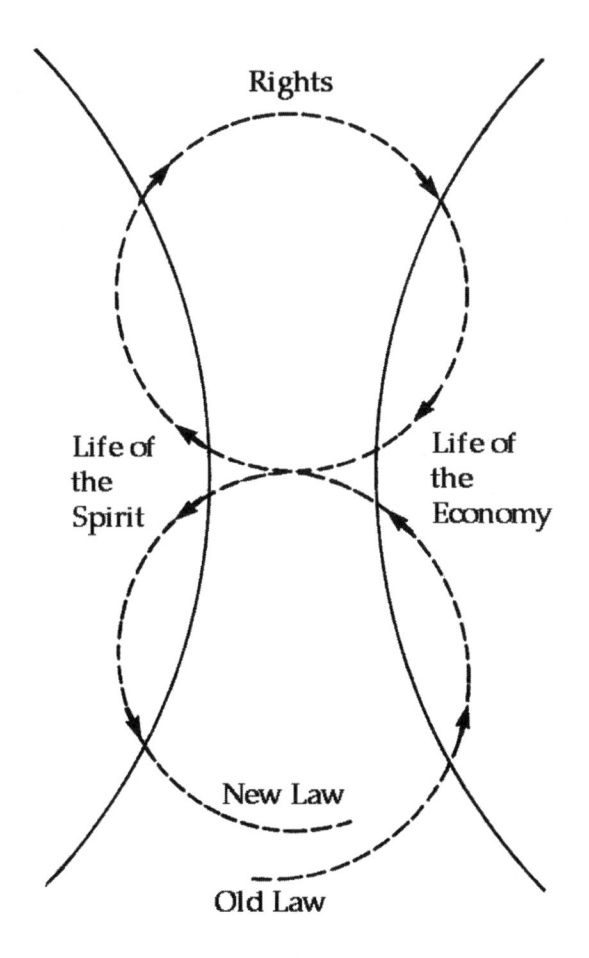

```
                    Rights
         _____
        /         - - -      \
       /       /        \     \
      /       /          \     \
             /            \
   Life of  ↙              ↘  Life of
   the      \              /   the
   Spirit    \            /    Economy
             ↖            ↗
              \          /
               \        /
                \      /
                 New Law
              - - - - - -
                Old Law
```

A new sense of justice can be created out of this struggle within the economic life and out of direct experience of the problems social and unsocial drives can create. This sense of justice can then be transposed to the life of the spirit to be consciously understood and clarified. After these steps one can enter into the economic life with new social initiatives, there to test and demonstrate the viability of what has been gained. Approval in the economic life will foster a justice that produces regulations and laws at a higher level.

The weakness of one's own social drive is not the only obstacle on this path. The prevailing custom and practice within the economy also bar our way. They constantly get in the way of a social attitude, or simply throw the "idealist" on the scrap heap to start with. Thus, we see more and more "communes" which are formed to put into practice what was understood to be right. These are communities of people who live together and form total or partial economic communities. The focus is to work for the other and guard him against consuming too much at the others' cost.

This path toward the source of justice is one of social development. But in this case the social question no longer appears in threefold but in fourfold form.

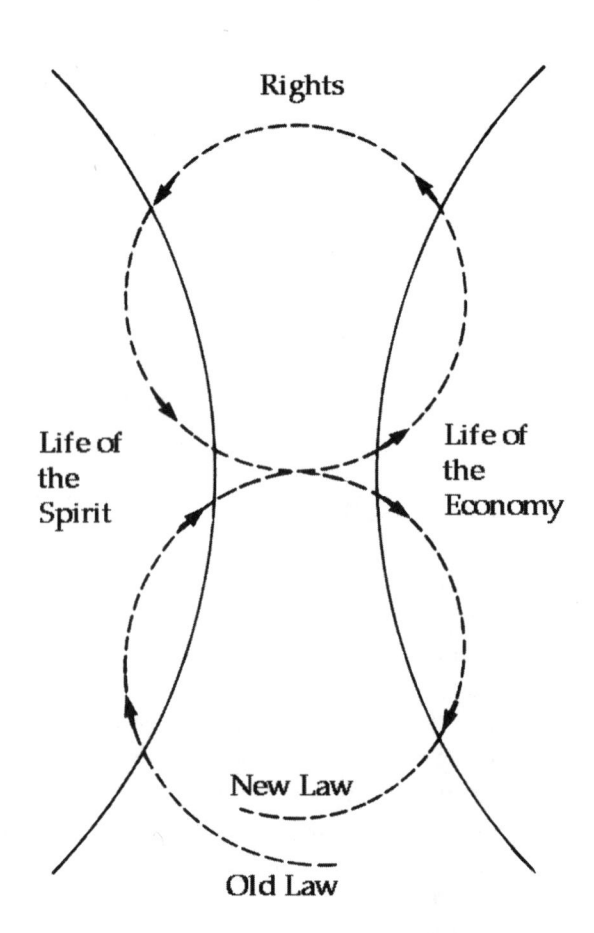

```
                    Rights

    Life of                    Life of
    the                        the
    Spirit                     Economy


                   New Law
                   Old Law
```

If we face our society as an observer, it presents itself to us as a jungle that must be seen clearly if human beings are to live within it in peace. Then society shows us its threefold nature, and it reveals soul forces that need their own spheres within which to unfold. The essence of the resulting threefold articulation is equilibrium: The three spheres must achieve equilibrium within the whole of society. The unfolding of one sphere depends on the unfolding of the other two. Yet equilibrium excludes oneness. The fact that equilibrium must be newly found at each instant raises the question whether such a threefold structure would not instantly fall apart.

The doubts are dispelled the moment I abandon the role of observer and experience myself as part of the social organism. Now I no longer control my own and other people's participation from the outside but experience that, although I exercise my humanity in several areas, I do so from the center of the social organism. I experience my ego as a controlling, combining, regulating and unifying force. It allows me to be active in the life of the economy one moment, shortly after in the life of the spirit, and perhaps on the same day in the life of rights, all this without losing myself in one of these spheres. This uncovers the new theocrat. In him the three spheres of the social organism find their unity.

The theocrat of old found the source of his inspiration outside the social organism. This divine source empowered him to mold the body social as something toward which he developed conscious knowledge as an object. Placing ourselves in the center of the social organism, we experience this source as a unique domain with which we have to develop a relationship, comparable to relations to the life of the spirit and the economy. A fourth spiritual domain thrusts itself into the social organism as the spiritual source of social reality. It looms over the three domains that form the earthly body social.

Now we have discovered a fourth structural element. Spiritual and economic life face each other on one side, and on the other, the source of justice and the life of rights. Let us say it in other words. Because I myself am an entelechy, I can no longer describe the process of society as threefold—purely based on its earthly appearance—insofar as I experience myself as part of it.

We approach the mystery of the human being. We have described how justice flashes up as human being encounters human being, and then how justice is born out of our ego. Now we can say: face to face with our fellow human being we encounter . . . ourselves. I am face to face with my own reality, with my own inadequacy. But this is not the end of it. If it is an encounter in the true sense of the word, a new light will dawn in my consciousness. I will see that the sorrow and want on the part of even the very last unknown human being are my sorrow and my want, even as I experience it as my inadequacy to transform this knowledge into action. It dawns on me that the want and pain inflicted on other humans is inflicted on them by myself, because I no longer feel the asocial and antisocial forces in society outside of myself but within me as my asocial attitude and my antisocial behavior. The encounter with the other person becomes the encounter with myself.[21]

Now we are able to see the image of the human being within the social organism. Our individuality feels how the asocial element rises up within us as a real force, a function stemming from the life of the spirit; it feels how it is trying to seduce us to arrogantly penetrate other human beings with our knowledge. If the individuality experiences this as an unclean act, then it senses at the same time the counteracting force of morality. This force has its origin in the fountainhead of social reality. In the same way, we can feel the antisocial element rise up within us as it operates within the life of the economy. We get the feeling of being convicted of theft. This feeling is counteracted by a sense of responsibility toward even the last of our fellow human beings. It stems from the same social fountainhead. Finally, we are able to experience how our individuality is being protected by law and order as it operates in the domain of justice. This protection shields us against our own striving for power as it reveals itself unmistakably within our individuality. Now we also feel how this shield of order and control needs to be constantly renewed by the forces of freedom, born from the same social fountainhead. The force that is here attempting to flow into the world of law and into the external legal state is the quintessence of human right. Depending on whether this force surfaces as a demand from the life of the spirit or as an entreaty from the life of the economy, it shows its countenance as justice or mercy. The trinity of morality, responsibility, and merciful justice is a creation of the ultimate social force of love, as it opposes like a sun the subhuman monolith of power, slovenliness, and theft. We have learned to know this monolith as immense emptiness within which the personality is being exterminated.

If one experiences the social threefold order within oneself in this manner, one also knows that it is no mere theme for specialists or politicians. Threefoldness exists as a real potentiality within human beings, as well as a path of inner development. Wherever and however far I create social reality from this potential, I work on the realization of the threefold social order. This may be in macro-social connections, or it may come to expression in the formation of institutions or within the life of the family. Whether I stand in the world as a creator of social threefoldness or not is not decided within the context of the social structure. The question is whether I create an island paradise or whether I act within contexts that move humankind as a whole, that is, as a social organism. In other words, either one person or a group faces me as representative of all humankind as I encounter them in a social or unsocial manner.

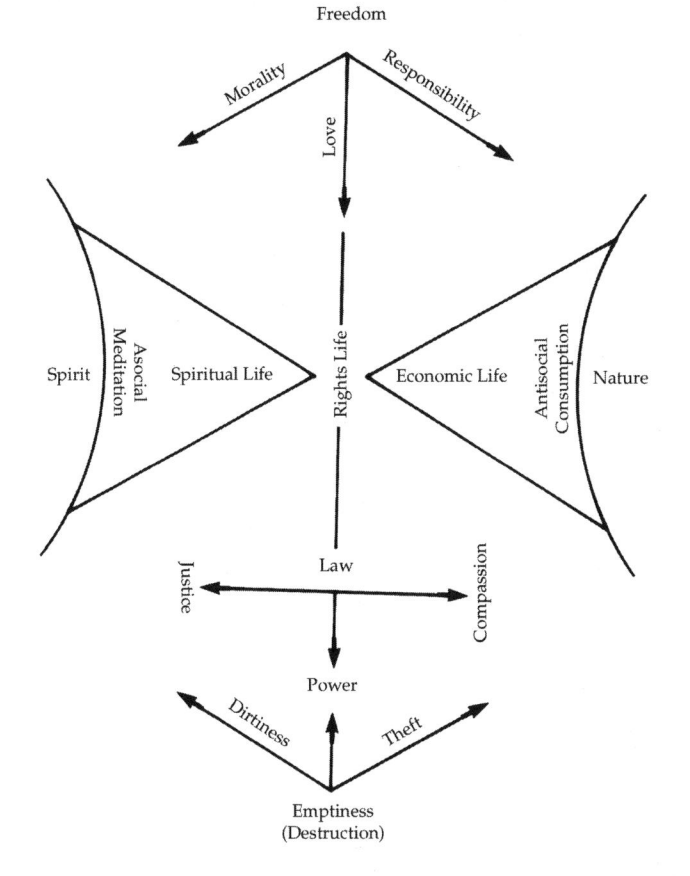

Endnotes:

[1] Benevolent love also has to some extent the character of an alibi. Runciman, a British diplomat, has demonstrated this in a classical and, in its cynicism, revealing fashion. In 1939 he was sent from England to the abandoned Czech Republic to act as go between during the time of the cessation of large areas to Hitler's Germany. He did this in such a neutral manner that the Nazis created a new song: "We do not need a Santa man, we have our Runciman." When the hard pressed Czechs finally approached him with the request to do at least some little thing for the Czechs who had been thrown to the Nazi wolves, he was offended and answered: "You will find my name among the donors for the victims of the conflict." (Gedye in *Fallen Bastions*)

[2] One could call this the homo economicus. Yet this being has the peculiarity that it lives exclusively for the best possible satisfaction of its needs. Even though science has thrown this being out the front door, it was brought back in by the back door by throwing non-scientific aims (freedom, play, self improvement) into the pot of needs.

[3] A seeming exception is the stock exchange. In reality this, too, is nothing but a well-organized but unimportant refuge for dying wasps, of no importance to the dynamics of the economy and harmless. What really can be done with stock is done by the big guys outside the Stock Exchange.

[4] With the same powers one knows how to prevent these happenings from reaching the mass media. In its time an industrial may look like an exception. Yet for the believers in our "free democratic order" such things are not a symptom but a deplorable accident.

[5] N. Koch, "Staatsphilosophie und Revolutionstheorie," (*Philosophy of State and Theory of Revolution*) p. 76.

[6] In his admirable analysis of the concept of revolution "Autopsie de la Revolution" ("Autopsy of Revolution") (Paris 1969), Ellul unmasks Marxism by showing it up as a confirmation of the reigning societal structure. "What does one do if events do not run the way Marx thought they should? ... As soon as this happens, orthodoxy had to uphold the opposite of the

facts as they happened either by interpreting them in this way or else by simply concealing them." (p. 159)

[7] C.J. Zwart in "Tussen harmonie en conflict" Assen 1975, p. 28.

[8] The striving of jurisprudence to become a science founders on the unwillingness to make this differentiation.

[9] A good example of this can be found in *Info 3* in the "account from Marx'stand."

[10] Compare this to the meaning of being a debtor within Roman law as recorded by Hägerström and Luntsted (in: "Die Sociale Frage als Rechtsfrage" 1/12 von H.G. Schwep- penhäuser [*The Social Question as a Question of Justice*]). A total reversal has taken place in the course of the development of human society. Roman law rendered the debtor unfree. He was completely in the power of the creditor and became his property as a pure object if he did not pay on time. If there were a number of creditors, it was permitted to literally tear him to pieces. Based on the realization of the truth (as in the text [transl. note]), modern consciousness of justice takes the role of debtor upon itself and thus achieves freedom.

[11] In A Konnen's "Denken over encyclopedie" (*Thinking over Encyclopedias*) Deventer 1975, p. 13, a new criterion surfaces: tenable over untenable. If one finds the definition of "tenable" more in the elasticity of the quantity (how much old-age pension, how many concessions may I make), then the "not tenable" has a qualitative measure. A law or a regulation that harms the dignity of a human being is inadmissible. The line separating right from wrong is razor sharp in such a case. For example, it is acceptable if, in consultation with colleagues, I omit certain contents from a lecture, even if I find them to be essential. It is unjustifiable if the same omission is made a condition or demanded by law or from a majority.

[12] One needs to bear in mind that Koch calls the law justice (right). This forced him to find another name for what here is called justice or right. By the way, many terms and shades of meaning exist for this. For example, Radbruch indicated what we call justice (right) with "Rechtsidee" (idea of right or justice). Extemporizing Goethe, this would be an idea that one could actually experience in society.

[13] It is remarkable that these values lose their individual qualities under these conditions. Forced tolerance, forced labor to fill the needs of others (taxes) are no longer social acts. At the same time coercion partially excuses asocial and antisocial deeds ("an order is an order"). I cannot agree with Koch's understanding that man's will to power flows into a specific form of the totalitarian state, the gray totalitarianism. Power is no more than an instrument that one can use toward the realization of one's (possibly pathological) will for self-preservation or one's fanaticism in whatever totalitarian tendencies. We shall encounter the essence of gray totalitarianism later as an offshoot of the state but precisely not of human passions.

[14] In *Spiritual Science and the Social Question* (GA 34/1960/191) Koch expresses the same thought from the economic point of view . "Wherever my work and my diligence are inseparable from other people's performance, their fruits are also inseparable." My portion of the yield can no longer be determined from a purely economical point of view. From a point of view of justice, it should not be separated.

[15] The Laws of Moses and the commandments may be an exception to this. Yet a forty-year-long excursion through the desert indeed demands adherence to them. One finds an interesting confirmation of this point wherever imperialism imposed laws for its own purposes but, exclusively for the natives, left the still well-entrenched native customs alone.

[16] This seems to be a bold statement in the face of the boast of our modern welfare state to have a social character. In reality our modern legislative practices are aimed at replacing personal behavior with automatic reactions. The latter kill any social activity on the part of the citizen, as well as the ability to make social judgments of those who carry out the laws.

[17] This seems to be a daring statement since our modern welfare state prides itself in its social character. In reality the whole striving of our modern social legislation aims at replacing personal social behavior with automatic procedures. These procedures on the one hand kill any social activity of individual citizens while on the other hand they also kill the social judgment of those who apply these laws.

[18] I speak of slave labor, even if the worker is being well paid. He is being exploited as long as society in reality excludes him from participation in the life of rights and spirit and as long as his position is reduced to "bread and spectacles (panis and circenses, the Latin for the ancient Roman custom of anestethizing the "proles," i.e. the commoners from such participation).

[19] GA 196/1966/133. The reason why Steiner uses the term "bolshevism" may be that in 1919 bolshevism was the only societal structure that already contained the germ of bureaucratic totalitarianism. At that time that was visible for only a few people. In the same way only few people understand in our time that bolshevism does not merely live behind the iron curtain but in our very midst.

[20] Money, i.e. the right of control over goods and work, has "eternal" validity within our present structure of society. The goods it controls spoil with time. This fact bestows institutionalized power on those with money. From a social point of view this is an injustice.

[21] What takes place here is impressively described by J.J. Loeff in his final speech "Het recht is der hoeder van de Ander" (Deventer 1973). I translate an excerpt: " The appearance of another's countenance subjects us to a judgment. Before we have become guilty by word or deed, we are accused and declared as unjust . . . the encounter is an act of teaching, emanating from the other. He teaches me; he is my master. Nothing about the other needs to be confirmed or negated. If one thinks that one can afford to do that, he becomes merely different. This is why the encounter with the other person is an experience in eternity . . . The other's naked countenance shows us, as it appears, not only the person who appears but every other human being as well. The other as HE commands in the name of all human beings who are in the same situation or could be in that situation.

Chapter II
Basic Elements of Social Activity

The basic sociological law

Of the four principles that weave throughout the social fabric, the one that Steiner described first and foremost, the basic sociological law, has been practically forgotten. This law can be found in two articles. Schweppenhäuser deserves the credit for pointing them out.[1] This law says: "At the beginning of cultural conditions mankind works toward the creation of social associations. At first the interest of the individual is being sacrificed in favor of these formations. Ongoing development leads to free the individual from the interests of these formations toward freely unfolding the needs and powers of each person." (Collected essays on culture and history, GA 31/ 1966/ 247 ff.)

We shall discuss the significance of this law in great detail in the next chapter, but some explanatory comments seem appropriate here as part of an overview.

Steiner speaks of a law. This implies that, just like the second law, the principal social law, this law has the same exclusive validity as a natural law. For the principal social law he stated this emphatically. Of course, one could object to this because our time certainly gives the impression of an increasing subjugation of the individual to the interests of the state when compared to the very liberal 20s of this century. We will examine the cause for this in some detail. Here we only wish to point out that we are dealing with a law of evolution, something that historically unfolds with time. Yet developments never proceed in a straight line; leaps forward give way to times of rest or even of regression. The evolution we are discussing covers millennia. As indicated by Steiner's formulation of the law, it dates back to the beginning of cultural conditions. We may assume this to be deep in the middle Atlantean period.[2] Although the end of this development is not mentioned, it is evident from further discussions that it lies in the far distant future. A few decades of regression have little significance within this framework.

What is the goal of this evolution? Only if we know the beginning and the end can we discover our current stage—and the direction in which we must work to avoid bucking the stream of history. Work on social questions must take the historic moment of our time into account if it is to be positive and sensible.

Finally, let us refer to the term "association." Further along the essay in question Steiner uses the development of states as an example, which is understandable because these essays are directed against Ludwig Stein's theory of the state. Yet the term "association" indicates every organized cooperation between human beings. The term "sociological" law also points to this. Sociology refers to relationships between groups in a general way. Thus, we shall have to look for the effects of this law on three levels, namely the macro, meso and micro levels.

The principal social law

The second law is the principal social law which is much better known. It is taken from the essays that appeared in Lucifer Gnosis in 1905/1906 under the title of "Theosophy and the Social Question" and reads as follows: "The less each person makes claim to the yield of his efforts, the greater the well being of a community of human beings who work together. This is to say that each one should give as much as possible of this yield to the others, and his own needs should be satisfied as much as possible from the efforts of the others."[3]

In contrast to the basic sociological law, which postulates constant change as time proceeds, we deal here with a static phenomenon, i.e., with a law of relation: the greater—the less. Hence, the sum of the yield can be larger or smaller, depending on the degree to which people work toward fulfilling their own needs.

This law has already attracted widespread attention and has led to practical ways of living together. Think only of the Camphill Movement or the living communities in Bochum, Germany, created with the help of the GLS Bank. For this very reason there is no lack of contradictive interpretations. It still remains for us to address these. We have to face another problem in the question of how it could come about that our unprecedented prosperity could be achieved in a society with a basic structure based entirely on the self-interest of the working people in contradiction to the principal social law.

In Steiner's formulation of the law we find nothing that confines its applicability to the macro sphere. Rather, it simply originates from people who actually work together. This is why we shall have to examine it on each of the three levels. We need to point out that this law does not imply any moral imperative just because it deals with human egoism. In the social life the law shows its results depending on how people organize their activities. An attainment of specific knowledge and work are needed to produce something in the economic life and both are free of the imperative "thou must." In the same way, an increase in the "well-being" of a group who works together depends on everyone's sharing spirit. However, one may not desire this increase or one may consider the result too trivial for the required effort. In this case one must be content with less "well-being."

The archetypal social phenomenon

The third element basic to social activity is very different. One can call it a law only from a specific point of view. It is a phenomenon. Steiner describes it a number of times but only once sketched it out with the concept as "archetypal social phenomenon"[4] in *Basic Social Demand of Our Time* (GA 186/1963/175). This assigns it to its central position in anthroposophical social science. "If one human being faces another, then one person is always trying to put the other one to sleep and the other one is constantly trying to stay awake. Yet, to speak in Goethe's sense, this is the archetypal phenomenon of social science."

One begins to feel the significance of this sentence if one reads it in conjunction with the social and antisocial drives, the main theme of the mentioned lecture. It really is possible to understand the other person only if one is "social" to the degree that one allows oneself to be put to sleep by him. Yet our antisocial drives will not permit this; they want to make us "put the other person to sleep." In our time the antisocial drive presents itself automatically. In contrast, the social drive—to provide the opportunity for the other person to be resurrected in our soul—is something that "needs to be consciously nurtured."

On one hand, this description points to the basis of social science: How can one understand a fellow human being at all? This problem creates the greatest difficulties in the theory of cognition and points to the first appendix of the *Philosophy of Freedom* (GA 4), which was published with the 1918 edition but in germinal form may also be found in the last paragraphs of the chapter "Individuality and Genus." On the other hand, this description provides access to the ethical source of all social questions. In our age, social action must truly be willed if it is to exist at all. We shall see that in such action the earthly workings of man's true spiritual essence finds expression. We are free to make the earth the civitas Dei (God's State) or the civitas diaboli (the Devil's State).

The combination of these two aspects—the cognitional and the volitional—leads to a true social science. Such a science encompasses a humanity which begins to be conscious of the ego in the social process, i.e. in willing to become social. This process of becoming an ego works within on all three levels. Like the archetypal plant and the archetypal animal for biology, the architypal social phenomenon becomes a benchmark and an organ for practical and theoretical activity in the social area.

The Threefold Social Order

Finally, we encounter the last basic social element, the threefold order. With a choice of words typical for him, Steiner has never called it a law. Again and again he pointed out that, unlike utopias, the threefold order is by no means a thing of eternity, only the key to the social question for a few centuries. "Now the demands of time have made the threefold order necessary. And again there will come a time when the threefold order must be overcome. But this is not our present time, it is the time three to four centuries from now. At that time one will have to think of how to replace it." (GA 192/1964/388). The threefold order, that is, an autonomous formation of the life of the spirit, the life of rights and the life of the economy, is in fact no independent principle. It is the principle that results when the person who wants to be social (archetypal social phenomenon) and the present relationships between work for the community and work for personal gain (principal social law) come into confrontation with each other (basic sociological law).

This shows that the threefold order does not carry any value in itself, no more than the dike that keeps the overflowing water from the land. Social initiative, the liberation of the individual, the increase in well-being, all represent values. True, the threefold order will always serve these values, but the way it is worked out will depend on the development of the group and the social capabilities of its members. Different solutions are even conceivable in identical situations. This explains why Steiner often seems to have made contradictory suggestions from one day to the next when practically engaged in social work in 1919/1920, but it also explains why he reproached his followers for taking "the illustration of the main topic for the main topic itself."[5] Hardly one of Steiner's many examples can be used as generalizations without becoming dogmatic.[6] Thus, the "Kernpunkte der Sozialen Frage" ("the Threefold Commonwealth")(GA 23) as well as the "Philosophie der Freiheit" ("the Philosophy of Freedom") are not teaching texts but exercises, the former for thinking and the latter, as we shall demonstrate, for social hygiene.[7]

Here we encounter a deep-seated problem of cognitive theory. We cannot deal with it in this context, but it should at least be identified. Based on the anthroposophical path to knowledge in general, and the "Philosophy of Freedom" in particular we proceed along strictly natural scientific lines. In the social area one can find numerous writings that "solve" social problems with cognitional thinking. These studies either satisfy only those who like to follow such trains of thought, or one finds recourse in them because one cannot come to terms with the social problems. They are almost useless for social action. One can go one step further and turn to abstractions that make much of the literature about the threefold order so boring. The statements are not wrong; they only have no connection to reality. Such discourse often ends with a sigh to the effect that (human) reality is not yet ready for the ingenious idea of threefoldness. Tragically, the end result is often nearly identical to conventional wisdom, only with a different prefix.

Social science is basically different from natural science because here man is not spectator, not observer, but "in the test tube" with the process to be studied. "Political economics are distinguished by the fact that we ourselves are in their middle.

Therefore, we must look at them from within. We have to feel ourselves within the political economic process like, perhaps, a being—so to say—in a test tube. Here something is being brewed over heat. This imaginary being in the test tube cannot be the analytical chemist, this being—I want to compare it to ourselves—would have to share in the experience of heat, it has to cook along itself. The analytical chemist cannot do this—to him it is an external event. "In natural science we stand outside the processes. No analytical chemist can experience it if the temperature rises to 150 degrees C. We must participate in the economic process with our inner being, and we must understand it within us as well" (GA 340/1933/52f). And on p. 14: "We have to drop the habit of constructing concepts that cannot be defined."

Here Steiner deals with the method applicable to the economic sciences ("merely" a matter of a metamorphosis of thinking). It applies in even greater measure to research of the social aspects of the life of rights and of the life of the spirit. "We destroy the social order if we try to intersperse it with the results of our intellect. Everything wherein thoughts must be active is dependent on this intellect, on the intellect arising out of chaos. Yet we must not use what emanates from chaos for social reform . . . we need these forces for our spiritual life, our free spiritual life. But these forces are useless if they join with the forces active in the social sphere. In this area the intelligence, useful and creative in the narrower life of the spirit, is harmful" (GA 199/1967/184). And Steiner clarifies these two aspects further: "Thinking socially is different than thinking out of the spirit. With the spirit all depends on the development of the individuality."

The path to knowledge of social matters goes through the encounter with the fellow human being, through the archetypal social phenomenon. There is no other way. True, social science is not founded on what I work out for myself, but on what the other person reveals to me. I will deal with this aphorism in detail when we discuss the archetypal social phenomenon.

It now becomes more apparent why Steiner's followers took the illustration for the essence. He enlarges on this in the already quoted lecture of March 9, 1922. Because this lecture is so difficult to obtain—volume GA 81, which will include it, has not yet appeared in print—I would like to cite it in more detail:

"This is the reason why, in what I had to explain, I held back with any utopian idea, refrained to state in any way what form capital or labor or anything of this sort should acquire. At most I presented a few examples of how one could think of a way that these things may be shaped in transition from the present conditions toward a near future. All this was merely stated as an illustration of how conditions should evolve. This evolution could happen in a manner similar to what I presented, when discussing the transformation of the forces working within capital in my 'Kernpunkte' (*The Social Commonwealth*), but it could just as well happen in some modified form. It was not my aim to paint an abstract futuristic picture but rather to articulate on what basis one could realistically come to a solution of the social question, a solution that is not based on a theoretical construction. It was not a matter of saying that this or that is a solution of the social question. I have indeed too much experience to try this sort of 'solution.' Hence, this was not what it was about, and the greatest misunderstanding that I encountered is that it was this sort of thing."

"I wanted to demonstrate that the solution of the social problem can only take place in a real way by itself—in no way can it be found by discussion, only by events, by action. Conditions for such action must first be established and I have tried to point to these conditions in my 'Kernpunkte' and other discussions."

"In this sense my book was an appeal finally to give up fruitless talk about the social question and to assume a standpoint whence one can take the solution in hand on a day by day basis. It was a call to those who kow how to transform abstract thoughts into action penetrated by thought."

"Above all people had the strong urge to have discussions about what I then wanted to found and am now attempting to put before you with these introductory words. The world was so strongly trained in abstract thinking with the result that one took this initiative from the point of view of abstract thinking alone, and one used what I used as mere illustration primarily for hour-long drawn out discussions. Yet it should really be a matter of understanding how the structuring of the social organism could daily be addressed in the manner indicated in the 'Kernpunkten.' Today it is not a matter of looking for theoretical solutions of the social question but rather to seek the conditions under which humans can live in a social manner. And they will live like that as soon as the social organism works in accordance with its three members, just like the natural organism works under the influence of its relative threefold order toward unity.

"Nowadays one must first explain how such things are meant. Even if one puts this into words people still demand to interpret whatever words one uses (after all one needs to use words) according to the intellectualisitc meaning given them in our time. That which is expressly not immersed in intellectualism is immediately translated into each one's intellectualism. Where my book discusses capital, natural resources for production and labor, a language is chosen which shows that the ideas are simply gleaned for life. In abstract discussions we can define things at length. This has actually happened. One party may say that capital is crystallized labor, labor that is stored up just as well as to say that capital is labor that has been saved. If one stops within intellectualism, one can do this with all national economic concepts. Yet these all are things we deal with not simply in theory, but issues we need to grasp in their living manifestation."

"An attempt has been made to arrive not at social ideas but at social impulses based on Anthroposophy. This is no superficial matter. I still remember the time when there was much discussion about this. I had to reiterate: I mean social impulses! People got very angry at this. Of course, I should have said social ideas or social thoughts. All these people had in their heads for such things were thoughts. They were terribly upset to hear me speak of impulses because they did not notice that I needed impulses because I meant realities and not abstract ideas. Of course one has to express oneself in abstract ideas."[8]

Steiner often speaks about the necessity to allow "social ideas" to flow into society from beyond the threshold, that is, out of spiritual science. This confronts us with the question of how this matches the above quotes. It would be an oversimplification to limit such ideas to ones of reason alone and to declare as applicable ideas stemming from Steiner's theory of knowledge. In this case all fits nicely with what one has always thought before, only one misses the essence of the matter.

We need to bear in mind that everything taken from spiritual science must be translated into thoughts and ideas to make it accessible to noninitiates. These ideas are a means of communication, and Steiner has articulated many such ideas, among them the four elements treated here. As such they are material for meditation.

It is another question whether we make progress in social work if we apply these ideas to practical questions. It is my opinion that the above quotations answer this question negatively. Certainly one can spread the "idea" of the principal social law. Yet if a solution has to have social validity, we must experience it as coming from fellow humans. The solution originates from our ability to handle the archetypal social phenomenon consciously. A solution purely based on an idea is always asocial. This is almost a matter of course. Spiritual life on earth is asocial. Its final permeation with the Christ being takes place through the social impulse as it lives in the archetypal social phenomenon. We like to be active within the spiritual life on earth and feel comfortable in the self-consciousness bestowed on us by dealing with our ideas. This is why Steiner's vehemence that the threefold order is an impulse and not an idea hurts us so much.

Here we begin to approach the problem that has divided the friends of the threefold order for many years. As soon as threefoldness is a law, it becomes impossible to be its spokesman any more than the spokesman for, say, gravity. Gravity is simply a fact, and the only thing that makes sense is to discover it and to point to its useful applications. Instead, we encounter people who are content to enlighten others and others who wish to "introduce" the threefold order (whatever this may mean). The former tend to dismiss the latter. If in contrast the threefold order is an impulse, a desirable alternative form of society, then it is necessary to stand up for it and to make it a reality wherever possible.

The detailed discussion of the principle of the threefold order will show that the question of its applicability has accidentally resulted in such contradicting points of view. A deeper understanding of the three elements is necessary to understand this.

Before we address these three elements, we need to revisit the question of the three levels. Proper understanding of the micro, meso, and macro level has confused and divided the threefold brotherhood. In this respect Kloss talks about functional and institutional (I think it is better to call it categorizing) threefoldness.[9] The former looks for the principle in the meso and micro sphere, and the latter points to Steiner's applying the concept of the threefold to all of society and so decisively dismissing its use in the meso sphere.

As in most quarrels, both parties are right. No proponent of the threefold order will deny that it has been gleaned from the essence of the human being. It follows that, because this essence is carried into every situation, the human being brings the threefold order with him as well. Looked at from this angle, there is no reason to look at the threefold order as an exclusively macro problem.

Anticipating later discussions, let us introduce them by saying that complete threefoldness is impossible in the meso sphere, that is on the institutional level. No doubt there is a life of the spirit in a textile factory—most visibly in the design of new patterns but also in every capability that is brought to bear, starting with tending to the machine all the way to coordinating the different production processes. Yet this spiritual activity has no real autonomy but has to be subservient to the end product. Inversely, the managers of a school have to bow to its spiritual goals. How and when their independence can be guaranteed, therefore, cannot be considered a matter of threefoldness. Autonomy of the three elements makes no sense in the meso sphere. The same is true of the micro sphere. No human being can divide itself into elements, but he can differentiate and behave in ways perhaps analogous to macro threefoldness. Thus, one may compare the prevailing problems on this level to the threefold order in the larger sense. We shall return to these questions.

Steiner's sociological writings present same problems. We can, in fact, find hardly a hint that threefoldness encompasses more than the macro sphere, that is, the entire social organism. He even reacted somewhat annoyed to the thought of introducing the threefold order to the Anthroposophical Society.[10] In contrast, he answered a question on this subject during the founding of the Christian Community: "In your community you have no need to theorize about the threefold order, you can bring it about."[11] All this makes me feel that it is senseless to quarrel about the term "threefold order." We have to note that social problems appear on the meso and micro level in the same way as on the macro level. The following chapters will show that these problems and their resolutions show up as well on the macro level, although their differences must be kept in mind.

A handicapped human being remains a human being, even if his legs are replaced by prostheses. In the same way problems on all three levels remain threefold, even if circumstances demand that certain functions have to be taken over by "social prostheses." Of course, special knowledge is needed to produce prosthetic limbs, and one must, of course, also expect that the "good will" of "decent people" alone is insufficient for "social prosthetic appliances." These questions will be our principal focus in the second half of this work.

Endnotes:

[1] Hans Georg Schweppenhäuser "Der sociale Auftrag der Anthroposophie und die sociale Verantwortung des Anthroposophen" (*The Social Task of Anthroposophy and the Social Responsibility of Anthroposophists*), Freiburg 1972 p. 38ff. He may have indicated this law earlier in his "Erfahrungen aus der Sozialwissenschaftlichen Arbeit ("Experiences in the Social-Scientific Field)" Berlin, p. 12.

[2] The statements in "Aus der Akasha—Chronik" ("From the Akashik Chronicle") (GA 11/15.—o.J./14ff.) indicate that the first formations of societies date to the second Atlantean period, whereas in the third the first states were formed.

[3] (GA 34/1960/213) also in different special editions under the title "Geisteswwissensschaft und die Soziale Frage" (*Spiritual Science and the Social Question*). By the way, the principal thought may also be found earlier in "Einleitungen zu Goethes Naturwissenschaftlichen Schriften" (*Introduction to Goethes's Natural Scientific Works*). (Pocketbook edition '62, p. 91)

[4] I encountered the term "Sociales Urphenomen" ("Archetypal Social Phenomenon") in the lecture of September 3, 1922, published in the "Blätter für Anthroposophie (Papers on Anthroposophy)," 1962/4. Steiner uses it in an illustrative manner, and the context makes it clear that this has no connection with the meaning alluded to here. In the sense of this lecture one could replace it with "Social Symptoms." This meaning would be impossible in a previous lecture of 1918.

[5] (GA 83/1950/203) and the earlier quotation from the lecture of March 9. 1922. Also see (GA 198/1946/14), that perhaps "not a stone will remain on top of the other" of all that has been said of the threefold order, but that "everything will take a different form."

[6] The "National Ökonomischer Kurs (the National Economic Seminar)" (GA 340) seems to be an exception, because it does not belong strictly speaking to the literature on the threefold order. It belongs to scientific seminars, because it deals with a socio-political (perhaps a practical social) theme.

[7] It is mandatory to examine the ideas of H.G. Schweppenhäuser to some extent when one gives an overview of the four elements of the social impulse. In his beautiful booklet "Der soziale Auftrag der Anthroposophie und die Soziale Verantwortung des Anthroposophen" (*The Social Mission of Anthroposophy and the Social Responsibility of the Anthroposophist*, Freiburg 1972) he in fact speaks of four laws. Three of these agree with the ones mentioned here: the basic sociological law, the principal social law and the threefold order. He calls the latter a "temporal law," not in the sense of the word but as treated here. But in place of the archetypal social phenomenon, there appears a law of social causality. He claims to have found this in a lecture of August 1922 in Oxford ("der Mensch in der Sozialen Ordnung" (Man in the Social Order"), Dornach 1979. Here Steiner deals with the question whether man is the product of social conditions or whether the social conditions are what man has made them. Steiner calls this a senseless question, because in the social field "one can make progress only if one thinks in spirals." Try as I will I cannot see a law in this—and Steiner does not call it one, but calls it an important methodological pointer connected with Steiner's remark about the test tube, which is yet to be discussed. On page 48 "If Schweppenhäuser means that in the social law of causality one can recognize the latitude for spiritual productivity of individuals which alone can overcome the social scientific agnosticism and the social fatalism," then I agree with him from a methodological point of view, that is, as far as the scientific treatment of social questions goes. For practical social work the latitude

for spiritual work must be given a very different reason as we shall see.

[8] I would like to translate a few sentences of A.H. Bos on this subject. These are taken from an article he wrote for the December 1982 issue of "Modelingen van de Anthroposofische Verenigung in Nederland." "The student of spiritual science can think about his idealistic images of the social organism, of the way that everything in the life of the spirit, the life of rights and the life of the economy should be arranged and of the relationship between these domains. Thoughts like these have a strong formative and organizing force. Yet, in spite of this, if one applies this force in the social sphere, it has dreadful and destructive results. Rudolf Steiner called Fichte a bolshevist, the same Fichte then also the philosopher of the ego, the man about whom he otherwise spoke with the greatest enthusiasm. These statements contain no contradiction. Fichte attempted to create social form, based on pure thinking and to impress them on reality. This leads to asocial and antisocial conditions. Social forms capable of being used by the community cannot be found by the personal thinking of the individual."

[9] Kloss "Vom Grenzverlauf zwischen Gliedern des sozialen Organismus" ("On marginal areas of the social organism") in "Beiträge zur Dreigliederung des sozialen Organismus (*Contributions to the Threefold Social Organism*), October 1975.

[10] GA 190/1971/210f and GA 192/1964/143. These passages show that Steiner particularly rejected exclusive forms when "one can be far removed from that which can be meant with real social thoughts."

[11] Also Heinrich Ogilvie in Info 3 /1981/7 as well as "Triune Social Research" III/3 with no source given: in response to the scruples of a Waldorf teacher whether the threefold order did not overreach, Steiner supposedly answered: "Tomorrow is too late, you must begin tonight" (in English). This can hardly refer to macro-threefoldness. Further, GA 332a/ 1950/114: it is "really possible to start at any point in life ... with this threefold order, as long as one has the will, if only one really understands what it means."

Chapter III

The Basic Sociological Law

At the beginning of cultural conditions mankind strives toward the creation of social associations. The interests of the individual are sacrificed to the interests of these associations. Further development leads to the liberation of the individual from the interests of the associations and to the free unfolding of the needs and powers of each person.
— *Rudolf Steiner*

These three sentences describe the essence of the most important chapter of the earthly development of humanity. Steiner describes how humanity was led by spiritual powers in pre-Christian times, how it gradually outgrew this form of leadership, and how a new impulse was bestowed upon the earth with the mystery of Golgotha. This impulse enabled the human being to gradually re-establish the connection with the spiritual world and regain his place in the spiritual order as an ego-being. Related literature describes this process as an individual one, that is, an event concerning the personal development of the individual person. When dealing with the basic Sociological law, however, Steiner emphasizes the social forms that go together with the development of an individual. In numerous passages he pointed out that an individual path to redemption is not impossible but is Luciferic and in the final analysis brings individual development to a premature conclusion. A survey of these passages makes it clear that working together in such social groups is a necessity for the future development of mankind. *It is therefore permissible to speak of a sociological complement to the description of individual development of consciousness.* The question has two components, namely, what social forms are created by the process of individuation, and, how can humanity create social structures that promote individuation in a timely manner, that is in accordance with the existing stage of development?

In both of his essays on the basic sociological law,[1] Steiner takes issue with Ludwig Stein's book *The Social Question in the Light of Philosophy*, Stuttgart, 1897, (Die soziale Frage im Lichte der Philosophie) wherein the author speaks in favor of subordinating the individual's interests to those of the state. Steiner explains the basic sociological law in regard to the development of the state: "Which form of state and society is the desirable one if all social development flows into a process of individuation?" His answer is not hard to find. A state and a society that regard themselves as ends in themselves must strive for domination of the individual regardless of how this domination is practiced, be it by totalitarian, constitutional or republican methods. As soon as the state ceases to regard itself as an end in itself but as a tool, it will cease its domination. It will constitute itself in such a way as to enable the individual to play the greatest possible role. The ideal of the state will be not to dominate, but to become a community wanting nothing for itself and everything for the individual.

The basic sociological law does not apply to any particular form of state. "If one understands the time we live in, one can well say that the most advanced people strive toward communities in which the individual's inner life is affected as little as possible by communal life. They are intended as means toward the development of the individual. Community consciousness vanishes. For example, the state should be constituted in such a way as to allow the unfolding of each individual's personality the greatest possible latitude."

I offer this quotation so we can avoid misunderstandings that would limit the broad significance of the basic sociological law. Yet if we wish to trace the validity of this law historically, we must follow the metamorphoses of state forms. Forms of community life in past times have been handed down to us only in very fragmentary form, as these forms were simply taken for granted in daily life. Even today it is greatly resented when sociology concerns itself with our daily, usually quite unconscious, habits. It is often distaste for the habits of other nations that impels us to take pen in hand. The numerous travel descriptions from the19th century are so biased that nobody notices how much sense a strange sounding phenomenon makes as part of the overall structure to which it belongs. Inversely, only a loving eye can confront a nation with its mirror image without the scandalous reaction that "this is how our enemies see us."[2]

It is regrettable that we have no history based on the basic sociological law. Although Hans Erhard Lauer's *History as Stepping Stones Toward Humanity*, Freiburg 1956, (Geschichte als Stufengang der Menschwerdung) provides an understanding of the liberation of man from the interests of the community, the basis here is the development of the individual, not the social conditions. Yet, if it does not find expression in a description of real historical events (at least in fragmented form) the basic sociological law remains a theory. Therefore, the historical layman can produce only a very rudimentary picture of this developmental aspect of society, convinced that it has the right slant, even if the details are fragmented. Since I am a layman, I write this description, as if it were.[3]

Former structures of community living are by no means clearly visible to us. In particular, regarding prehistoric cultures only hypotheses exist. Most lack convincing justification but rather they serve as proof of the Darwinistic orientation of their originators. (See GA 60/1959/372 ff.) For example, the domination of the prehistoric horde by the will of the strongest has never been substantiated even among the most primitive tribes. Not only does it appear that this has been interpreted into the tribal way of life but, if the practice ever existed, it was introduced by its "progressive" conquerors. Indications point more to a magical prehistoric time when co-existence was prescribed by taboos with variations in response to situations of the moment.[4] A leadership position may have been based not on physical strength, but rather on a greater capability of using talents hidden behind appearance (medicine man, shaman). This impulse toward shaping society can hardly be explained based on present-day documentation. Furthermore, it is questionable if Steiner looks at these societal forms as "cultural conditions" in the sense of the basic sociological law. After all, culture is the end result of the division of the original integral consciousness into that of the subject and that of the object and of man's creative power to transform the outer world into an expression of his inner world.

The oldest documented forms of community living are those of the delta-cultures. Yet even here the description of their highest flowering is lost in the realm of legends. During the times of the first written signs, pointing to a past "golden age," the structure of the community is expressed merely as a claim to a form but not an ideal. This form is known as theocracy. At the head of a community we find a personality, priest and king at the same time. This person does not derive his position from his own capabilities but is the tool of higher powers. As the lowest point of an inverted pyramid, this person receives the inspirations by which he/she is meant to fashion the people into an earthly pyramid. This then represents the mirror image of the spiritual pyramid (Fig. 1).

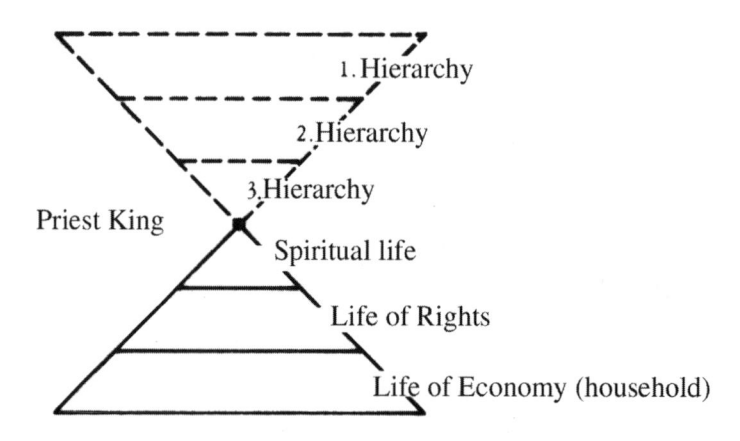

Fig. 1. Egypt: the theocracy on earth as mirror of the spiritual hierarchies

In the words Asia, Lowest Heaven and *Tenno*, Son of Heaven, (the term for the Japanese emperor) we find a last reflection of the dual pyramid. In those theocracies the spiritual life was understood as the expression of the third (the lowest) hierarchy, the life of rights as expression of the second, and earthly conditions, which we would call the economy in our times, as expression of the first hierarchy. The structure of the community was an expression of the higher laws because in this way one felt oneself to be the expression of the spiritual world. For this reason the population by and large conformed willingly to these structures. In the words of the Basic Sociological Law it sacrificed its own interest to the interest of the community.[5]

One may be inclined to consider this pyramid a wishful construction of history had not history presented us with a rather accurate example of this community structure. When the Spaniards under Pizarro conquered the empire of the Incas, there were scientists and priests among them. What the Spaniards found was so foreign to them, even the most mundane customs of daily living, that they found it worthwhile to record their observations. Louis Baudin collected their reports and published them in abbreviated form under the pregnant title *The Socialistic State of the Incas*. In light of Steiner's comments, as contained in our two essays, these seem of special significance. ". . . When all social democratic ideals are realized, all individualities will be suppressed."

The Inca empire has not, or if so only minimally, become a part in our cultural picture. Rather it had come to a halt. Perhaps it may not have been a pure theocracy; it is questionable to what degree the sources of inspiration were still flowing. Yet the social form clearly indicates theocracy. Land and humans were the property of the Inca who disposed of them, not according to his own judgment, but in conformance with the religious cult. Religious life permeated all communal order in a realistic and highly practical manner. Life of the spirit, which included what we would call handicrafts, was a cult; the life of rights served the cult, and the economic life (agriculture and cattle-breeding) made the cult possible. Thus, the entire life of society was dictated by the cult. Deviations, even mistakes and errors, were blasphemy and could be punished by death. Daily routine followed exactly prescribed forms. These could only be changed for pressing reasons via the hierarchy, e.g. in catastrophic emergencies.

The entire harvest belonged to the Inca. Roughly eighty percent of it was distributed. This part of it served to provide for those who worked in the sphere of the spirit, as workers in the building of temples, or spiritually, as priests. It also served social actions. Grain was rapidly distributed using wheelless conveyances to areas of famine over a system of roads. There were many such areas of repeated famine in this huge kingdom with its volcanic landscape. Only twenty-percent of the harvest was left for the local population, but not as private property. This harvest was stored for about twenty years because grain was only then considered ready for consumption. After this it was distributed. The monolithic states of our time are increasingly concerned with the problem of how one can gain control over the last remaining free area of the economy, namely the consumers' ingrained habits. The Incas existentially solved this problem in the above manner. Illegally acting individuals and those who produced for themselves were found out; all dwellings had to be wide open during meals so that the supervisors could detect any possible excesses of consumption.

The life of rights also served the common good and not that of individual subjects. Legal tenets with high moral requirements prevailed. Stealing was most severely punished, but if somebody stole because he was hungry, not that person but the next higher one in the hierarchy was punished, as the latter should never have allowed the suffering. Marriages were not private matters but a concern of the community. The philosopher David Juscamaita reports that in Peru even today the following procedure is used. Young people who want to get married are assigned an apartment and a piece of land. They are allowed to live together and to work for one year. After this period of time, the community decides whether the marriage is a positive element within the community. Only then is the couple allowed to marry and continue to use the apartment and land.

Documents from ancient Egypt complete this picture. The entire yield of the harvest belonged to the pharaoh who gave part of it to the area administrators for distribution. Legions of supervisors descended at harvest time to collect and count the prescribed number of sacks of grain from each acre of land. Goods brought in from abroad by traders belonged to the pharaoh, who took part of these for himself and left the remainder to the traders.

In addition to the land and goods, the lives of his subjects belonged to the ruler as well. There are reports from ancient times of the custom to exterminate a vanquished people who were of no use to the league. When the individual was only a member of the whole, only a tool to accomplish the ends of the theocrats, the human beings were totally programmed, to use a contemporary expression. (See also GA 102/1974/114.) Nowadays we have discovered what an effort is needed to free a brainwashed person from his programmed reactions. It may have been a completely impossible task to reprogram a whole people to fit into the victor's principle of order. It is easy to imagine the depth to which a person's etheric organization is affected by the theocratic organization if one thinks of the wanderings of the Jewish peoples in the desert. For generations this tribe had been adapted to the Egyptian theocracy. It took forty years to rid themselves of this program and turn to their own task.

We find a final echo of this old theocratic situation when Genghis Khan seriously considered the extermination of the many millions of Chinese after the subjugation of China. The reason: they were unfit for saddle and war. He was two thousand years behind his times. King Kyros (sixth century BC.) is famous for his great goodness because he did not exterminate the army he had vanquished but merely partially mutilated its warriors. According to Peter Bamm, Kyros was the world's first ruler to practice religious tolerance.[6] At this point the human being starts to have significance as an individual self, not just as a member of a people. With the end of the Egyptian period the time of justified theocracies is over. The eighth century BC marks the transition to new values with the founding of Rome.

We are able to observe an evolutionary process even during the Egyptian period. The life of the spirit is granted a degree of freedom, a space wherein the thinker is no longer the total pawn of the common interest as a matter of course. The theocratic ruler surrounds himself with councilors who gradually gain a certain degree of independence. (Think of the position Joseph had with the pharaoh.) This is symbolized by the move of the pharaoh's residence from Memphis to Thebes and by the fact that instead of the one palace for the priest king, two are built, one for the high priests, another for the pharaoh. Worldly and cultic matters start to be separated.

This structure came to its flowering later in Greece. After the birth of philosophy (Thales), independent thinking developed, and the life of the spirit gradually assumed its rightful place. Steiner writes (GA 18/1924/ part 1. p. 24): "Prior to this, (referring to the times before the Peloponesian wars), each individual was firmly locked into social connections. The community and tradition were the measures for his actions and thinking. The individual personality had meaning and significance only as a member of the whole. Under these circumstances the question of the value of the individual's worth was mute."[6]

Theocracy in the narrowest sense, i.e. the social structures wherein all life is ordered hierarchically, ends at that time. In this connection Steiner points to the appearance of "the kings by the grace of God," Solomon in particular (GA 93/1979/235).

Yet, considering the Greek city-states, very different from each other, one can speak more about a tendency rather than a full realization. In Athens the first free life of the spirit developed in the sense that the philosopher and the artist were no longer tools of the theocrat but were allowed to represent (or carve in marble) ideas that opened a multiplicity of possibilities. In contrast, in Sparta, the spiritual life remained a matter of the state determined by theocratic considerations, e.g. how many strings a musical instrument was to have.[7]

Councilors existed even before that time. Required to give advice within the societal model and from its perspective, their task was very different. Thus, they remained tools, and, if their counsel was bad, if it had unfortunate consequences, they lost their heads. In Athens the philosopher, scientist or artist was a free councilor, allowed to broadcast his ideas freely, as long as he carefully recognized the hierarchy in other areas. The legal relationships, and above all, the economy remained matters of the religious cult. They were rooted in the strictly hierarchically-ordered religious life. Those active in the spiritual life were able to enjoy certain freedoms. They individually headed a pyramid that had its assigned place within the social one. As masters of the house they were mini-theocrats, whose word was law and whose slaves cared for their daily needs. During a regressive phase of Athens, Socrates demonstrated with his death that, as he subjected himself to the theocratic laws, he was willing to die for the freedom of the spiritual life. The human being was gradually freed from the interests of the associations in one of the social areas (Fig. 2).

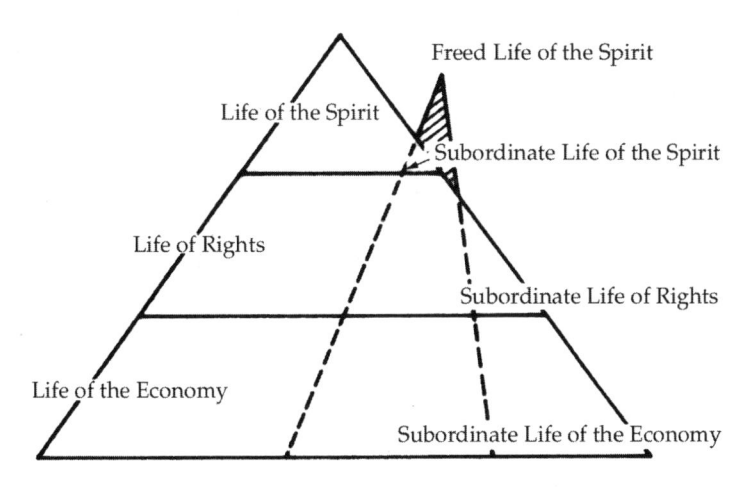

Fig. 2. Greece: the freed life of the spirit separates from society. At the apex of a domestic hierarchy and within the societal hierarchy, it dominates a subordinated life of the spirit. Example (domestic artists), a subordinated life of rights (administrators) and a subordinated life of the economy (slaves).

This freeing was accompanied by another phenomenon, which we shall encounter later on, namely the usurpation of the newly emancipated domain. It tends to spill over. We can read Plato's *Republic* with this in mind. He announces the goal to employ philosophers as (almighty) statesmen. In the spirit of those days we can understand the emancipation of the spiritual life only as though this spiritual life were supposed to take over the theocratic domination of the past.[8]

The challenge to sketch the typical structure of Greek society lies in the fact that the emancipation of the life of rights had already started during the so-called flowering of Greek culture. This happened in the same way as did the emancipation of those portions of the economic life which originated in the life of the spirit (crafts and free professions) or the life of rights (commerce). Thus, we have to go back to the so-called mythical times of Greece to a description of the epoch when spiritual life exclusively achieved a degree of independence.[9] Yet documentation of societal structure of those times is unreliable; as is so often the case, documentation only starts when decadence has already set in.

That segment of the population, active in the sphere of the life of the spirit, was emancipated from the sphere of the state in ancient Greece. At the same time we see how in the Roman Empire, after the reign of the kings, the rights of man (*jus*) took the place of the divine right (*fas*), but here, too, only for part of the population. The workers within the economy, the slaves and plebeians, remained firmly within the theocratic structure and had no rights of their own. Only at a later date were they represented (indirectly) by the people's tribune.

The emancipation from the community can be shown also in the development of personal rights. First, the right to property appears, in particular the right of ownership as an absolute right which grants the owner total power to dispose of his property for use or abuse. Within a narrow and personal framework, we may see this as a transfer of the divine-theocratic power to dispose over earth and man. The deification of the human being is still conceived after the theocratic model. In this respect there is a juridical controversy which continues to the present day. This involves the question of whether the right to property represents a relationship between owner and object (thus a religious question), or whether it constrains the right of disposition relative to other people. In this latter case it would be only here that the actual question of rights would arise. All our present property rights are still full of old magical and fetishistic qualities (because these are now outlived). "Is there still anyone in our time who feels that, if one speaks of 'people with possessions,' the word has a certain connection with being possessed!" (GA 190/1971/66)

The human being is emancipated through covenanted relationships of people to each other within the rights sphere of obligations.[10] If a person accepts obligations, he gives birth to rights in agreement with his fellow humans. This takes the form of regulations wherein both parties declare to be constrained and which they expect to have protected by the state, even if these regulations go against the interests of the state. Man has progressed to the stage of free responsibility; he now lives with self-generated rights and obligations.

During the Middle Ages in Europe, important traits were added to this emancipation. This was a time of rulers without a state. On the surface of history we experience how, in the battle between emperor and pope, the emporer usurps the right to nominate bishops, based on his "by the grace of God" status (battle over investiture). The pope bases the right to bestow royal crowns in representation of God. Both do this based on theocratic tradition. During this battle against the pope the emperor was increasingly estranged from the old Germanic principle of justice which recognized the emperor and other nobles merely as the first among equals (*primus inter pares*). The emperor himself assumed increasingly Cesarean/popish features. The novel principle by which the office of leader (*princeps*) is no longer determined by blood but rather by abilities was to fall into a long Sleeping Beauty sleep. The structures of society became totally polarized. One belonged to either one or the other pyramid (See Fig. 3).

Both theocracies lacked the substance which had formerly justified the hierarchy. The upper inverted pyramid was gone. Even when invoking Christ as the governor or rule by the grace of God, these merely served as legalistic justifications for worldly power. Under these circumstances the life of the spirit could identify with the theocracy; after all they both abused the life of rights in order to exploit the economic life. This prepared the way for a process of retardation described in the following discussions.

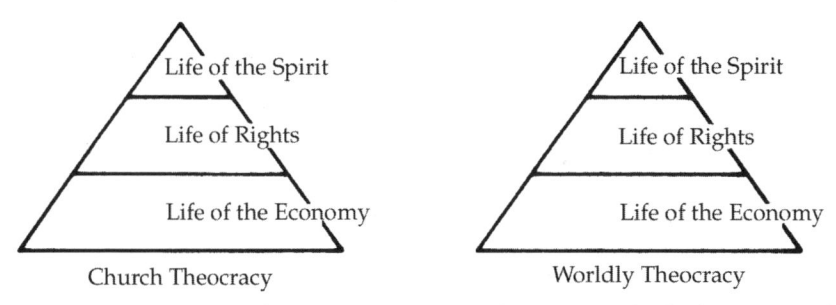

Fig. 3: Rome: the battle between emperor and pope created a dualistic societal structure. People were made to fit into a worldly and a church "theocracy."

Yet quite different things took place in the shadow of this battle. During the true Middle Ages, that is, prior to Roman law, a system of mutual dependencies had evolved from the Germanic concept of law. Although the population remained economically subordinated to the feudal lord, a new element, mutual obligations surfaced: the obligation of the population to provide natural products, that of the feudal lord not only to protect but also care for the well being of his subjects. At this time the Irish monks appeared all over Europe. They worked without any kind of power, purely by example. This complemented the emancipation of the life of the spirit based on the four old Greek tendencies. If one adds this to the picture, one gets an inkling of the trend of those times toward a life of rights which culminated in a great flowering (Fig. 4).

Around the year 1200, devastating regressions occurred and served to formulate our one-sided picture of the Middle Ages. When it came to emperors, consider the case of Frederick II. He re-introduced old, established oriental forms. And, as far as the church is concerned, consider the destruction of any form of tolerance, as evidenced, for instance, in the crusades against the Cathars *cuius regio eius religio* ("the ruler imposes the religion"), which dragged on up to the French Revolution.

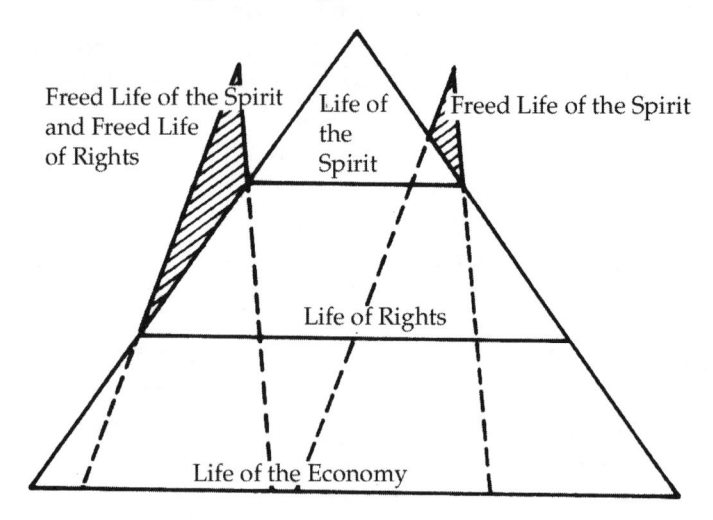

Fig. 4: The Middle Ages: the regulation of mutual rights and obligations enabled an emancipation of the life of rights and the life of the spirit.

These regressions were unable to prevent the process of emancipation. Starting during the flowering of the Middle Ages in Northern Italy, in the Languedoc, in Flanders and in certain German cities the liberation of the economy joined that of the spirit life, and rights life. Increasingly, more and more people no longer placed their talents at the disposal of the feudal lord, but established themselves independently. Sometimes they covenanted with lords of the world, sometimes with the lords of the church. If necessary they crawled in the dust, but after each massacre this movement resurrected itself. A new type was born, the economic human being, the entrepreneur. His existence was no longer dependent on the good will of his ruler but on his customers, on his ability to adapt himself to their needs, his expertise, his achievements and his feel for business. Soon he created his own organizations more or less after the model of the existing societal structure (guilds, Hanseatic union).

This quick description is not intended to supply a complete picture of social history over several thousand years. The intent is to describe the starting points toward social structures in the respective epochs as they were taken up by human evolution, refined and incorporated in the social life. If one omits much that is essential for a thorough consideration of history, one can call the social structure prior to the storming of the Bastille a *society with three estates.* To be sure it was crisscrossed everywhere by theocratically-oriented absolutism, yet three areas are clearly distinguishable:

1. A life of the spirit existed, consisting of learned clerics, artists, as well as free scientists. It was independent but not allowed to engage in matters of law or economic matters.

2. The nobility administered a life of rights. This had to take spiritual and economic matters as given facts.

3. An economy existed of citizens who were allowed to take part in the life of the spirit, as long as they acted as passive consumers and who were allowed to use the legal apparatus as long as they "knew their place," did not question the justice of the laws, did not rebel. They were not to be disturbed in their economic activities, except, of course, the usual bleeding by taxation. In this way each person was confined to his part of the whole, to his estate.[11]

Yet it is really incorrect to talk of the three estates because among these three layers there was a fourth one, expelled like the pariahs of India and, thus, as far as the others were concerned, no "estate" at all. These were the more or less enslaved peasants and agricultural workers, the servants and the proletarians. They had practically no rights at all and were unable to participate in the life of the spirit, even had they been admitted to it. This life of the spirit was hardly more than the ruins of Greek culture upon which it was based. Mainly from the standpoint of education the workers lacked this base.

At this point we can speak about a society with three estates in an ideal and typical model. The life of the spirit was the same for all (*cuius regio, eius religio* "who owns the kingdom, owns the religion"). People of other confessions were, at best, tolerated. Within its own organization the life of the spirit even had its own set of laws (e.g. church law, the courts of honor of free trades) and its own economy based faithfully on the model of the old theocratic principle. The area of law and state had acquired relatively total autonomy. The nobility no longer allowed the clerics to have any say regarding political aims, although the political structures continued to have largely theocratic characteristics. (The nobility usually dominated a large part of the economy through property ownership. In some cases, as in Great Britain and Scandinavia, they were already crisscrossed with democratic elements.) And finally the economy was more or less liberated from an overall social point of view, however theocratic its institutions may have been. This was true as long as the economy was not subject to clerical or feudal domination. (Fig. 5)

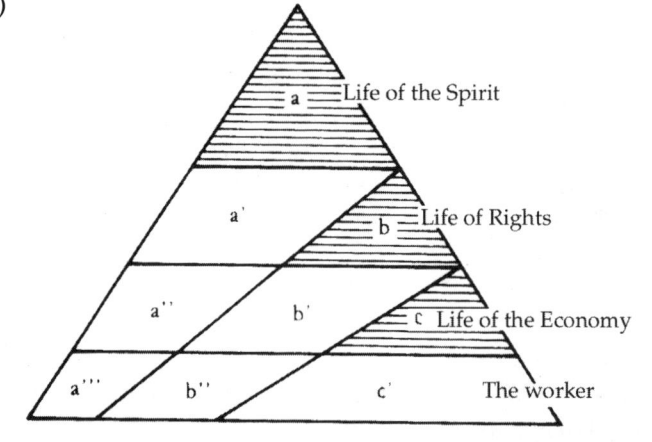

Fig. 5: The three estates: (crosshatched: free areas, white: theocratically dominated areas). The life of the economy is free only within the economy(c), but dominates the proletariat (c'). The life of rights is free within the law (b), yet it also dominates parts of the economic life (b') and workers (b"). The life of the spirit is free within itself (a) but dominates also parts of the life of rights (a'), of the economy (a") as well as the workers (a"').

In no way can one yet talk about a real threefold order, as rooted in historical evolution. The division in three parts here denotes the ideal-typical society of three estates where the three estates are quite autonomous and each person is held in his proper area (Fig. 6.).

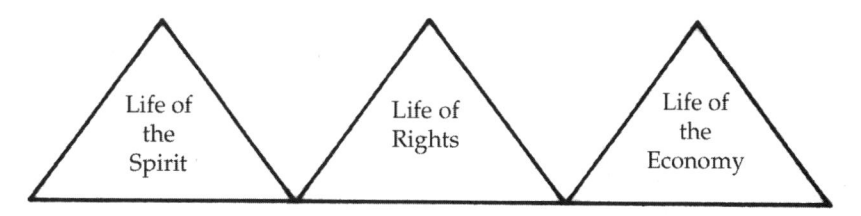

Fig. 6: The ideal model of a society with three estates

This society of three estates was in danger of collapsing, due not only to the autonomy of its parts but also to the striving for freedom of its citizens who were waking up to independence. It was being held together by the last remnants of theocracy. Its agents, being rulers "by the grace of god," claimed that they provided leadership in the areas that had become relatively independent and brought unity to what tried to move apart. Responsibility for all the people legitimitized inroads into the life of the spirit (censorship), the life of rights (outlawing societies), and the life of the economy (protective duties). This was possible as long as the disposition of the old theocratic soul was still present within the smallest social circles, that is, as long as any sense of being a subject still existed. When this was no longer the case, archaic sentiments were externally grafted onto the people (the principle of nationality, "blood and soil," and so forth) and reinforced with the concept of sovereignty.

When the French Revolution eliminated the last (huge) feudal structures, the three estates were set free of their immediate dependence on the interests of the community. Yet the last "estate," the proletariat, the original peasants and slaves, was only set free in theory. In reality it continued to be the base of the three pyramids as workers, house-servants for the city dwellers, lackeys for the nobility and servants of the academicians. Based on historic precedent one could expect that, like the three estates, it would make itself independent and create its own areas of activity. Yet what role in society remained for it?

Steiner explained in his work *The Threefold Commonwealth* (Die Kernpunkte der Socialen Frage) that, due to their origin, the proletarians had no access to the life of the spirit. The life of rights was fashioned for the interests of the ruling classes, and they had to sell themselves to the life of the economy with their labor. Consequently since they had no access to any of the social spheres, nothing tied them to the interests of these estates. To use a socialistic phrase, they had "nothing to lose except their chains." The proletarian was not bound either to the content or to the structure of the established order. He had nothing to offer except himself. Therefore one could look on him as predestined to play the role of one who places the human being at the pinnacle of the social structure in a mighty upheaval, no longer a slave to tradition in his own sphere or an immature dependent in both the others. Within such a structure each individual could freely make a contribution to all three spheres. Thus, these spheres would not make the human being into a functionary, a tool, a player of a "social role," but, inversely, human beings would shape these areas according to their individual potential. The self-conscious ego sends its personality to each one of the three spheres where it can participate as it sees fit (Fig. 7).

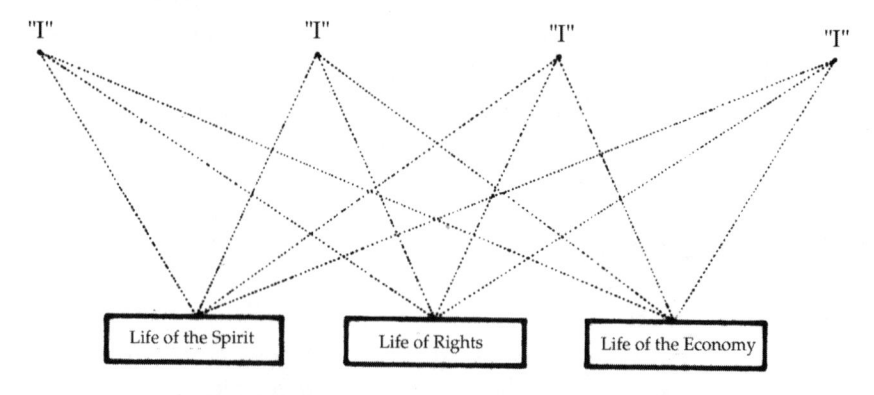

Fig. 7: The liberated human being. The self-conscious ego sends its personality to each one of the three spheres where it can participate as it sees fit.

On the eve of the French Revolution the threefold challenge flowed into this constellation (GA93/1979/280), namely the demand for Freedom, Equality, Brotherhood.[12] With hindsight we can recognize these ideals, when properly understood, as structural elements of a new form of society. After freeing him from the prison of his own particular sector, these ideals would have permitted man dominion over all three areas. Each person would be in a position to develop all the potential of his or her manifold capabilities in the different spheres, and everyone could learn to promote the development of one area without subjugating another. Thus, one would face the total change indicated in the article quoted by Steiner above. Having freed the individual from the interests of the associations, these interests now serve the development of the individual. Yet, before we can turn to this picture of the future, there are a few more aspects to consider.

We all know that the French Revolution failed to bring this turn-around. It wiped out the past without creating anything new. Of the three watchwords *freedom* and *brotherhood* were turned into political slogans, and *equality*, an ongoing struggle in our times, brought with it the *"machine d'égalité,"* the guillotine as a sinister omen. Helpless in the face of the revolutionary upheaval, one added the alternative *"ou la mort"* (or death,) to the threefold watchwords. As if it emanated from the depths of the people's instinct, the image of the totalitarian state emerges with its extinction of any sort of human development. The youngest son, the liberated life of the economy, was triumphant as in the fairy tale, yet unlike in the fairy tale, it ruthlessly tied the life of the spirit and of rights with its fetters. It proceeded to bring about a "radical extermination of all consciousness of the spiritual foundation of the social structure. . . ." (GA 184/1968/44).

In so doing it brought the state back on stage.[13] Starting with the assumption of corrective measures and proceeding to the establishment of competitive institutions all the way to today's monopoly covering almost all aspects of social life, the explosive development of the state represents a short circuit back to the oldest social form, theocracy. As citizens of the state the modern technocracy assigns our place as tools of the commonwealth in the same way as the former subjects. The former priest-king felt himself inspired by a spiritual pyramid, and, in the same way, today's technocrat thinks that he acts out of his own abilities, yet he merely obeys technical necessities—one thinks that one is pushing and one is being pushed. The theology without God was added seamlessly to a theocracy without God. In this process one imagines modern sociology as a complex of anonymous forces, more or less as did Karl Marx. "In no dimension does it take the human being as an individual but rather as a link in social development. How a person thinks, acts and feels is all taken as results of social forces by whose influence each one is being guided."[14]

The nationalization of society has quite often been described in all its horrible, implacable logic. Above all I would like to point to Jacques Ellul's work, "La technique ou l'enjeu du sciècle" (Paris 1954).[15] Technocracy, however, does not invalidate the basic sociological law. After all, the steamboiler does not invalidate the characteristic of water to expand when it turns to steam. We know that our state boilers are barely able to withstand the pressure of individualization. Here, too, it appears that the passing of a threshold is, like a sociogentic basic law, once again accompanied by theocratic forms.[16] For our purposes we can ignore the questions that arise from this. We shall also leave open the question of whether this theocratic nationalization of social conditions may be regarded as one of those setbacks, explained by Steiner as necessities in human history (GA36/1961/92) or, more probably, the deterioration "as a world kamaloka still below the Kali Yuga." Finally, Steiner's remarks about the goals of the anti-forces open a vista of very different perspectives: they are striving to prevent Christ's sacrifice from bearing fruit by furthering theocratic structures. (GA 184/1968/XV)

One may consider the following works a testament of the time prior to the darkening which started after the year 1800: Goethe's "Märchen" (Fairytale), for the entire social structure, Schiller's *Letters Regarding the Aesthetic Education of Mankind* (Briefe zur ästhetischen Erziehung des Menschen), for the life of the spirit, and Humboldt's *On the Limits of Effectiveness of the State* (Über die Grenzen der Wirksamkeit des Staates), for the life of rights. It was a bad omen that brotherhood in the economic sphere found no champion. When one finally appeared, his work "Das Kapital" (*Capital*)was not marked by the blessings but rather by the devastations which "free" economic life had brought about. These devastations caused the author, Karl Marx, to create a caricature.[17]

Up to now we have dealt with social structures on the macro level, that is, huge organizations wherein the individual remains anonymous. To my knowledge little that touches the sociological basic law is known about on the meso level, which deals with institutions. We know there were schools in ancient Greece, notably schools of philosophy. How may these have been organized? It is highly improbable that associations within the areas of the law or the economy existed. In ancient Rome, too, the different factions probably formed around influential or charismatic personalities rather than around institutions. We also know about the guilds of crafts people of the late Middle Ages with their strictly hierarchical but externally constrained conditions (guild regulations) and something regarding the early capitalistic textile industry. This is fragmented knowledge, and more importantly it fails to include what was then routinely understood. Yet just that interests us most. Instead of this road of inquiry we look in the opposite direction. We ask ourselves which meso social structures correspond to the macro structures as they succeeded one another. If we find these meso structures in our time, we can, somewhat cautiously, conclude that these were paramount in "their" time. All that once existed continues its life in one form or the other. As we experience the institutional forms around us, our understanding for historic forms keeps growing.

This part of our considerations cannot bother to address how appropriate for our time some contemporary formations are. We shall find out that every kind of structure may be justified from one point of view or another because the meso-structures are undergoing different phases of their respective development.[18] Here we are dealing exclusively with recognizing again what we have found on the macro level. We shall let the phenomena guide us in this and take particular care not to be guided by statutory or constitutional regulations. These may in fact be interesting as declared intentions of the founders or, as a necessary, albeit unpleasant, way of adapting to legal requirements. The reality of interplay in the institutional realm has, as a rule, little to do with these matters in the short term.[19]

The theocratic structures stand out most clearly. We encounter them in all realms of society. For example, we come to an automobile repair shop. Whether they can do anything for us, when and how the boss (or repair manager) decides. He is being called in when the problem is uncovered and then gives instructions. If he thinks that something better and faster can be done, he pushes the mechanics aside. One can see the structure even more clearly observing the employees. They ask for his decision at the least question. He is ever-present. Should two workers have a dispute, the affair is immediately settled as he firmly puts his foot down without bothering to hear the arguments of both protagonists. It is no different on the farm or in industry, even though in the latter areas much may appear muted due to laws and work protocol.

In the area of the law we have similar experiences. A local party conference[20] may be engaged in a heated discussion but, the moment a great personage enters one could hear a pin drop, and all eyes turn expectantly toward him. Anything discussed before this means merely that one side feels confirmed in its stance and the other gives in. There are always only two matters at stake, namely that theocrats exist in an institution (this in itself would present only a micro social, personal relation problem) and that these persons are acknowledged by a pyramid, be it a formal or an informal one. Added to this is a third aspect, at times more and at other times less important, that the superficial forms can further such a structure or make it possible/impossible. The best example of the first matter is the internal constitution of government agencies. The minister is formally responsible, down to the last employee of his ministry. His authority extends to his coworkers, be they appointed by him or by someone acting in his name, all the way to the base of the pyramid. This is macro-theocracy. Yet the effects of this carry over to the meso-sphere by way of the boards. For the functionary, every one of his decisions, however unavoidable it may be in a given situation, has its risks. If the superior fails to agree after the fact, the decision was wrong. If one does not want to burn one's fingers, then the reign of the mandarins is at hand. The bourgeois counterpart to this has exactly the same effect. It is the weekly coffee klatch at Dr. Liveright's wife's. She owes her title solely to her husband, but the authority to her own personality. She decides who is to talk with whom and about what, arranges friendships and breaks them up, sets tone and manners. Her small circle of so-called intimates broadcasts the intentions of the queen as a matter of course. The personal ideas of these intimates are of no consequence. For example, it is sufficient to whisper to a new member, "Frau Dr. does not like to see that."

Let us complement this example with one from the life of the spirit. The medical doctors with their therapeutic practices and the artists with their special schooling are not the only ones who rule over their specialties like priest-kings. The following picture of a school may elicit a "sounds familiar" from some of my readers. Just before the schoolday starts, two rows of grown-ups stand behind the door. Their conversations come to an abrupt halt. The expected authority enters. Now one request follows the other, as do the answers, in rapid succession. Concern after concern: an afternoon off, the drafting paper is used up, request for an advance in pay, a pain in the neck of a mother, may this or that society use the hall, may little Lizzie have time off from school to attend the wedding of a cousin and so on. By the way, here, too, the outstanding or domineering personality is not necessarily the rule of the day. It is rather a matter that he or she is acknowledged as such by all. That we are dealing with a charismatic person is recorded elsewhere (on the micro-social pages).

Incidentally, we should not recognize this theocratic structure only in its formal and informal variations. We find it disguised in democracy as well. Every reader knows of clubs whose presidents set agendas for the annual meetings to make decisions about the most important matters. Yet everything has really been decided well in advance. This is scantily hidden behind the standard question asked by the moderator, if anybody has any more questions regarding the matter on the table. It is hidden behind the chairman's astonished and defensive look when a question is of a critical nature and also behind the routine of asking who is against rather than who is for an issue.[21] The hand that goes up at this point most certainly belongs to a negativist.

These examples are real. They are described here in larger than life caricature as I felt it was more important to highlight typical embodiments of structures than to produce a picture of reality. In real life they appear only rarely. Either they are masked or mixed with other structural elements, either from conviction or because domineering persons make claim to authority. This in itself does not result in a theocratic structure, only in a sickly example of one. It happens when co-workers tolerate the behavior of the person in question because they do not want to rock the boat or because they are afraid of being fired. A true theocracy requires acceptance of the mission of the theocrat by the entire society. We shall investigate the anomalies and impure forms of social structures in Chapter VIII.

In its essential elements our cultural life is still based on the accomplishments of the ancient Greeks. For the most part this is also the basis of the social structure in the meso-area. We find this most prominently—and there almost without exception—in industrial organizations. It is called the "line-staff" organization: staff functions are fitted into the strictly hierarchic edifice, the "line organization hierarchy." This forms into more or less independent groups or committees who advise those responsible in the higher echelons. In this way one fits a segment of spiritual life into the economic life, and provides those responsible a wider view but, most of all, in order to achieve an honest exchange of proposals or criticisms. The subordinates within the hierarchy are either forbidden or not expected to provide this exchange. (Fig. 8.)

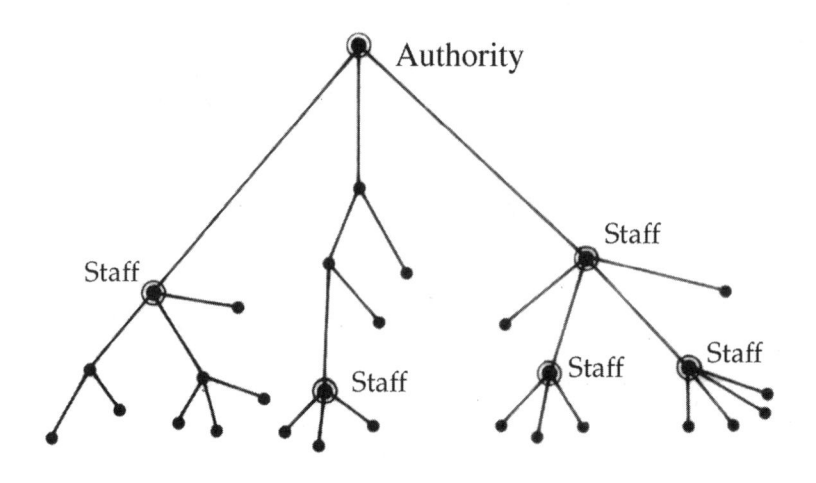

Fig. 8: The line-staff organization. Almost exclusively existing forms or organizing work are based on ancient Greek social forms.

Characteristically, this structure has only been perfected within the economic life, the very area that took no part in the theocratic age. In the area of rights and spirit, the ancient Greek structure always tends to degenerate. Government officials, particularly ministers, frequently surround themselves with committees, of ambiguous purpose. Does one require an independent opinion, or is it a matter of getting carefully picked representatives of the spiritual life to bolster up one's own opinion? Perhaps the purpose is merely to palm off a sticky problem to a committee in order to avoid an unpleasant decision for the time being. But woe to one who attempts to introduce genuine counselors into the the bureaucratic hierarchy. In this case the structural hierarchy resists most vigorously. Newcomers pose not just a danger to the promotions of the veterans, but more so these "bulls in the china shop" of artificial formal curlicues and oriental etiquette threaten the china of smouldering feuds for position. There exists within officialdom an area—again, an economic one—where the ancient Greek structure has surfaced. From time to time one allows, for economic reasons, an investigation of the effectiveness of entire organizations by independent bodies.

As we have seen in Ancient Greece, how important the liberation of the spiritual life is for the state is highlighted by a strange institution: the ruler gets himself the fool, whose "fool's freedom" makes honest expression possible. This dates back to the absolutistic time when the hierarchy was being reinstated in such an exaggerated way that even the most exalted personages no longer dared to speak their own opinions but only that which they assumed would match the opinions of his excellency.

The life of the spirit is no stranger to the Greek structure, but often assumes unstable forms. The top of the hierarchical triangle either surrounds itself only with people who agree with him ("Anyway, one cannot talk to others about anything worth while"), or else he values free advice so much that he is willing to have others take the responsibility. Now we are back in "Rome!" The ancient Greek structure has the best prospect of emerging in the teacher-to-pupil relationship. As an example, in my dealings with a firm of tax consultants, I had the following experience. The tax attorney involved young academicians in the most difficult cases, ones he was handling personally. He did this not only because he wanted to train the young people but also, primarily, so he had access to their unbiased thinking, as yet not corrupted by experience. The day to day activities of these newcomers was, however, under total control of the hierarchy.

A custom frequently found in hospitals is another typical example. Within a strictly hierarchical structure there exists a small group who not only acts as a counseling resource but even has the power to make decisions within their own specialty. This group usually consists of doctors (seldom therapists, never nurses or social workers), and as a committee, they have this special privilege. But exactly as in ancient Greece, it applies only in their own specialty. The moment they question the organization of the working conditions, a conflict with the hierarchy arises, namely with the chief. Nowadays this no longer ends with the hemlock cup but rather with being fired.

To find Roman conditions in today's institutions is harder than one would suppose. Where do today's institutions really release a person from their own interests when it comes to the sphere of justice? Where are the factories, societies, shelters, etc., where co-workers are granted rights when claiming these rights may go against the interests of the institution? Where are the special courts of justice, staffed with judges who were chosen based on personal credentials, who could be called upon to pronounce valid judgments when it comes to a conflict between the worker and the institution? Since such judges do not exist, one appeals to the existing statutes in order to at least get some protection in this way. But seldom can the existing statutes, lost in macro social abstractions, do justice to the real needs.

This lack is understandable. The law always and everywhere tends to split in two.[22] This is why the symbol for justice is the scales. It leans either to one or the other side, and a continuous effort is needed to maintain balance. It is rather easy to lose the mid-position. In this case justice can no longer bind together but separates both parties. Then they start to wage war against each other as can be seen in the macro-social sphere. Emperor fights Pope, and so forth. Institutions do not want war. They want to grow and become more encompassing—until they encompass infinity. This is why they avert bestowing rights to their workers. Such rights would lead to an unbalanced, insecure condition. One needs to learn to deal with ever changing hybrid conditions. After all, not only one person's rights are at stake but the other one's as well. The right of one is the obligation of the other. From the point of view of development, those are steps backward, not growth but dying off.

In the life of the economy, also, we rarely find Rome, except in a degenerated embodiment: the management against the union, executives against the shareholders. It is degenerative when one strives to find not an equilibrium between natural opposites but rather domination of one over the other. It is degenerative because in the fight for power people are not freed from the interests of their associations but are being drawn more deeply into their sphere.

Hence, just as with ancient Rome, we need to pay more attention to the formative stages than to the fully realized social forms. If we do this, we can see how a tendency to create equilibrium lies in the antagonism between management and supervision. The supervision should bind the management's autocratic ambitions in a manner similar to the life of justice, where equal weight of executive and legislative have aimed at creating a balance between community (executive) and individual development (legislative). In the life of the spirit the directorate stands for the rights of the workers next to the board of directors who represent the ideal-theological side (theocracy). Yet, whatever form it takes, the Roman structure remains a martial one, a system of achieving equilibrium based on power (checks and balances).

We also experience examples of feudal practices. Who does not recognize the men and women in large institutions, each with his or her own following? The obligation to stand up for the interests of the followers is matched by the adulation and apron strings of such heroes. Here we find conventions of honor and tournaments, wars and alliances like in the Middle Ages. Here we find harmonious relationships as well as cliques.

If we look for the corporate state in the meso-sphere, we find, surprisingly, all sorts of experimental structures. In the macro-sphere more or less utopian ideas of a corporate state may be found ghosting around in people's heads. In the same way we find a "threefold order" of classes ghosting around in any number of progressive experiments.

There exist corporations with a threefold governing body within the their pyramidally-oriented structures, where the commercial, social and research interests are represented. In actual fact the commercial side dominates and, often, represents the entire company (theocracy). In our modern national governments also the assignments for ministries of commerce, social action and cultural affairs are joined by the ones of minister of state, foreign affairs and defense in some sort of superior capacity. It is a common characteristic of such forms to have a degree of freedom within each area, as long as this is possible within the the framework of the overall strategy.

The same can be said for threefold formations within anthroposophical institutions: "organs" dealing with the life of the spirit, the life of justice and that of the economy. These are theoretically or actually peopled with specialists in each area. The great spirits within the spiritual organ find themselves to be more or less representative of the entire spiritual life of the institution. The economists (most often the financial experts) find that they are the specialists in the organ of the economy. And a few ladies may be found in the organ of rights who are responsible for the beauty of the rooms and the cozy atmosphere around the coffee table. With closer observation, this has little to do with the threefold order and everything to do with the three estates. Even in places where the "threefold" structure has been defined down to formalities, we can find a fourth organ, more or less in the background. Sometimes it has become an institution, and at time it exists simply "as a tradition." Its function is defined in different ways: as a coordinating body where questions raised by the three sectors may be aired, sometimes as an organ of perception, able to sound the alarm in case of emergency. When the authorities demand a partner in continuous dialogue, it may become an organ or representation. It may also be an organ that is normally dormant and wakes up only when the other three can no longer work together, thus endangering the existence of the institution. In actual fact this fourth organ turns out to be the remnant of theocracy which holds the rest together like in the old state with its estates. It is possible that, like a good mother, it allows the little ones to play by themselves in their room, of course, only until it "gets to be too bad." It is also possible that this fourth organ is in reality the gray eminence which guides the institution from the background.

In the meso-social area we can indeed find progress in the structure to the effect that new forms are being created which grant the workers more freedom from the interests of the association. Yet we find, at the same time, that the old forms continue to exist, often with justification. Within the micro-sphere this is even more the case. Theocrats exist and so do people who look up to them. There are people of the type of Frederick the Great, who believed that everyone was allowed to be happy in his own way as long as he obeyed all the laws and statutes. And there are people who do not mind being pushed around as long as they can devote themselves to the aspect of spiritual life dear to them. Others demand independent laws beyond this and are even prepared at times to allow such rights to others. In spite of all macrocosmic developments, a growing number of people strive to be part of any decision in any field that even remotely concerns them. We are living in the midst of the struggle for this increased interdependence. This is the starting point for the new world. How can any institution grant the freedom demanded by the sociological law to every worker without losing its own identity? The question cannot be answered directly from within this law. We shall return to it in Chapter VI.

From the point of view of institutions and workers, we find four social stages of development of each (Fig. 9). Since each type of worker can encounter four different types of structure, we arrive at sixteen constellations, setting aside for now different shades and mutations. Only four of these are harmonious, namely those wherein the worker faces a structure appropriate to him, for example, an "ancient Grecian"-oriented person working in a corporation with a line-staff organization. We can also understand that the possibility of dissonant constellations grows by leaps and bounds as mankind goes through another stage in development. Increasing numbers of people are working within a structure that does not agree with them. No wonder we have social unrest.

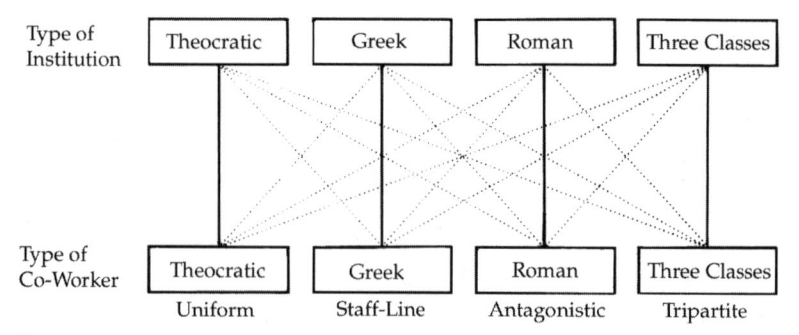

Type of Institution	Theocratic	Greek	Roman	Three Classes

Type of Co-Worker	Theocratic	Greek	Roman	Three Classes
	Uniform	Staff-Line	Antagonistic	Tripartite

Fig. 9: Institutions and their workers, identified by the four stages of development, taken from past stages of society's development. As a rule they only work well together in cases where institutions and workers correspond (vertical lines). Different combinations produce social discord.

Now let us take another look at the basic sociological law. Perhaps the goal of freeing the individual from the interests of the institutions has not been reached; yet it is within reach. The development of the individual has brought the structure of society to this point. Does this mean the end of development? Is all that remains that we harmonize what we have gained?

Merely reading Steiner's law may create this impression. Continuing study raises questions. "As soon as the state does not see itself as an end in itself, it will create a formation wherein the individual will receive the greatest recognition. A society will exist which wants nothing for itself and everything for the individual citizen." If we take on the full meaning of these sentences, we can begin to understand that we stand merely at the beginning of a development. Humanity has gained freedom from the interests of the institution and now faces the task to organize the state. We do not do away with it. On the contrary, we have to transform the former tyrant into the tool of freedom from domination. He shall limit his task to guarantee each individual's freedom. We do not incorporate the institutions into the state since this would force the individual to conform to the community. The state will have to see to it that working within the institutions occur only in freedom.

We know from the Soviet and British examples what socialized medicine looks like. We even know this, although somewhat masked, from the medical associations in Western Europe. As a tool of life without rulers the state will have to see to it that each person is allowed to seek the help they consider appropriate. It must also guarantee a school system wherein pupils (or parents) look for teachers who, in their view, are most desirable for their own development. The impulse to freedom will work down to the meso-sphere from the macro-sphere because the "associations" which will form will emanate from the real striving of real people. This freedom will also set boundaries to monopolistic tendencies that, as an example, might be allowed to dispose of the village's only gymnasium or the town's only stage.

Is there a law that also governs this functional change of the state from a tool of domination to one of help to the individual? If the answer is yes, is this law the same as the basic sociological law only projected with more consistent thinking? Does it apply to the state alone or quite generally to all social doings?

If we turn our attention to certain symptoms of our time, we can approach the answers to these questions. At present hardly a beginning is visible of the (total) liberation of the individual from the interests of associations. Yet a further step is apparent. Just as there are stragglers, there must be pioneers. The future (almost always) announces itself with its shadow: the new creation starts off by revealing its negative aspects. The striving for housing- and life- communities, or for communes, may appear to be a reaction to the reactionary unified state. Yet, with all its—at times sordid—accompaniments, it may be the first inklings of a principle which only the future will reveal in its true form. As an impulse it deals with more than the liberation of the individual from the interests of the community. Then the community will stand in for each individual. If the commune is to be worthy of its name, one will have to arrange it so that "the individual is of the greatest possible importance."

One reason why such experiments fail is often the lack of a structure. This keeps them from taking hold, and they collapse like the American colony of Robert Owen or the Dutch one of Frederic von Eeden. The formless edifice reaches out too far and is sure to fall back to antiquated theocratic forms. We can even understand Leninism in this way. One shies away from this form because it has always been the instrument of tyranny. And one does not yet know that the form that brings us together will transform us from within and no longer from the outside. "Mankind would indeed have to go through a kind of anarchy if no one were to exist who can grasp these inner connections and who would bestow ideas to the spiritual life of mankind. Such ideas would take ideas into account which are capable of dealing with these changes, dictated by the natural cause of evolution." (GA 172/1974/81)

The importance of this blind striving is more visible as we encounter more clearly defined beginnings. Groups are forming to take care of a mentally ill person—perhaps a schizophrenic, maybe a criminally insane one—and include him or her in a living community. In a sense they sacrifice the community's excess of substance and make it available to the needy ones. This is not done to educate nor to create a feeling of superiority but simply to make life again possible for a human brother or sister, for social healing, one could say. Steiner mentions how such groups are in a position to redeem a person's karma. "In this way whole communities can help a person who has committed an injustice." (GA/123/1978/218) Making such excess of forces available does not merely impose great demands on personal lives; it calls for structures, simply because a vessel has to be given a form if it is to hold a content. "Just as the form without spirit is useless, so too spirit that fails to create a form would be without action."(GA 10/1955/105)

What such communities are attempting, in essence, is the reverse of what Steiner describes as applying to the beginning of cultural conditions. The individual is not made subservient to the demands of the associations; rather the community is offered up to the interests of the individual; it may even be founded for that purpose. No member of the community is asked to give up his freedom. Instead one personally decides to offer up part of one's freedom for the sake of the fellow human. Sacrificed freedom is love.

Within a community of like-minded people there is a danger when it comes to creating a community around the task of helping oddballs to rejoin the society. We can imagine how such a circle of like-minded people could gather around a person, and proceed to throw out his ego, and, using the emptiness of soul thus created fill the person—made functional in the process—with ideas dictated by the circle. The frightful black magical results of such a practice remind us of brainwashing. Brainwashing is used as a psychological method to destroy opponents, as standard practice by sects, as motivation to growth or consumption. This danger lurks wherever groups of like-minded people show mercy to a person. In milder form it is a constant danger in institutions devoted to ideologies, especially when they deal with feeble personalities (children, old people, and sick people). Yet it is hard to imagine the formation of such a group if it consists of such like-minded people who not only tolerate opposing ideas but even experience them as a supplement to their own onesidedness.

Yet, as Steiner has repeatedly described it, this image stood at the inception of our so-called fifth cultural epoch. Using the title of Sigismund Gleich's principal work, twelve representatives of the "entire orbit of all the worlds ideologies" placed this image at the disposal of the thirteenth, namely the initiation of Christian Rosenkreuz. This motif of the multiplicity of truth and of its many levels is intended to flow into our present epoch so that it comes to bear in the next. In the future, total freedom of thought becomes a need for every human being who stands at the pinnacle of his time. "Within that part of mankind of the sixth cultural period which then will be the civilized one, there will be an end to commonality of belief as it still exists in so many places, commonality of belief as it still reigns in different ways within various human communities." (GA 159-160/1967/103) Today we still need the liberation of the individual from domination, that is, from the ideas imposed by associations. Later on we can transform the association into the tool that enables the image of the other to be mirrored in each individual's soul. The individual will then be able to live off the power of the community. (GA 40/1961/256)

Only at this point can we see the true dimensions of the basic sociological law. Freedom from associations is only the prelude. Only from a starting point of freedom can we begin to create a planet of love. Only in freedom can we make the decision not to leave our human brother behind but to feel the despair of his soul as our own.[23] Here we find continuity with Steiner's saying that in the future humans will sacrifice their sheaths for souls who have suffered damage to their own. (GA 218/1976/176f) What hides behind the basic sociological law is the Christianity of the Manichees.[24]

At this point we can understand that the law has been fulfilled when the individual has really been freed from the domination of the associations. What comes after this can no longer be considered as a law in the sense that succeeding steps *must* come about as part of the history of evolution. From the point of view of this liberation the evolutionary step reached at this point is an end result. Something new may follow or not. Man is now free to create new types of associations which serve neither his own wellbeing nor the wellbeing of the group, but rather the wellbeing of a particular member. (see GA 102/1974/195 f)

Yet it is understood that human evolution is capable of such growth and that if one refuses it there will be consequences. Reaching the stage of development when the individual is left to his own devices also opens the door for the striving to become conscious of one's own ego in its true form. The other plays a decisive role in this process. "He (man) feels that every discord between himself and someone else is the result of an ego that has not fully awakened."(GA 7/1924/21) If man fails to form the institutions capable of harmonizing these discords, the chasm between predisposition and social reality will grow wider and wider. The resulting social chaos will end in the social catastrophes whose beginnings we are witnessing today. "Realistic observation will show that all evils which can rightfully be called social, stem from the deeds of humans." (GA 34/1960/203) We are far removed from anonymous social forces.

Let us return to the present. We can neither plan nor program what the liberation of the individual will create in the future. We can only create a basis. This requires a society in which the state is charged with the task to create the liberties for the individual out of which the love-forces can begin to grow. "The state cannot liberate the human being; this can only be done by education; however, the state must see to it that every individual finds the soil on which his freedom can thrive." (GA 30/1961/235) This implies that the form the state assumes must fit the changing needs of the individual so that no one within that state is forced into a strange environment. "Every organization with a *predetermined* character must necessarily suppress the free development of the individual in order to assert itself as a rounded organization." The social ideal is logically called by Steiner, "anarchistic individualism."

This raises the question if, in such a society, there can be an ordered communal spirit with regard to supplies of needed goods, human relationships, service activities, and so forth. This paradox can be resolved in the same manner as the supposedly exclusive three freedoms of the French Revolution.

We have examined the historical process of giant steps whereby mankind has arrived at "the free unfolding of needs and powers" in the three areas of social life. This does not imply, however, that the individual requires, or should indeed demand, the same unfolding in these three areas to exhaustion and all at the same time. Indeed "every kind of domination of one over the other" is an abomination; yet the possibility is there for everyone to voluntarily take upon oneself duties, and perhaps constraints as well, if he wishes to make this sacrifice for the sake of mankind. Plainly spoken, this means that one cannot produce shoes if every worker wishes to develop him or herself before all else during the process of production. The economy imposes limits to the realization of the law of individualization. Chapter VII will deal exhaustively with the "how."

In the area of justice the realization of this law also has limits. These are not due to some legal process but exclusively to the fact that the unfolding of one personality may cause the suppression of another. The person who is willing to terrorize his surroundings with a radio or moped in order to unfold his personality dominates others no less than his hated landlord who considers his ostentatious consumption at the cost of his fellow beings a prerequisite for *his* development. Here justice will have to limit freedom in order to realize the basic sociological law.

In *Philosophy of Freedom* (GA 4/1921/198) we find the philosophical basis for such limitations. "Laws assume the form of general concepts only if they prohibit actions, but not when they demand actions. The unfree spirit has to be given laws regarding what he has to do in very concrete form." Here we may think of people who have not yet reached the timely stage of the basic sociological law—"Laws take on the form of concepts to prevent actions."[25] Without hurting their fellow man, human beings can unfold only in the life of the spirit. In this article Steiner demands ruthless acknowledgement of one's own views. How much of these views is true should be left to the future to decide and not to the judgment of some group of people. The basic sociological law counts on the gradual release of the person from the hierarchy. This is being accomplished in the life of the spirit. If today's humans are still spiritually dependent it lies with them not with any associations. The light no longer comes from outside.

"The great historical moment of history demands that all humans can enter history as individuals." (GA 305/special printing 1979/46) But as soon as we are set free from the hierarchy of society, the task of finding our place in the spiritual hierarchy faces us. This corresponds to the second phase of the basic sociological law. Although we must have achieved freedom to realize this second phase, we must also realize that the alternative is to succumb to the Luciferic temptation to abandon our human brothers and sisters. At one time the hierarchy of society was created after the model of the spiritual one. What still holds it together after a fashion in our time are the last stunted remains of this. Additionally the individual is no longer gifted with social inspiration ever since our liberation from the social hierarchy. Future spiritual life will depend on individuals finding each other and forming communities. "In this way human associations are the mysterious place where higher spiritual beings descend in order to work through individual human beings, in the way the soul works through the members of the body."[26]

Nobody will be able to force people into such communities. But if they fail to form in freedom, the spiritual life will dry up and culture will freeze up. Luciferic upward development of the individual will have delivered mankind to Ahriman.

The basic sociological law then proves to be the essential developmental law of spiritual life. Indeed the life of the spirit is the sphere wherein the human being develops and unfolds its life of the soul. (This has already been discussed in the first chapter, but we shall return to it more thoroughly in later chapters.) To this end we need freedom from outside influences. The question is how each individual comes to terms with himself. Every person can answer this question, provided that he is not hampered by all possible communities. Every person can, at his own discretion, transform this freedom into an inner one. Nobody, and especially not the state, should interfere with this process. One must be able to live the freedom of spirit with no restraints. A problem arises if he takes part in the life of justice or works within the life of the economy. In this case he cannot leave his spiritual life at home because in these areas, too, he is present with that part of his personality that calls for free unfolding. The question is how this unfolding can be reconciled with the requirements of the life of rights and of economy. The reverse of this question also applies. If he is not to remain a bookworm, a person organizes life institutions (e.g., a school or in the macro sphere as a participant in a circle of researchers). Then economic and legal questions arise within the life of the spirit, and these by their very nature interfere with free unfolding. The search for solutions to resolve these contradictions in a manner appropriate for the times—that is the actual social question.

Endnotes:

[1] Contained in the "Gesammelte Aufsätze zur Kulturgeschichte 1887–1901" (GA 31/1966/147 ff). If not otherwise mentioned, all quotations in this chapter are from the two essays.

[2] "Vom Genius Europas" (*About the Genius that Is Europe*), Stuttgart, 1963/1964.

[3] This overview demonstrates the errors in viewing the basic sociological law within a narrow time frame. It may be impossible to document progression from the original social forms to Atlantean times with exoteric history. However, I could not discover an argument in favor of H.G. Schweppenhäuser's idea that the Basic Sociological Law would be different when applied to pre-Christian cultures.

[4] See studies of islanders and Indians "Patterns of Culture" by Ruth Benedict. N.Y. 1946. The factual material presented in this work is simply being ignored in our theories of culture. In the following text there is much discussion of structures. I would like to state here that in my terminologies structure and form relate like Goethe's primeval plant, to a particular type or even to a concrete specimen. There are many *forms* of society, yet these can be identified as variations of a small number of formative *principles*, i.e. structures.

[5] Regarding the concept of theocracy see Steiner GA 11/o.c., 8/32; GA 54/435/ 1961; GA 145/1962/14; GA 305/ special edition 1979.1. This last lecture contains most important references about how the life of rights and economy emerge from theocracies, without dealing with the relationship to structural questions.

[6] Peter Bamm "Alexander oder die Verwandlung der Welt," Zürich: 1965, p. 107.

[7] See the beautiful book by C.M. Stibbe, *Sparta*, Bussum 1949

[8] By the way, it is interesting that Theocracy no longer appears among the forms of state of Aristotle. He confines himself to the description of six succeeding structures; three healthy ones and three sick ones. Here, too, we experience the mighty leap in human spiritual history from Plato to Aristotle. I recommend Karl König's "Über die Dreigliederung des sozialen Organismus" (*The Threefold Social Organism*) 23.3. (private printing) as a source of appreciation of the Aristotelian central concept of the human being as "zoon politicon"—with an interpretative reach from "political animal" to "group forming living being."

[9] I would like to assume that Steiner thought about that time when he remarked in the Greek "Polis" there was no trace of a concept of law (GA 100/1967/140). The conceptual grasp of the law was kept for the Romans. Pre-Roman Greece had already made essential contributions to the practical application of the law.

[10] As regards to the birth of justice out of theocracy, see the significance of the emancipation of labor, in GA 305/ Special edition 1979/14.

[11] Exceptions demonstrate this best. For example: in pragmatically oriented Austria it became customary to knight citizens who promised to become important statesmen. That authorized them to be active in the life of rights. The continuation of such customs may be observed in clubs today. Shortly after World War II an economic scientist of renown in Holland, a man with humble background and widely known by a popular nickname, was to be promoted to a high diplomatic position in connection with a restoring diplomatic connection in Washington. The minister of foreign affairs demurred; he literally answered: "We do not know this name."

[12] See Karl Heyer "Aus dem Jahrhundert der Französischen Revolution" (*From the Century of the French Revolution*) Second edition 1956, in particular p. 37 f. 13. One can, from a certain point of view, depict the managed society as a new structural achievement. It certainly has features different from the societies of Louis IX. Yet Frederick II himself created, as we saw above, the first genuine bureaucracy, the east Prussian State of appointed nobility. He imported oriental theocratic customs to Europe. A new element introduced by the French and American revolutions has been pointed out by Jacques Ellul in his significant book "Autopsie de la Revolution" (Paris 1969, pg. 99ff). At this point in history, freedom was not to be gained by opposing the state; rather the state was assigned the role of protector and promoter of freedom (and other rights): "*C'est maintenant le pouvoir, qui condamne, qui exécute, guerroi au nom de la liberté.*" To this subject and to the connection with Marxism see also GA 18/1924/174.

[14] GA 18/1924, part 2/173. Also compare this to GA 21/1976/126. Passages where Steiner points to the state as the modern God, in some sense equating to theocracy and technocracy, are GA189/1946/60, GA 333/1971/90 and GA 328/1977/91.

[15] I have addressed this problem in the following essays: "Die Dreigliedrigkeit unseres Steuersystems" (The Threefold Nature of our System of Taxation) and "Das dreifache Antlitz des Terrorismus (to appear shortly in German translation). Also see J.W. Ernst "Das Schicksal unserer Zivilisation und die Kommende Kultur des 21. Jahrhunderts" (The fate of our civilization and the future culture of the twenty-first century) Freiburg 1977, p. 73: "When the royal puppets of the 20th century had finally fled, the remaining republics transferred the Godking aura even to the boring formation of the bureaucratic state." See also the introductory chapter by Walter Abendroth "Rudolf Steiner and Today's World" (Freiburg 1977).

[16] The biogenetic basic law, formulated by Haekel, shows that in the evolution of every individual being the evolution of the tribe is repeated in concentrated form.

[17] Of course it is possible to describe the emancipation of society from various points of view. In view of the relationships to be described we treated this here from the point of view of structure as this also corresponds to the basic sociological law ("liberty from associations"). It is, however, of interest that Steiner treated the same process based on social activity, probably in deference to the British character (Oxford lectures of August 26, 1922 (GA 305/special edition 1979/I). Here he describes how, as culture migrated from East to West (Theocracy), the evolution of what is warlike and legalistic happens along with ambivalence of spiritual life which relapses either to theocracy or, as theology, assumes a legalistic character. This creates a twofold situation until the pressure of the industrial revolution causes an independent economic life to form the third part at a later time.

[18] This applies only conditionally to macrostructures. Structures overtaken by world events may have had a degree of justification, perhaps due to commonalities of peoples living on different levels of consciousness. Since the year 1879 we have entered a phase in human development in which demands for a structure appropriate for the times are arising everywhere.

[19] It would be a mistake to conclude that statutory regulations are of no importance. Sloppy dealing with forms for which one has freely voted not only indicates a tendency to deal in a highhanded way with the rights of coworkers, but more importantly, it robs one of a tool for social education. Faithful conformance to statutes is in the meso-sphere what politeness is in the microsphere. They share increased effectiveness when applied without fuss.

[20] Parties only appear to belong to the macro level. Most party members know each other as little as would citizens of any state. In reality a small circle of party leaders decides all questions, and party conferences serve only for propaganda purposes. This elite is the actual structure of the party and belongs to the meso level. (See GA 177/1966.277.) This is the reason why in our democracy of political parties even county elections never exceed the meso level. The vote is a formality because the delegates have already been appointed.

[21] See Chapter VIII regarding the problem of voting.

[22] See the discussion of the correspondence between the three fold order and the human organism in GA 219/1976/XII.

[23] See GA 109–111/1965/199: "The law, self-understood in the Devachan—that one cannot be happy at the expenses of others—that law shall be realized as a mission on earth."

[24] See GA93/1979/76 dealing with Mani as the preparer of future forms of society. Note to GA 218 that here Steiner connects the sacrifice of the sheaths with the atonement of personal debt. If, however one remembers the spiritual law that every step upward is bought with others being left behind, then the debtor relationship is always a given fact.

[25] Lapidary Joseph Wörner in "Jederman" (January 1981): "He who tries to command being good becomes evil himself." See also GA 30/ 1961/ 65: "It is a fallacy to think that the human being can act according to other then self-created laws." We shall see that the path of social knowledge and that of the *Philosophy of Freedom* are not identical at all. One can even state that this surfaces certain tensions. Yet in we are particularly close to this path when it comes to the Basic Sociological Law (see, for example, GA 4/1921/92, 118. 171. 178). One could really call this the *Philosophy of Freedom* applied to practical life.

[26] GA 54/ 1966/ 179 ff. also GA 154/1973/42: "One will have to get used to the fact that, what one has to look upon as direct healing force of spiritual science, has to be made effective by human society."

Chapter IV

The Principal Social Law

> *The welfare of a community joined in common tasks will increase in the measure that the individual decreases his claim to the proceeds. This means the more of these proceeds he gives up to his coworkers and the more his own needs are satisfied not by his own efforts but as a result of his coworkers' efforts.*
> — Rudolf Steiner

With this law we enter a totally different social world. The first impression could be one of incompatibility with the Basic Sociological Law, because it suggests detaching the person from the domination of associations and connecting him to interrelationships to achieve social results. If one were to label the Basic Sociological Law the unknown (if not indeed the ignored), one can perhaps identify the Principal Social Law as the misunderstood. One is close to the mark if one considers the motive underlying the interpretation of the Principal Social Law to be the desire to come to terms with an unpleasant truth regarding one of our strongest motivations, namely income. Taking a look at three widespread untruths or half-truths regarding this law can help us to a better understanding.

The Principal Social Law postulates that men work for each other. This is actually a spiritual rendering of what in economic science is known as the consequence of the division of labor. This interpretation contradicts Steiner's explanation: "This law is alive in concrete reality if an entire group of people succeed to create institutions that assure *that nobody can ever make claim to the fruits of his own work,* but that these in their entirely are used for the benefit of the entire community."[1] To make sure that no one thinks that by the fruits of labor he means the product, Steiner then specifies "that our fellow Men work and that they get a certain income are two totally separate things."[2]

Secondly, the Principal Social Law is intended to be outmoded and absorbed in the Threefold Order. Steiner supposedly mentioned this during the period of the Threefold Commonwealth (19191922). Züricher Vorträge [Zürich Lectures] were published in 1977 (GA 328), the sources of the Threefold Commonwealth (GA 23) and the threefold movement. Here he refers to the "fundamental social law."[3] "This Principal Law applies to social life with an exclusivity and necessity equal to any natural law in regard to any area of natural science."

Thirdly, Steiner describes an ideal condition which would only exist if humans were ripe for it in the sixth cultural period. He contradicts this statement in the same essay. "One should, however, not think that it suffices if one ascribes general moral validity to this law, or if one were to translate it to the attitude that everybody works in the service of his fellow human beings." He calls the belief in the goodness of Man as held by Robert Owen "one of the worst illusions." He counters with Man's bad nature as the reason for "regulations," and the establishment of institutions. This applies not to the future but to the now: "Already in our day there exist certain human communities where the germ for this sort of thing is being prepared. These will make it possible for mankind to perform a leap in social development, as it were, in a sudden jerk. . . . Yet everyone can work within his own sphere in the sense of this law." It makes no sense at all to wait for better times. On the contrary, "he who works *for himself* is bound to fall prey to egoism. Only he who works exclusively for others is able gradually to become an unegoistical worker."

Having seen what the law is not, let us examine its meaning in the strict literal sense. In contrast to the Basic Sociological Law, a law of development, the Principal Social Law is a law of a timeless condition. The degree of resulting good depends on the behavior of people. Their actions can increase or diminish it.

Here Steiner addresses the criteria of economic life: people working together, fruits of efforts, satisfaction of needs. The three archetypal processes of the economy give content to the law: production (working together), barter (yield of efforts), and consumption (satisfaction of needs). A.H. Bas shows in "Triodos Berichte [News from Triodos]" #21-26 (1928/83) that the threefold formulation of the law is in fact a direct expression of the three aspects of the economy—capital, work, product. However the results, namely either the social product or wellbeing, are in no way intended to be the yardstick of modern economic science. It is the "health," i.e. a state expressing a wholeness, a state of not being damaged, in the therapeutic sense. The law has a therapeutic effect on those who work in its true meaning. Arrangements that contradict it will "create some misery and trouble." Steiner uses the word "wellbeing" to clarify his meaning. "Clearly this law affirms nothing less than the following: the wellbeing of mankind is greater to the degree that lesser egoism is present."[4]

Indeed, we are dealing with the basic law of social economic life, just as we recognize the Basic Sociological Law as the one applicable to social (earthly) spiritual life.[5] Objectively, there can be no products of effort in the life of the spirit or of justice; therefore, the law cannot possibly be applied to these spheres. The results of the work of teachers, doctors, priests, and so on, are the results of human abilities (the person realizes his talents, gets well again, finds himself) which cannot be considered as products. This is true also of the results of those working in the sphere of pure law, for example, working out a proposal. Rights, too, can be called products only in a perverted sense. Two examples can demonstrate this.

If one were to measure the efforts of a physician purely by their economic results, one would have to conclude that the yield would be relatively small if he heals a sick person, but optimal if he kills an incurable sick psychotic child. In the latter case, if one applies conventional economic thinking, he increases profit by reducing the costs which the community would have to spend yearly on behalf of the child.[6] Likewise, a tax official could increase his output by conveniently overlooking a mistake to the disadvantage of a taxpayer. But a society arranged along these lines contradicts our ideas of justice and human dignity.

The influence of economic practices may encourage one to think that all human values can be expressed in economic terms. However, this way of thinking fails when stood against the feeling, and increasingly, the consciousness that efforts in the realms of spiritual life and law cannot be quantified. This evaluation severs the connection between effort and result, and also the connection between effort and product. It has long been known that work pressure does not help achieve thoroughness or the precision required by the formulation of laws. This is why the state undertakes to look after its officials and does not pay them according to their output. More and more, we consider that employees working in the area of spiritual life burn out or get derailed under the pressure of output quotas.[7]

In no way does this mean that the Principal Social Law means nothing to the spiritual life. Wherever it is institutionalized, where work is done together toward a purpose, it reaches into the life of the economy. *To the extent to which* work is modified by its main cultural concern, it, too, is subject to the Principal Social Law. Further discussion of this theme will be taken up later.

That the welfare of mankind increases as a function of decreasing egoism places the Principal Social Law in direct contradiction to classical economy. The latter bases general wellbeing on individual egoism. It is the invisible hand which, according to Adam Smith, transforms individual striving for profit into the good of the whole society. Mandeville characterizes this peculiar goddess more accurately in the saying, "Private vices are public benefits." This straightforward concession to antisocial behavior has since been discounted. Yet subconsciously social Darwinism ghosts around to replace it (market survival of the fittest). It has long been acknowledged that there is something wrong with this. Wellbeing is in part a fruit of the spiritual life, which increased the production of goods through the Industrial Revolution and division of labor. In part it is the result of the exploitation first of one's own workers and later those of other countries. With this we are back to the Principal Social Law: "All institutions within a community of human beings which run counter to this law must, in the long run, produce misery and need somewhere."

To describe this law as based on historical development is not as easy as to do this with the Basic Sociological Law. Where can we find it in practice? Where do we find the historical traditions that "in communities of human beings who work together" the individual satisfies his needs only from that which the others bestow on him? Are we not forced to go back to life in cloisters, to the larger family picture or even to what we found as theocracy with the Incas, where all the yield of the soil had to be delivered to society? Are we not speechless as we face a law which seems to contradict modern development and, furthermore, individual development?

The question becomes more complicated, because in the course of sociological development the law becomes concrete reality in ever new forms. Coercion, which at one time welded the community together, is no longer accepted. "If Owen had had the power or the will to force all the people in his colony to their assigned work, the whole thing would have had to work." Questions which theocracy—and a lot of theocratic institutions to the present day, such as the armies—solved by force, today require solutions under very different assumptions. Almost all examples from the past, and even those of the present, need to be taken more as examples of how coercion *no longer* works. This is the central question of this book and the focus of Chapter VII.

Even in situations where men are working for each other, we are dealing with hybrid forms. Without a measure of working for each other, communities are unthinkable. "Every community would in fact crumble if the work of the individual were not made available to the whole. Yet since time immemorial human egoism has crossed this law." We find this in the family where father gives all his pay to the whole, after keeping a part of it for his individual hobbies. Mother follows his example and asks for two receipts for the irresistible dress she has bought, one for the real amount and one for half of what she paid, in case her purchase meets with objection at home. And both parents violate the law in the same way when father gives Johnny and mother gives Liz a few dollars for washing the car and doing the dishes.

The hybrid forms continue in the factory. What is being distributed is not the common profit; most co-workers are paid an indemnity, a wage, "earnings." They did not come for the sake of working for their fellow human beings but in order to earn money. All else is for those in power, except what they designate as "for all the workers" as a reserve, or what the revenue service takes for "the population at large."

This continues on the larger level. The national community would fall apart if no work were done on its behalf. Because one does not do it voluntarily anymore, laws see to it that obligatory taxes are collected so that the state can provide the public needs (order, safety, roads), without which the whole would fall apart. Even here those in power can abuse the system for their own benefit. Inversely, as another part of the picture, the tax-supported state loses its power where communities work for one another in the sense of the Principal Social Law. In this case the state's points of leverage are missing: income, property, changes in personnel.

It is not our purpose to discuss the anomalies of the economic life. These only make understanding of the Principal Social Law difficult at a time when the life of the economy already often shows itself in its corrupted form, with contempt for freedom. The law is taken from spiritual science, as Rudolf Steiner emphasizes in the three essays. It is founded on " a deeper understanding of the human being and the world." We are still obligated to to investigate this law in the reality of the present social life. Indeed, Steiner has repeatedly pointed out that one cannot deduce occult results from sense experience, yet that, once expressed, they can be understood by all participants and will deepen that very sense experience. Still, we have the problem of cognition when it comes to the social realm, because one cannot understand an economic problem in the abstract but only on relation to economic activity. Conventional economic laws are valid only within an abstract world. They need to be populated with specimens of "homo economicus," and much that is being deduced for the life of the economy from Steiner's writings requires "homo anthroposophicus." One can carry out experiments in thinking in the spiritual area if one can think that this will lead to the truth. In contrast, what takes place in the economic life depends on how real people, who are producing, marketing and consuming, react to the actual and real conditions here and now. As Steiner puts it: it is impossible to figure out the prices people have paid in the market in Lausanne; rather one needs to ask for information.

In the same way one cannot prophesize based on logical deductions how the wellbeing of a community that acts in the sense of the Principal Social Law will compare to one who works within egoistical relationships. One must wait and see how people fit in the process of work if they renounce the results of their labor right from the start. Are they going to do as little as possible for a given wage in accordance with the classic laws of the market? Here this means to perform nothing themselves while having their own needs satisfied by the efforts of others. Or would they, once freed of matter of enough pay for their own work, really start to work hard?

The results of experiments conducted prior to World War I point to the first possibility, to loaf at the expense of others until they too lose the inclination to work. And when the funds ran out, the experiment disintegrated. In Steiner's view such experiences in no way contradict the truth of the Principal Social Law. Indeed, he places one such failed experiment center stage of his explanations, that of Robert Owen, who set forth that human being's antisocial inclinations are not only a natural trait but also many times stronger than their social skills. This can cause great social faults and has led to the economic warfare which, since the beginning of our present age has repeatedly destroyed vast economic treasures among other things. This premise demands the creation of conditions to hold this egoism within bounds. Traditional regulations which force specific work output will certainly still be required for some time in the macro sphere. This will be the case as long as liberty is abused. In the meantime a social vanguard will have the opportunity to try out arrangements which could enable the victory over the antisocial tendencies to a certain degree.

The words Steiner dedicated to this question are terse and clear: "Of course it is not merely a matter of understanding such a law. The real praxis starts with the question: how can we make it become reality? Obviously the law says no less than: Man's wellbeing is greater, egoism is lesser. This indicates that when this is to be translated into reality, one is forced to deal with people who can find a way out of egoism. This is totally impossible as long as the measure of weal and woe of the individual is determined by his work. He who *works for himself must* gradually fall victim to egoism. Only he who works entirely for others can gradually become unegoistical."

Furthermore, "a precondition must be met to bring this about. If someone works for another, he must find the reason for his work in that other person. If somebody is to work for a community, he must have a feeling for the character and significance of that community. He can arrive at this feeling only if the community is much more than a vague sum of individual people. It has to be filled with a spiritual reality which each member shares. Each one has to say to himself: the community is as it should be, and I *want* it to be that way. The community has to have a spiritual mission, and every member wants to contribute to the fulfillment of this mission. All the conventional unfocused and abstract ideas of progress cannot take the place of a mission. It is not sufficient that one individual here, or a group there, will work, without an overview of why their work is helpful except that they and their fellows, or even their pet interests, gain something in the process. A spirit of the whole community has to be alive down to each single individual."

It is not a matter of gathering to work together only those who want to become social, who are not strong enough by themselves and therefore seek the support of an association or institution. One could compare it to an association of (former) alcoholics who know that alone they are too weak to resist temptation and, for that reason, look for help. The comparison may be justified if one views economic egoism an addiction in our time.

A union of those who have good (social) intentions is also not enough. Rather, two conditions must be fulfilled. One is the existence of a mechanism which stops the individual from realizing his antisocial drives in the area of the economy, something comparable to the sphere of rights in the threefold structure. The other is the "spiritual mission."

To legislate this mission externally would be a relapse to theocracy. It would be a step back in our development toward world economy to demand a closed (self providing) economy. If we founded economic units with people who shared identical views of the world, this would also be a relapse in liberation from ties of blood and nationality. Surely this can not be the intended meaning of the spiritual mission.

People working in the field of the economy have two aims. One is the work and the product, the other is to earn income. These are "the dual arrangements common to all human communities." Therefore, if one were to remove the income motive, then the performance must have a meaning or value beyond working for one's existence. Where can we find this reason?

In theocratic times work had a meaning because one knew oneself to be part of an organism. People within communities understood each other because they shared a common spiritual bond. (GA 73/1973/315) Liberation from the associations, as described in the previous chapter, was a first step toward being estranged from the meaning of work. Thus, the economy's organization of work was elevated from being determined by instinct to being determined by inner motivation. (GA 36/1961/75 f/)

Yet people could still find pride in their work — in their own skill and in every product. We think of the pride of the medieval artisan when his creation left his hands. "The heartwarming bliss lies in the product itself." (GA 119/1962/22) It is a matter of course, in the present day and age, for artists and other creatively active personalities within the sphere of spiritual life. The joy of creation bestows a meaning which transcends the pay. "The further back you go, the more you find that working and vocation are two quite different things." (GA 56/1965/245) It is, therefore, understandable that increasing numbers of people are departing the humdrum life in factories and offices and turning to the alternative scene of pottery, hand weaving, cheese making, and so forth. Nothing should be said against this, but we should realize that this can only happen when an economy based on the distribution of labor produces cheap utilitarian items, not just for their own needs but for the needs of their customers as well who can save up the purchasing power to afford handmade articles. "Back to handicrafts" does not provide a solution for society.[8]

It is no longer possible to look for the meaning of work in the joy of making the product. As Steiner states in more detail in 1908, this phase is irrevocably over. The distribution and dismemberment of labor has, in general terms, seen to it that nobody creates a finished product anymore. "The joy of the product must be replaced by the joy of working for fellow human beings." (GA 56/1965/237 f.) For the first time a self-imposed goal for work comes to the fore.

In the long run individual workers may not be able to summon up the will power to perform and produce unless, behind the product, one sees the consumer, the human being, whose needs get satisfied. It is the human brother who appears here and whose earthly trouble, earthly need, evokes our interest, our presence, our involvement, our compassion.

This is easy to understand in the abstract. One knew the needs of the fellow human in the medieval cities, in the village up to about sixty or eighty years ago. Nurturing brotherly love for others was a virtue. In the Middle Ages the church encouraged it as a road to self development. Today we know little about our neighbors and, even if we should be confronted with their problems, we would certainly think of an appropriate agency. Knowledge and outspoken dialogue are rampant equally among statesmen, union leaders, princes of the church and journalists. In industrial production the workers remain abstract fellow citizens, and, even if they assume flesh and blood, "one cannot help them" who "don't deserve it," who will proceed to breed more children anyhow, and so on. Our human brother has indeed moved far away. Only where one can experience the trouble, close up and personally, may there arise still a remnant of experiencing the brother in the fellow human being. There still exist doctors who forget their income when a sick person visits them and teachers who forget that their eight-hour day is over when a child needs help. But how can one expect the work for an anonymous person who buys the product in an anonymous shop to fill anybody with enough enthusiasm that one is willing to work for it without pay?

Perhaps we can get a step closer to this "spiritual mission" which allows us to choose this difficult path. What are we told by a spiritual concept of the world to counterbalance the materialistic concept of adding another kick to a suffering person because it will help the survival of the fittest along and thus the wellbeing of the human race?

At the end of the previous chapter we pointed to the perspective of the basic sociological law. Communities will look after people with retarded inner development because the communities' progress is achieved at their cost. Our own wellbeing is secured at the price of the earthly misery of our contemporaries. In the final analysis it is not tolerance, forgiveness and goodness that lead us on the path to social action, but rather the recognition of debts we have to pay. "Earning" needs to transform itself into "redeeming the debtor," into the deliverance of the spirit in the sense of gnostics. Chapter I dealt in great detail with this indebtedness: my consumption is always at the cost of others. Whosoever thinks this through to the very end encounters the archetype of the earth as the body of Christ. He has given it to mankind so that they can eat of if as brothers. Against this background, is there anyone who fails to feel the debt to our human brothers produced by appeasing our own appetites? Does anyone continue to help himself from this table while there are still hungry guests?

In our time individuals are drawn to institutions that offer social training. They do this partly because they acknowledge the debt and partly from a vague, unconscious urge. They do this in spite of the fact that they are embarking on a challenging path. Not only will the fight against their own antisocial drives become very real, but "the successes can, under certain circumstances, be measured only by very small partial victories." (GA 159-160/1967/302 f)

According to Steiner this social training is a necessary prerequisite for that condition in which those in the sixth cultural period who stand at the pinnacle of their time will literally experience the misery and need of their fellow humans as their very own. For this condition to be brought about, true idealism will have to be implanted into the economic life. To this end mechanisms that prevent working for oneself will have to be established. "The Principal Social Law is all about the *fundamental principle of a social order* which can be realized only in institutions which exclude egoism as a regulating principle."[9] Once we feel the other person's misery as our own, we no longer need the crutch of institutions. Then we shall work for our fellow human beings out of our own misery as we assuage our own pain.

This challenges us to create the appropriate forms.[10] Yet it is not the task of this author to list or sort institutions in relation to the Principal Social Law, rather to sketch a few attempts toward these new forms as indications. A further description of specific failures of such institutions will be part of the discussion of anomalies of social life in Chapter VIII.

I am not aware of any experiments on the macro level. I emphasize this because there are more than a few voices to the effect that the welfare state is aiming toward the realization of the Principal Social Law. In actual fact the division of work and income is on the increase today. Yet, at the same time, in my opinion a dark counter-image is forming in this area. More than ever those who work aim at the satisfaction of their own needs, and at least some of those who do not work are idle not because they cannot work but because they do not want to work.[11] We are dealing with two symptoms of the same phenomenon, namely egoism. In one group they work too much in order to consume too much; in the other group, they do not work because they can consume without work or because their efforts would not affect their rate of consumption. These attitudes fit right in with the classical theories of economic science.

Today Western economics is in the pincers between these two groups. For example, here is an incident which took place within a large industrial corporation. Union leaders asked Management to declare a worker ill a week after his sickness started. The manager was a sly dog. He stated that the decision really was up to the workers themselves. He called for the foremen, who without hesitation answered, "You don't think for a minute that we will allow these shirkers to eat the sausage from our bread?" This characterizes today's social conflicts: the refusal of those who work to work for those who do not (children, elderly, ailing people, unemployed).

This is not offered as criticism of either the unions or the politicians. It is possible that their motives are noble. (GA 177/1966/163) Their politics have nothing to do with the Principal Social Law. The workers are totally unwilling to let go of anything; something is being taken from them. The fact that this is done for a social purpose is another story. Reality seldom respects good intentions. "The very efforts toward material well-being of people without a spiritual orientation must result in increasing egoism and thus gradually produce need, misery and poverty." Here in 1905 Steiner has already described the welfare state.[12]

Whether this spirit exists will first be seen on the micro level, in the way that individuals behave in institutional life. One can carry out effectively the sense of this law wherever one happens to be active, even in surroundings where the opposite is being practiced. In such cases it is much harder because the supports of established conventions are missing. To be sure, those who fail consciously to seek the community structure simply pocket wages, salaries and even profits derived from more or less blind forces within society. Yet in social life spending rather than earning is the important thing. Each one can decide how much to accept of the output of his fellow human beings (which comes to him in the form of income to satisfy his needs and wishes) and how much to put at the disposal of others. This is his very own moral decision. Is it deplorable to allow the right to the efforts of others to be determined by those who are the source of one's income? Is not the supposed freedom, gained with income, in reality a coercion to consume?[13]

Everybody can use any work as a means to serve fellow humans instead of as a means of income. Where this is actually impossible, for example, when speculating on the stock market, there is also no work involved. Unfortunately, the people who work in this sense are conspicuous. At the end of Solzenytzin's *Cancer Ward*, a cleaning lady puts so much love into her menial and dirty work and is paid a mere pittance. For the first time the phrase "ward nurse," up to this point only a horrible euphemism, grew for me into a concept. As we encounter such human beings, we ourselves become better humans.

Here, too, it is only on the meso level that we come close to the measure of a human being possible today—he stands between the macro social goings-on into which have descended in the subhuman sphere and the rare saint to be found on the micro social level. We have already shown, according to the Basic Sociological Law, that it is in the institutional sphere where people who want to can still have the latitude to regulate their social interfaces themselves, all the way down to the structure. The task at hand is then, in our case, to bring them into harmony with the Principal Social Law. Nowhere has Steiner pointed so strongly to the meso social as when he talks about the Principal Social Law. If one looks beyond the institutional level to the world at large, where in our time is there a "total community" with a "spiritual mission," the fulfillment of which "each individual" wants to contribute? If, on the path to making this law a reality, one is limited to dealing with people "who find the way out of egoism," one can, in our time, think only of small communities for whom "this all-encompassing community is more than an indeterminate sum of individual human beings."

At this point one needs to consider two things. First, communities such as these are not dependent on altruists or even saints. On the contrary, it is only in the working for others that one learns to overcome egoism. "Only he who works exclusively for the other person can gradually become an unegoistical worker." Secondly, we should consider that work in the surrounding society is oriented toward self-interest and that the door to a bourgeois lifestyle remains open. After all, an institution can order its own life only with its statutes, and even then only partially. Hence, institutions based on the Principal Social Law tend to be unstable. Members of the community can withdraw at any time. This increases the temptation to counteract the "good life" with an antiquated hierarchical connection which contradicts the Principal Social Law.

I have good reason to place the "good life" in quotation marks. It is questionable whether bourgeois life contributes more to the "joy of living" than living in such communities, even in a very superficial sense. Research by Tibor Scitovsky ("The Joyless Economy," London 1976) shows that most of the work-saving consumer goods cease being used for enjoyment and, in a short time, become an addiction; they are used to alleviate the displeasure brought about by their absence. Many of the stimulating items of consumption (art, culture, sport, danger) are, in contrast, inexpensive or even free of charge. Furthermore, it would be a misunderstanding to believe that working for others is the same as working for a smaller income. Rather, one can conclude from the Principal Social Law that the exact opposite is the case, namely that the welfare of the whole community increases, including the material base as well. If we can see the Principal Social Law as the principle of the economy, it is logical that this includes good management. In the background is the concept that "only those can work together who have confidence in each other." (GA 36/1961/22) As egoism increases, distrust becomes more obvious and the work becomes shoddier. If distrust is eliminated, performance improves, but the increased yield does not go (directly) into the pockets of each individual but becomes "income of the whole community." The very people who strive to free themselves from egoism are the first ones to reduce their own desire for income in light of the present multitude of needs. This is more or less a side effect.

In this connection we shall describe several budding and ongoing efforts as concrete applications of the Principal Social Law, two examples from the sphere of the spiritual life and one more or less from the life of rights. Sadly, I know of no such effort beginning in the life of the economy. Experiments in this arena have been either too invisible (small alternative shops), or have, in some circuitous way, reverted to the more prevalent wage system. This is understandable, since all enterprises are intimately woven into a world economy, and it is difficult, due to competition alone, to take a single participant out of the established commercial system.

The oldest institution which follows the Principal Social Law is the Camphill Movement.[14] This is where I first encountered the Principal Social Law in action. I asked Karl König (in 1956) how he could find so many coworkers who were willing to work and earn no income. His reply was, "Well, indeed they really don't earn a single penny. But if I thought they had no income, my opinion would be quite wrong. All coworkers get food of great quality. Where else in the world does such a thing happen? They live in really beautiful houses with tasteful furniture. Who on the outside can afford that? They can attend numerous, superior cultural affairs. Where else is this possible? There is enough money for everyone to have wonderful, if not luxurious, vacations. And, furthermore, some married couples live here who can send three and even four children to the Waldorf boarding school. In England on the "outside" one would have to be a millionaire!" This is how I suddenly learned the concept of income as real income.

Basically no one in a Camphill community "earns" anything. Each one satisfies his needs from the "profits" of the community. The community may encompass one house, a few houses, or a whole village, as the case may be. The individual's income vacillates between two poles: what is available in the community and what he needs. Neither is a given. Needs are in constant flow, even from day to day. A fixed income is, therefore, impractical, not even an "advance" which is often used to mask the wage system. The profit of the community is no fixed sum, not even where the state pays sustenance for each child. There are houses with many children and few coworkers — these have a large income of money. The ones with few children and many workers, with elderly people and invalids, have little money to distribute. One does not aim for equality. The Principal Social Law as economic law aims at brotherliness. Inequality demands brotherly help. And as one sees the brother in the other person, inequality teaches us to overcome envy, the greatest enemy of a healthy social life.

Within the total community the needs of each person are not subject to scrutiny. Each coworker has a checkbook, apart from the incidental change everyone carries. Thus, each one can pay for supplies. With regard to larger expenditures, sensible and thoughtful housekeeping demands that one ask first whether this or that is within the present financial scope of possibility and reason. Total visibility of the finances is an indispensable condition. Often a bursar is available to discuss extraordinary expenditures or mediate touchy situations. But it is always possible to refer to the house unit which constitutes the basic financial unit.

We will not address further details here but will revisit the Camphill movement as a model in subsequent chapters. In summary with respect to their main goals, the Principal Social Law is successfully in place in most Camphill establishments. Steiner's prerequisites are fulfilled insofar as regulations really exist to the effect that nobody can ever claim the fruits of his own work and that every person who joins his or her existence with Camphill places themselves in the service of the "spiritual mission" of the community. The result which Steiner ascribes to the law, namely greater well being, is truly being achieved. Within forty years Camphill has grown into a very rich movement in the material sense, not rich in the sense of profits or invested capital or that the members live in affluence. Rather the members are rich in real income, in satisfaction. As a movement Camphill is rich in the sense of the Templars: it owns large estates with high theoretical monetary value. These are, however, not available for egoistical exploitation but for meeting the needs of human beings.[15]

One can experience in the current structure of society that the Principal Social Law is being squeezed from two sides. As we have seen, it cannot be managed in its essential area, namely the economy because therein it is surrounded by profit-oriented institutions. In the cultural area the subsidizing state intervenes in the working conditions with its requirements, for example, to pay the salaries which have been included in its calculations of the degree of support. In doing so it includes the coworkers in the obligatory insurance scheme and, on the other hand, forces them into a wage earning situation. This makes the wage question: "Do you intend social or cultural activities?" when it actually comes to the spiritual sphere. Activity in the social area means a return to extremely primitive conditions—incentive pay is eliminated and those involved are long since thoroughly excluded regarding such extra pay. Thus, the temptation to choose the second (cultural) purpose looms larger. It would be a mistake to reproach anybody on this course of action. Yet one should be honest enough not to justify one's choice with social excuses.

It is interesting to note that, in institutions when the simple pocket money has been replaced with larger sums, this is construed as "underpayment," often causing envy, discontent and rapid turnover of coworkers.

We discovered another attempt to advance the Principal Social Law into new territory on the part of various therapeutic institutions in the Netherlands over the past ten years. The basic model is always the same: the therapists, including the doctor or doctors, work purely on their therapeutic task, without remuneration tied to achievements. The circle of patients decides to carry the cost of the therapists livelihood and all other community expenses.[16] Since this working community is not a joint living community, the money issues are of a different nature as the coworkers take money home. To avoid the traps of the traditional wage system is not an easy task—the danger of a masked wage, a regular advance which could become habitual and grow into a demand, and here we are with a wage system again.

In actual practice, such therapeutic institutions have remained viable only if the doctors join the other therapists as equal colleagues. For the patient this means that he is not only supporter but also patient of the whole institution. From our vantage point this shows that, even after the fact, one cannot tell how much one or the other person has earned. The process of therapy results from a common effort—starting with the diagnosis and extending to the final interview. Wherever the doctor is the highest level, the therapeuticum tends to fall apart into the two camps of the poor brothers and the rich fathers, and the "social structure" is merely window dressing. Incidentally, let us repeat that the distribution of income in no way reflects the law of equality. Thus, the doctor may claim to have greater needs than the consulting hour receptionist. Yet I know of at least one medical office where this is the other way around.

It is impossible to answer clearly the question of whether the "welfare of the community" has risen due to these ways of working together. State intervention obscures the situation too much at present. The contrast between brothers and fathers may well be a replica of the conditions in a society which bestow the power of making the decisions and a higher income to the doctor and allows those who fail to practice pocketbook therapies to shrivel up on the border of minimal existence. Since one is not in a community that lives together, it is difficult to avoid this unsocial layering of the society. Certainly a degree of financial equalization is possible and with it a degree of improvement in well being. Experiments like these are relatively recent. Social forms need (much) time before they yield results.

Finally, though working on common tasks, living in separate quarters impacts the workers' thorough exposure to or immersion in the "spiritual mission." It is tempting to look for the spiritual mission in a shared view of the world or allow it to shrink to nothing more than a close karmic connection. Rather the spiritual mission really has to arise from a social impulse, working for fellow human beings out of love. Actually, this can be easier in therapeutic vocations than in most others because the suffering brother is so concretely present.[17] Here we encounter some of the challenges to implementing the Principal Social Law within the life of the economy. The vocation of the therapist is in fact part of this life in our society.

A final example brought in this book is the banking communities established by the GLS-Gemeinschaftsbank and its sister institutions in Bochum. In a community bank, up to fifteen persons who know each other well combine forces. Each member pays all his earnings into a communal account. Each one can withdraw what he needs to cover his own requirements, up to an agreed upon maximum. Often it is also agreed that no one is allowed to dispose of the portion in the account which he had deposited himself. The account statements show each participant how much he has paid in and withdrawn himself. He can also see the sum of what the others have paid in and withdrawn, but not the individual amounts.

Although these income communities have taken their inspiration from the Principal Social Law, they are mentioned only in the broadest sense of our present context. They are not communities of people who work together. Rather, each one pursues his own vocation separately; he may study or lead a financially-poor existence. Such communities have their home not in the life of the economy or the spirit, but rather in the life of rights, namely the (pure) relationships of person to person. These communities are in no way devoted to the "increase in welfare" but as gathering places for experiences with the "me" and "you." We shall investigate this aspect in the next chapter.

We must remember that these experiences do not refer to public institutions but to private initiatives. There one stands on the border of the meso social and the micro social. One can conclude that here too a positive influence on the well being of all the participants finds expression. A new and, at times, increased consciousness arises of what one's own efforts on behalf of fellow humans signifies for them. (Refer to the second part of Chapter I.) This results in a more economical handling of the means to achieve satisfaction. This again leads to financial surplus. An increased respect for life is nourished in the participants when aims are addressed which, in their eyes, are valid for the future and thus are transformed into gifts of money. The participants know that they can become part of the stream of human progress. Perhaps one may say that the lack of working together is balanced by an increased "spiritual mission."

Such are the small and primitive beginnings. Those who are practicing them will be the first ones to agree. But these beginnings are what it is all about. "Good results are reached wherever this Law makes its appearance, wherever someone works according to its spirit as far as is possible for him on the spot where destiny has placed him in human society. This is true, even if at times only in ever so small a measure. The healing progress of the whole of society can only be built up from individual efforts brought about in this way."

Endnotes:

[1] The quotations in this chapter all refer to the essays in Lucifer Gnosis 1905/1906. These appeared under the title "Geheimwissenschaft und sociale Frage (*Occult Science and the Social Question*) as special edition and in GA 34/1960/ 191 ff.

[2] See H.G. Schweppenhüser "Fallstudien" (*Case Studies I & II*) (Freiburg 1980).

[3] This lecture appeared as early as 1943 in the Swiss magazine *Gegenwart*, but due to the war it was hard to obtain. But then the lecture of December 21, 1918 had already been published in 1921. In it Steiner also makes reference to the Principal Social Law. (GA 186/1963/305. also GA 185 a/1963/60), first published in 1919.

[4] See also GA 54/1966/96 f: "Trouble, misery and suffering are nothing but a consequence of egoism. We need to understand this sentence to be a natural law . . . the struggle for existence is the actual source for misery and suffering insofar as they are of a social nature." Here we find the distinction from suffering of the soul which is the basis of the Basic Sociological Law. "Wages for work done are nothing else than the conversion of egoism into the economy."

[5] I am in agreement with this. Christopher Budd writes in his book *Prelude in Economics* (Hoathly Hill, 1979), p. 13: "The ideas of men change with their consciousness, but the essence of economics is eternal."

[6] One does not express this "output" of the physician's as part of the so-called social product. Nevertheless, this degenerated utilitarian mind set has a subconscious effect on medical practice (GA 127/175/20 f.) For example, a professor at the Erasmus University bases his claim for grants on the monetary savings to the community brought about by timely abortions when certain examinations of pregnant women discover brain damage of the unborn.

[7] Civil service salaries will not solve this problem.

[8] Industrial work sharing and its consequent mechanization, i.e. automation forces a steady decrease of workers needed for a

given end product. This creates a space for fewer work hours or dropouts. Those latter provide a not to be underestimated contribution that makes it even possible to live in our society. Yet this fails to solve the problem of those who are active in the industrial apparatus without whose output we could not exist. It is certainly true that much mass production is not justified by demand and can be replaced with smaller project groups who yet conform to the work sharing concept. But here the question of motivation reappears again, in a form different from handiwork. For now motivation can still be found in the consciousness of making a contribution in the fight against counter-cultural and inhuman profiteering. Yet in the long run it is unlikely that we can continue without a positive motive, a "spiritual mission."

It is quite another question what the decreasing need for work hours will mean to the individual. The freedom from the fight for survival has two sides to it like all accomplishments. I would doubt that the negative side of this can be solved by more leisure time for spiritual development. Leisure tends to be opposed to such development. To work on social problems and new social professions is closer to the mark. The more the state depersonalizes social help the more the will to work in these areas increases in more and more people and the more the need for this type of work increases.

[9] Hans Erhard Lauer "Grundgeheimsnisse des Christentums" (*Basic Secrets of Christianity*). Dornach, 1964, p. 64. Referring to Steiner's *Fifth Gospel* (GA 148) Lauer explains that the formulation of the Principal Social Law . . ." means nothing less than the *answer to the remnant of the temptation* of Christ by Ahriman which at the time *had remained unanswered."*

[10] In GA 93/1979/75 Steiner challenges us to create such forms in our time. The humanity of the sixth archetypal race will transform these into spirit. This form must appear earlier because it has to exist so that Christian life can flow into it. This form has to be distributed by people who will create it so that true Christian life of the sixth archetypal race can root in them. "This form of society must spring from Mani's intention, from the small group which Mani is preparing." We encounter the Manichaean principle again, as we did with the future form of society of the basic sociological law. The

basic sociological law is less concerned "with the nurture of inner life - life will continue in other ways as well—but more with the nurture of the outward form of life."

11. Another aspect is that not only is the work which they don't perform not paid but at times they are punished by the withdrawal of their social help money. R.J.A. Janssen ("Emancipatie ten janzien van de arbeid" Deventer 1982) points out that we should really not speak of being out of work but of not having a job. Even the wording lets us experience how the actuality of our No.1 social problem is being veiled. It is not a natural catastrophe but a problem of our social structure.

12. A quote from 1917 (GA 35/1965/349) can substantiate this. "To the degree that human beings regulate their social life together from their ordinary consciousness, forces intervene which work against the sense of development salutary for mankind." It may in fact be the personally tragic fate of many a politician, and it is above all characteristic for our time, that the most frightful measures have often been decided with the best intentions. This is not meant against social security for all. Our present sense of justice demands that we assure everyone's existence, even if and exactly when, he is so ill that he cannot work although he could do so. This amounts to coerced work via rewards for it is not only moral sour grapes, it violates the Principal Social Law, as we shall see. "It is important that each individual is capable of respecting and translating this principle (separation of work from income) into actual life in total freedom. This total freedom would not be there if the right to income would depend on willingness to work. Yet, if it is established that one *cannot* work for one's own income, this freedom would no longer be in the way." Here Steiner is decidedly against the idea that the separation of work from income, in the sense of the Principal Social law, were a given fact with salaried office workers. Besides, even from an economical point of view a guaranteed existence is preferable to today's controls via social security, because this latter rewards slyness instead of willingness to work. This is demeaning for those actually involved and burdens the firm with expenses and expensive, unwilling workers as well.

[13] In the literature of threefoldness the custom of ignoring the Principal Social Law has led to two symptomatic aberrations from the factor of freedom. In GA 73/1973/178 Steiner called this factor the fundamental concept of social life. Wilhelm Schmundt "Zeitgemässe Wirtschaftsgesetze (*Modern Laws of Society*)," Achberg, 1975, pg. 18, wants to obligate workers to work when the owner offers pay (also Leber, as mentioned above, only based on the moral concept of willingness to work). Lothar Vogel even goes so far as to oblige the recipient of money to be "unconditionally obliged" to "buy goods for the same amount."

[14] It was founded in 1939 by the physician Karl König in Scotland with a few coworkers. At first it dealt with therapeutic schools. Later so-called "villages" were established, places where coworkers lived together with adult handicapped individuals, thus building an economic basis for such a community. Later farms, work with environmentally damaged individuals, teaching pulpits for handicapped as well as "normal" Waldorf schools and training establishments for special education, Eurythmy, etc., were established The individual structures are different not only from place to place (in the meantime there are communities in a dozen countries), but they also change as time goes on. We can sketch only a few features here. I gave a detailed recognition of this social striving in *Info 3*, 1977/6 to 8.

[15] By the way the comparison goes even further. The Templars were rich; the brothers owned nothing. The wealth, or only a tiny portion of it, did not consist of gold, as Philip the beautiful found when he burglared them. It consisted of estates and, above all the confidence the order enjoyed and the fact that for the first time a worldwide organization which extended over all of Europe, Asia Minor and North Africa: "enabled others . . .") See also A.H. Bos "Die Templer (*The Templars*), Stuttgart 1982.

[16] Regretfully I have to bypass the interesting *associative* aspects in this connection. They add to the question of needs, based on the Principal Social Law, the question of satisfying external economic requirements (GA 73/ 1973/ 197). This leads into the macro social area.

[17] Here one has to distinguish two community forming factors, namely the community forming power of ideas, because the "world of ideas, active within me is no other than the one in my fellow men" (GA 4/1921/170); this world lead us to a common understanding of the Principal Social Law. If this world become the basis of action, sectionalism arises. The concrete effectiveness in the sense of the Principal Social Law arises from the "selfless dedication to the object . . . the idea has to reside in the science, love in the performance of our tasks" "Einführungen zu Goethes Naturwissen- schaftliche Schriften" (*Introduction to Goethe's Natural Scientific Writings*), Pocket edition 1962, p. 91.

Chapter V
The Archetypal Social Phenomenon

When human beings face each other, one person is always trying to put the other to sleep and the other one is always trying to stay awake. To talk in Goethe's sense this is indeed the archetypal phenomenon of social science.

— *Rudolf Steiner*

In the lecture cycle "Die soziale Grundforderung unserer Zeit" (*The Basic Social Demand of Our Time*, GA 186/1963/IV and VII), Steiner describes the human encounter in great detail, particularly so in two of the lectures. If one person wishes to understand the other, he needs to be prepared to allow himself to be "put to sleep" for a moment by that person. In so doing, socially he lets go of his own consciousness, and the being of the other person fills his soul. Almost immediately, his antisocial drive makes itself known, throwing the other one out in order to reassert his own self in his consciousness. The other resumes being opposite again, an object. Steiner calls this oscillation between a social act and a resulting antisocial moment the "Archetypal Social Phenomenon." To my knowledge this expression has not appeared in anthroposophical social literature until recently.[1] In fact, within the plethora of Steiner's social-scientific publications, it is only found this one time. Yet he stresses that this expression has the significance of an archetypal phenomenon in the Goethean sense.

Let us address it now. One can approach this challenging expression from various angles: as the result of spiritual scientific investigation, from a philosophical point of view based on the "Philosophy of Freedom," or as phenomena. In observation, as a young child listens, he appears to take the other person into his own being as his mouth drops open and afterwards does not recall what was said. A common reaction on the part of the adult is angry words of "do pay attention" when actually "don't pay such close attention" would be a far more appropriate reaction. For the child takes far more naturally to a social attitude than does the grownup. He simply "forgets" to throw the other person out again. One can also study this phenomenon with adults who become, literally, "captivated" by a speaker. If they stay awake listening (which does happen from time to time), they are so "carried away" that afterwards they can only report, "It was wonderful." The contact has slid directly into their unconscious because they were so captivated that they missed the asocial reaction.

Let us first examine this archetypal phenomenon of going to sleep and reawakening in the light of Steiner's descriptions of wakefulness and sleep in different contexts. Before I begin there is another interpretation, which has some appeal, yet does not seem appropriate. This explanation holds that there are three different rhythms: a long one of dying and being reborn when we withdraw the etheric body, astral body and ego from the physical body; a shorter one of sleeping and waking when we leave the physical body with our astral body and ego; and finally, the rhythm of conversation when only the ego leaves us in the process of becoming social.

Steiner does not refer to this interpretation at all in the two lectures. He talks about inducing sleep, a short period of sleeping and re-awakening. He does not comment that this is meant allegorically to illustrate a new concept. Yet, given Steiner's precise descriptions, this would have been his usual habit. Even when addressing parallel phenomena regarding death and sleep, he would never equate the two concepts when clarifying something about death by referring to sleep. For that reason alone I consider it improbable that we may be dealing with a third "death" rhythm in this case.[2]

Furthermore, in my opinion, we cannot call the very person social, whose ego (only) has left him. We all know this condition only too well since it is most common. A human being not permeated by his ego-consciousness is controlled by his instincts and drives. Such a person is incapable of a typical social action.

We need to make a distinction here. Steiner knows of at least two methods of inducing sleep. These are dealt with in sequence, certainly not accidentally so. They are found in a lecture of November 1919 and appear in the appendix in volume IV of "Die Geistigen Hintergründe der Socialen Frage [The Spiritual Backgrounds of the Social Question]."

One way of inducing sleep takes place through hypnosis using a medium. The subject's day consciousness is taken away. "What does one achieve by removing a person's usual capacity? Through hypnosis one arrives at an external method of observation of the person which allows him to appear not as a soul-spiritual being but in his very subhuman existence, in that which makes him more like an animal than he would be in ordinary waking life." This "descent into animalism" in no way lives in a human being the way it would in an animal. "Experiments such as hypnotism or mediumism bring to the surface what still lives in today's human being from past human conditions and what does not belong to this earthly sphere.[3]

Earlier in the same lecture Steiner contrasts this with a way of inducing sleep which might be called "the social principle," the social impulse of modern times. When we can transpose our lives into another person's life with our soul we meld into the other person. One might say that we leave our own bodies and enter into the body of the other. "As we do this, our life's experience allows something to arise from this act of sleeping into our fellow human, like the dream of repeated earth lives."[4]

Steiner states that we are social only when we sleep and at other times only when we rescue something from sleeping into our day consciousness (GA 186/1963/162). "Instead of our ego, which is now outside us, we have in us the spirit which otherwise permeates the entire world. We drive it out with our ego when we are awake, yet the ego is part of it, too" (GA 202/1970/176). The same is true for the astrality of the world in relation to our astral body. "All who live around us are still totally one with us in their inner being's essence (GA 54/1966/206). On the level of this world-spirituality and world-astrality, we are totally one with our fellow humans in death as well as in sleep (GA 239/1975/133). As long as a human being is not an initiate, his astral body, when moved out during sleep, mixes in with that of the others" (GA 100/1967/200, compare also to GA 181/

1967/VII). This process begins as soon as two people encounter each other. "When two humans face each other, it is a facing off of two astral bodies in love or hate, in good will or dislike. . . . The interchange between human beings consists of a constant exchange of conditions and relationships of the astral bodies." (GA 93/1979/144. See also GA 65/1962/479 and 652, all dealing with the tendency to assume even the outer shape of the other.) As Loeff describes the meeting in the article quoted in Chapter I, this is the reason that, for the socially gifted person, "the appearance of a human countenance subjects us to a verdict" (see Chapter I).

We get closer to what happens in an encounter as we read in GA 187/1979/80): "[In our time] human beings experience something from their ego only indirectly. This is when they relate to another person and karma unfolds." Once again we are being led to the connection between inducing sleep and karma. "When that magical relation to Men or environment which we call compassion or sympathy surfaces, we become especially aware of our ego. . . . This is because we feel something that takes place out there in the world, what is being experienced or thought about, is also taking place all over again within us. We share within ourselves a soul-spiritual event which is happening outside of us" (GA 124/1963/144). If the encounter deepens to "sleep," the ego rises to the highest level of its spirituality.

In sleep the consciousness of subject-object ends. We meld with the other being. Perceiving the "other" bestows on us a sense that makes it possible to feel with another being in such a way as to be one with it, to experience it as though it were oneself. If one perceives the ego of the other by means of thinking, living thinking which he or she bestows on one, one experiences the ego-sense" (GA 170/1978/110).[5] And only "when he grasps not only his own ego but the other one, when within himself he fully grasps a human being, only then does he belong to the human race" (GA 104/1979/198).

We learn more about the connection between the sense of ego and the Archetypal Social Phenomenon in GA 243/1932/127. "We can do this thanks to an organ, namely the sense of the ego. This organ is organised in such a manner as to probe the ego of the other, albeit not with an action of the will when awake but when asleep. The result, obtained when asleep, is then rapidly transformed into knowledge.... In this way I can really call the perception of the other an act of cognition. I must, however, recognize that this act of cognition is only a metamorphosed event of the sleeping will.... We do not consciously live in all cognition which we experience in sleep."

In summary, the listening human being can be filled with the speaking one because he goes to sleep for an instant. What lives in the speaker can in this way be transferred to the listener. This is no less real if it does not always takes place in full consciousness. Quite the opposite is true: the process is stronger under those conditions. A simple example is in advertising: sequences of images flit so rapidly past us that our day consciousness cannot take them in, but sales figures prove this technique is far more effective than directing messages to our day consciousness.

Let us take a closer look at the activity of speaking and listening. "What appears a simple matter of judgment that 'a person is speaking', is in fact the result of very complicated processes. These processes culminate in the experiencing of another ego in a sound wherein one experiences oneself.— The entire mystery of compassion with a strange ego expresses itself in this fact.—One feels one's own ego in the stranger. If he in turn hears the sound of the stranger's ego, his own ego lives in this sound and thus in the stranger's ego.—He who listens to the sound of another human bestows his ego on another ego, but when listening to the sound of a lifeless object, he bestows it only on the sound per se" (GA 45/1970/160f). The process is enhanced if one faces the speaker with veneration. "If one sends the thought of veneration toward someone else, one gives him or her the opportunity to let his or her own being stream into this empty space" (GA 93/1979/248 f). In contrast envy is a totally filled form "with no more room for anything." To what degree the social process succeeds depends totally on whether the listener has "already brought the word to his own judgement before it entered the soul" (GA 165/1981/224) or whether he hears it with tolerance (GA 54/1966/196).

In his lecture series "The Threefold Organization of the Social Organism" (Brachenreuthe 1964, private printing), Karl König calls the human ear the organ of the human being as a social being which lives in our three highest senses. We perceive our fellow man with the sense of language, the sense of thinking and the sense of ego. Here we find the basis of Christianizing the three spheres of society. The Archetypal Social Phenomenon takes place when we perceive our fellow Man.

After this brief glimpse at the findings of spiritual science, we return to our starting point: the social act of falling asleep and the antisocial act of awakening. What takes place in the soul of the two who act out the archetypal social drama? We reference the lecture of January 30, 1921 (GA 207/1972/59 ff).[6] "In a certain sense you have to abandon yourselves, surrender yourselves to them [the words of the other person], so that you perceive the being of the other person in what you hear." At the moment of falling asleep there stands, always just for a moment, our future before us, and at the moment of awakening, always just for a moment our entire past, both reaching into vignettes of past and future incarnations. Although these are erased so quickly, they have a powerful effect on our day consciousness.

Both experiences also occur if one person really puts another to sleep in conversation. Again, we encounter reincarnation in the social process. If the speaker fills the one going to sleep, not only will his future and past surface for him but those of the speaker as well.[7] When the words of the speaker span his past and his future, real understanding is possible. We manage to retain a faint afterglow of this into our day consciousness as "having understood." Only this understanding makes a response possible.[8] Otherwise we "talk past each other."

We can only grasp the full significance of this phenomenon if we look for it not only in conversation, which represent the normal occurrence, but in every human encounter. As Steiner puts it, what has here been expressed for conversation has validity; it is basically true whenever another human being appears before our eyes.

There exist, in fact, people who, whenever they enter a room, fulfill those present to such an extent that they are no longer "themselves." One talks of charismatic personalities. Such phenomena in extreme cases lean toward the pathological. For that very reason they are instructive, and we shall get back to them.

Thus, we have globally retraced the process of mutual understanding between two humans as it transpires from spiritual science. This shows that only a person who has achieved continuity of consciousness, who experiences sleep with full ego consciousness, can participate in conversation without discontinuities. The question arises whether anything can be gained for social praxis beyond pure knowledge of these things. In other words, since the understanding with our fellow men takes place in sleep, what good is this knowledge for us with our discontinuous consciousness?

We have already pointed out that, even with only partially continuous consciousness, a corner of the events taking place in sleep is grasped with every communication. Knowing this can be the source of inspiration or confidence for practicing two capabilities: striving to prolong the social gesture of going to sleep while the other one is talking, i.e. to fight the sudden antisocial awakening, and, secondly, to grasp consciously, at the moment of awakening, what is hidden from our consciousness during sleep.

This brings us back to a comment made in Chapter II, when we discussed the philosophical basis for what is social: the Archetypal Social Phenomenon is our social organ of cognition as well. If, practicing it, we bring it more or less to our consciousness, we really do not change the process. Yet we can increase opportunities to be socially active by the measure to which we succeed in gleaning more or deeper insights from the other's words. The object of social science lies within us, not outside of ourselves. The vista opened up by this experience can make understandable the archetypal social phenomena that take place outside of our immediate experience.

Now we shall illustrate how human beings strive to communicate. We shall encounter much that we know from experience. The theoretical explanations above are much closer than we think to what we already feel. We start with the basic discourse, or conversation, ideally the form of communication when address and reply are fully consummated, as shown in Fig. 1.

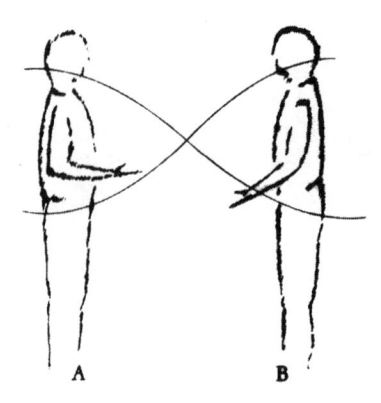

Fig. 1 The Archetypal Social Phenomenon in person-to-person discourse, the basic encounter.

B puts A to sleep. "Going to sleep" affords A insight into B's intentions, the future. A fills himself with it as he sleeps. He takes it along to the "midnight hour" of "sleep," in other words, the point when every night in sleep we are totally spread out into the cosmos (in the picture the point when the lemniscate turns back on itself). This is where B's words find their place. From there A takes it back, and, in waking, what has motivated B dawns on him, namely the past. In this way what B means is transferred to A in its essence. A is now in a position to answer based on B's essential being. The process repeats itself: A puts B to sleep. B gets to know the intent and source of what A has spoken and can, on his part, give answers out of A's essential being.[9]

In fact a communion of spirits takes place here. The conversation reveals its esoteric character. Goethe divined this in his fairytale of "The Green Snake and the Beautiful Lily." (We shall deal with its special significance for the anthroposophical social impulse later on.) As mentioned above, this process can occur in every encounter and in the same manner. The response need not be verbal. Recognizing the other in "sleep" leads to the recognition of his soul or biological need and can result in a helping word or deed.

We have seen that a large part of the process of communication takes place in most people's subconscious. Yet do varying degree-waves of the process penetrate ordinary day consciousness? We know those exceptional persons who are capable of listening and responding. They personify Steiner's words to the effect that we are social only when asleep and otherwise only if we can salvage something from sleep to day consciousness. We are, however, social not only when asleep but also when we allow others to put us to sleep. Being social happens as the result of sacrificing consciousness. Here again we find a parallel to Steiner's description of the workings of the Christ in our time, namely Christ's sacrifice of consciousness for the benefit of the free unfolding of the human being. (GA 152/1980/44 f)[10]

There is a further parallel. As we accept the other person within ourselves while we sleep socially, we add his self in a certain way to the evolving stream of karma. By so doing we reconnect it to mankind. In this way we can accomplish, on a much smaller scale, what the Christ brings about after death, by joining the "socialization" of our ideals to the totality of mankind. (GA 155.1960/39)

Finally, we find a third connection of the Archetypal Social Phenomenon with Steiner's Christology. It involves the moments when we see in the way we deal with another human, if it is grasped with sufficient depth, the realization of what Steiner describes as the two paths to the Christ (GA 189/1946/29 f and GA 193/1968/58 f): to go with the other's thought and to act out of idealism. Thus, the basis in common for two actions is provided by the Anthroposophical Social Impulse: to bring social content to the basically asocial life of the spirit and to the basically antisocial life of the economy. This occurs when a fellow human's need of the soul or body becomes the motive of our actions. Chapter I was dedicated to elaborating this thought.[11]

Now we return to another theme from Chapter I. Social processes are death processes. Part of our ego-relatedness has to die and more than that. What is social is so difficult for us because we do not want to die. In GA 73/1973/178 Steiner considers the dying processes (in contrast to the growth processes) as in organic nature, "a bridge between that part of nature that we understand and the social spheres of life that need to be understood." The death of the plant brings about the seed for the future. Thus, our social future is brought about at the expense of our social death processes. These occur at the beginning of the Archetypal Social Phenomenon. If one perceives the process of falling asleep, then one "learns to understand the significance of dying for the human being." As we allow another to put us to sleep, we therefore "die." Physical death removes our sheaths one by one. Similarly the social process is one of progressive disposing.[12] Steiner cites Max Stirner's words in GA 30/1961/144: "Only when nothing is said about you and you are merely named are you recognized as you; as long as something is being said about you, you are merely being recognized as something." As we awaken in the other, we have an experience which is repeated and magnified in dying. When you have passed through the portal of death, "you are forced to live in the other person, if I may express it in this way." Then one experiences what one has done to him, and this life outside of oneself "makes the future compensation occur." (GA 236/1977/102 f)

Let us get back to our schematic image of an encounter. In the two lectures about the Archetypal Social Phenomenon mentioned earlier, Steiner emphasizes that we are of necessity both social and antisocial.[13] He states that in our time being unsocial comes naturally and tries to totally dominate us, whereas we have to nurture and purposely practice being social.

We can observe this when two people talk to each other. The impulse to put his partner to sleep is stubbornly resisted by that person's unsocial attitude not to allow this to happen. In this way the meaning of the speaker never reaches him. Some single expression which evokes mental associations penetrates to him. The "reply" is a train of thought which has little or nothing to do with what has been said. No conversation takes place, but two monologues are being declaimed.

One can perhaps picture this process schematically by showing that A and B in fact try to reach each other but fail. (Figure 2)

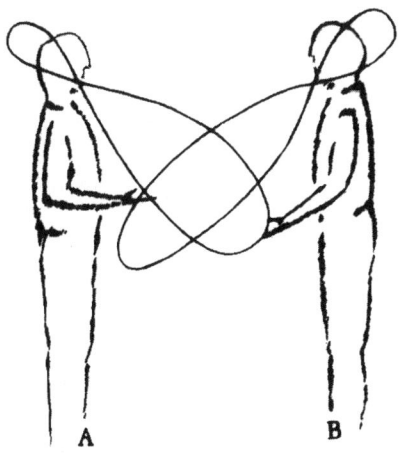

Fig. 2 The partners do not reach each other.

It is also possible that B does not really address A but talks over his head. We all know this from personal experience when somebody wishes to show that he knows everything. The most obvious examples occur in politics. We hear speakers obsessed with structures and generalities to such an extent that they are totally uninterested in the constituency before them. People who agitate in the meso- and macrospheres with their models and programs for a better society belong to this same category. In this case A may be ready to open up, but B never reaches him. One "talks over the other's head." (Figure 3)

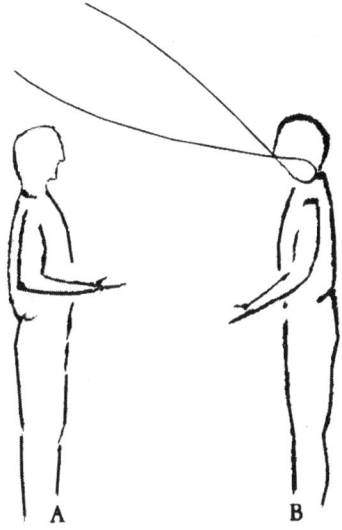

Fig. 3 B talks over the head of A.

The next digression is intellectual banter. Here it is no longer a matter of understanding the other person, but rather the goal is to twist the speaker's statements around or to show up his contradictions. The listener does not allow any train of thought to enter his head but only key words which he could use to formulate a repartee. Any semblance of allowing himself to be put to sleep is out of the question. (Figure 4) One avoids this, since, God forbid, one could be convinced.[14] One can even enjoy this sort of thing in casual company when the mood is light and nobody is taking anything seriously. Applied cleverly, it can defuse touchy situations because one can use it to elevate matters gone too far to an innocuous surface level. However, it is deadly and boring if used in all seriousness. In this instance, one can speak of an "academical debate" at best, or, at worst, the decline of parliamentarism.

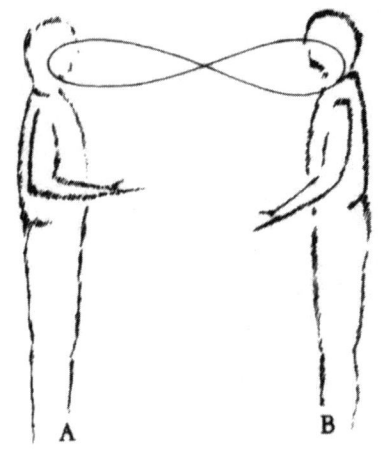

Fig. 4 Intellectual banter: no trace of any inducement to sleep.

The next lower level aims at the emotions of the partner. A picture of "just let the ego hang out" can illustrate this level of encounter. (Figure 5) A gets into a dream state of sorts, and he excarnates somewhat as a result of what B is saying, or simply due to B's presence. Typically for the meso sphere this can be accompanied by affirmative as well as digressing emotions. These are easily recognized in everyday life. On the one hand, we spontaneously like a likeable person, sometimes more so than we really wish. On the other hand, we are predisposed to criticism of statements made by one we dislike, even if later, after more thoughtful consideration, we actually share his opinions. One does not let oneself be completely put to sleep, but only to snooze. The wave of sympathy or antipathy rebounds too quickly and tends to fortify the positive or negative response.

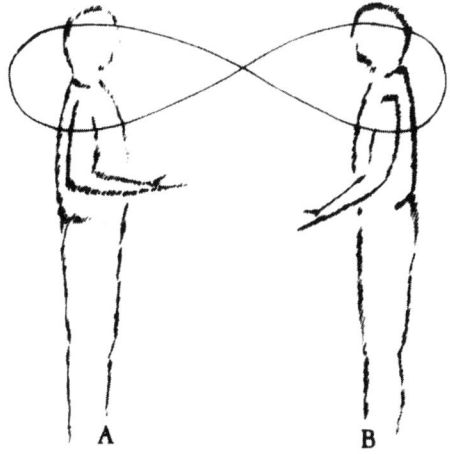

Fig. 5   One addresses the partner's emotions.

Yet another, even deeper "communication" has already been pointed out: B puts A to sleep, and A does not wake up again. A remains filled with B's content. His "response" is, at best, a repetition of what B has said. This is hypnosis: A becomes a tool. An example of this dynamic can be found in modern jazz sessions, as it were, a mass psychosis on a macrosocial level. Another example is when a whole audience is driven to a warlike frenzy. (Figure 6)

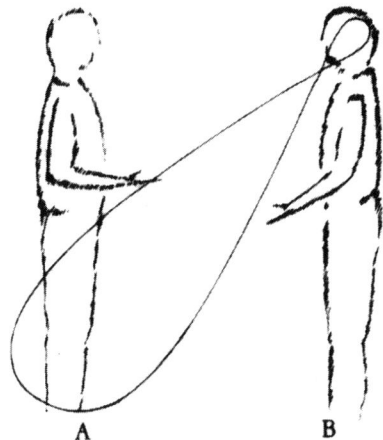

Fig. 6 Hypnosis: the listener becomes a tool.

Yet even beyond this level of sub-human response, further stages may be observed—all the way to the trance-state. The aforementioned possibilities suffice for our purposes to this point. I have the impression that the Archetypal Social Phenomenon, when properly understood and elaborated further, may become the basis of a new science of communication.

The Archetypal Social Phenomenon harbors another eminently social question which clearly illustrates a connection between the social and moral spheres. To what degree is it appropriate to put the other person to sleep and to fill him with one's own content? Because the action of putting the other to sleep is inherent to every social communication and, thus, with being human, it is impossible to get around this question.

The inviolability of the body is a fundamental human right; in other words, nobody has the right to interfere with the body of another person. In the present connection it is not as important that this right is being trod underfoot by police actions, in prisons and in hospitals, but rather the lies and the sophisticated distortions of the law, which deny the fact, that are of greater importance. The denials show how much importance we assign to this right in our times. Our rights are clearly stated that, as for example one formally expressed in Dutch law, a doctor can only physically intervene with a patient's express permission. When there is reason to believe that a patient's state of consciousness does not allow him to make his own decision, it is not the physician but the patient's next of kin who is allowed to decide on behalf of the patient.[15] Likewise corporal punishment in the schools has been discontinued in more progressive countries. Should this be different when it comes to the soul?

This is certainly true in practice. We know of prohibitions only in very exceptional circumstances, such as the imperceptible advertising of hidden persuaders or brainwashing. It is, after all, one of the "freedoms" of speech to not be stopped from trying to persuade another person. But is it altogether impossible to imagine a ban against persuading the other party? And indeed one cannot forbid being influenced. These are areas beyond the law. For this very reason they have great significance in the sphere of rights in a larger sense, in interhuman relations. It is more than mere politeness, when, standing before a door, one knocks and waits for the "come in." In the same way a person with true inner tact feels an appropriate restraint when facing another's soul, only to a much greater degree.

Herein lies a connection to the core anthroposophical works of Rudolf Steiner. For example in *Knowledge of the Higher Worlds and Its Attainment* we read, "Not for one moment must we think that another person could be a mere object of observation for us." (GA 10/1955/66) In the *Portal of Initiation* (GA 14/1920/44) we read that evil fruit could come from your desire to wake the light in others which lives in you yourself. (Ruth and Hans Pusch translation) A passage in *The Story of My Life* (GA 28/1925/320) comes close to this: "Spirit vision should not be abused to research the innermost intentions of our fellow Men without their own wish." The same chaste attitude should be observed when it comes to penetrating into another with one's own ideas, not to speak of attempting to convince him. Alwin Alfred Rudolph, in his *Memories of Rudolf Steiner in the Workers Training School* (second edition, Basel 1955, page 56) writes about Rudolf Steiner: "But never did he correct anyone's spoken opinion." This question was extensively explored in Chapter I in discussing what is asocial. Here we encounter it again as it comes to giving content to the Archetypal Social Phenomenon.

A socially sensitive person will not leave to his own judgment the permission to put another to sleep with his thoughts, feelings and impulses. Such a person will wait to be invited in by the other. A healthy sense of restraint will induce him even to hide his greatest need until he is certain that the other is indeed ready to accept this need within his own soul.

And when the invitation is offered, he will make modest use of it. He will not strive to extend the "sleep" of the other, but rather allow him to return to the unsocial, the "wakeful state" in a timely manner. Since the listener, in contrast, has freely decided to allow himself to be put to sleep, he allows himself to be filled by his partner's concerns. He accepts a great responsibility, namely to answer not based on his own opinion but on his fellow human's situation in life, possibly on the common vision of past karma and future possibilities.[16] His own view ("myself in your place ") is appropriate only when his fellow human asks him to share the problem from his point of view, in other words, when he invites him to put him, in turn, to sleep.[17]

Translating this into the concepts outlined in Chapter I, he who allows himself to be put to sleep (socially) affords the other an opportunity to be asocial, i.e. to follow the instinct to resurrect himself in the other person. The other extreme is to allow the one who has been put to sleep to wake up, that is, to be antisocial, i.e. to face the other as an object. This swing of the pendulum is the basic process inherent in all social events. We have now reached a deeper understanding of why Steiner always waited for the question, whether in everyday matters or in the installation of the new mystery school.

This way of dealing with our fellow man can stand before us as an ideal of being human. It can also be seen as an archetypal image of social hygiene. Today we succeed with this gesture only in rare cases. In its conventional sense hygiene is a way of dealing with the material world where, for example, we either leave dirt where it is or take it where it belongs. Social hygiene is the way of dealing with fellow humans in a similar way. It gives them the space to which they have a claim because they are human.[18]

It is essentially impossible to trace the Archetypal Social Phenomenon on the meso- and macro-levels. We are dealing here with the individual and with the freely chosen initiative which each individual can bring, or not bring, to social life. We can represent this initiative only as entelechies, as spiritual beings, in various establishments or perhaps in even broader connections. Only individuals, not institutions, can be free. In the act of accepting that the other puts us to sleep, freedom and love are both involved. Surrendering our consciousness is a sacrificial deed of love: it can only be offered up in freedom. What flows out of the other remains just as open as does the response, the fruit of this sacrificial deed. We accept the other within us in the place of the Christ. Not I but the other within me. It is soul therapy for both. "Compassion and love enable us to come free of ourselves and to live within the other being." In the same way "it should appear as a mystery that he can, as it were, pour himself into the being of the other soul" (GA 136/1960/65 f).[19]

Strengthening the social component within the Archetypal Social Phenomenon must be practiced. Again, let us point to some practical examples. It is no happenstance that the two examples have already been mentioned in our discussions of the Principal Social Law. Again we encounter the communities inspired by the GLS-Bank in Bochum. It is only possible to endure that other people freely dispense of "my" income if I consider their life as my own, only when the "love thy neighbor as thyself" becomes a reality. The economic life, i.e. the Principal Social Law, commands one to allow the other person to be resurrected in one's own life of wishes and desires, to face his actions as we would face our own.[20]

What happens in this respect in the Camphill movement is, in a way, more typical, because it is more specific. Every Saturday evening everyone comes together in a Bible meeting. The meeting has two parts. The first consists of a conversation about a random theme, often simply about current events. The second is based on a Bible text. From a social point of view both are of equal importance. Whatever is placed on the table is accepted in the sense of the Archetypal Social Phenomenon, regardless of whether it comes from the highest spheres or simply from the heart, whether it be long known or quite serendipitous.[21] One attempts to allow oneself to be put to sleep, to be completely filled with the soul content of the other person and to reply thusly. All criticism, all contradictions, are outlawed as they would rob the Bible evening of its meaning. The intent is accomplished if each participant takes part with the aim not to further oneself (to hear something new, have problems solved), but rather to be a resource for the development of the other persons. Part of the experience of a Bible evening is to respect the point of view of another person even if it destroys one's own. The other aspect, the silent appearance of the other as a person in need, is acknowledged by the sharing of an almost symbolic meal during the first part of the evening. We can imagine what this means for an initiative, and beyond this for all of mankind, if this waking up in the other person were to become a weekly practice.

In conclusion let us briefly address the question of where the Archetypal Social Phenomenon is housed. We have seen that the Principal Social Law is a benchmark for the economic life, and the Basic Sociological Law a guideline for the spiritual life. Is the Archetypal Social Phenomenon then a guideline for the life of rights? Yes and no.

We answer "yes" if we understand the Archetypal Social Phenomenon to be the basis of all that is social, the "I" and "you."

After all, justice is nothing other than the answer to the question of what is due me in relation to the other person. However, we we say "no" by picturing the Archetypal Social Phenomenon as the driving force in the economic and spiritual life as well, unless this is no more than a Robinson Crusoe or a hermitís tale. As I have described in Chapter I and intend to elaborate in Chapter VII, the Archetypal Social Phenomenon comes to expression in the Basic Sociological Law, in the life of the spirit, and the Principal Social Law in the life of the economy. It is both the driving force and the realization at the same time only in the life of rights. The intuitive feeling for what is right answers the question of what is due to the other person as soon as we perceive him. "As soon as a person has recognized something as being right and the opposite as wrong, no external power in the world of the physical plane can convince me that what I see as right within me is wrong" (GA 136/1960/53).[22] This social intuition alone is, however, insufficient for the meso and macro spheres. The principle has to incarnate into the structure and, finally, all the way into the form (the law). The spirit creates its own vessel. To this end we now must turn to the fourth element, the Threefold Social Order.

Endnotes:

[1] Karl König makes special mention of it in his lecture of December 1964 "Der Mensch als socialis Wesen und die Mission des Gewissens" (*Man as a Social Being and the Mission of Conscience.*) This appeared only in a private publication.

[2] See also GA 181/1967/VII, where Steiner describes becoming one with other people as the result of the ego and astral body removing themselves. Yet a contact below the threshold takes place if only the astral body connects with the object. This is evident from GA 127/1975/38.

[3] The following quote also shows us the difference to "just being out a bit." "There is merely a difference in degree between the one acting in deep hypnosis and the conventional scholar whose thinking is not based on the action of his own ego but on what the principal wants to see." (GA 30/1961/339)

[4] See Karl König as another source regarding the connection between the sense of the ego and what is social. "The sense of the ego is the archetypal social phenomenon within us."

[5] As regards the ego-sense and what is social see also Karl König "Der Mensch als sociales Wesen und die Mission des Gewissens (man as a social being and the mission of conscience.) (Private printing) There we find on page 7: "The ego-sense is the Archetypal Social Phenomenon in us."

[6] See also GA 239/1975/238 ff.

[7] This fulfilling, this becoming one with the other, actually represents the stage of intuition which is the basis of the knowledge of reincarnation. To the theme of intuition and social process, see also GA 114/1923/I.

[8] According to Kienle and Knipping in a lecture given in Dornach, "The times in relation to Raphael and Michael." "If in a dialogue one manages to express ideal connections, this is often due to the spiritual being of the partner in the conversation whose individuality merely uses one as an organ of expression."

[9] "One cannot grasp the will if one fails to understand it based on the act of falling asleep." (GA 73/1973/169) "The will is that of our soul being which we carry through the midnight hour of existence, which then lives in us as feeling." (GA 207/1972/77) Feeling is where past and future meet in man in the truest sense. Finally the power of waking up is the one which makes creating mental pictures possible for us.

[10] See also Valentin Tomberg "Die vier Christusopfer und das Erscheinen des Christus in Etherischen" (*Christ's Sacrifice and His Appearance in the Etheric*) private printing of his lectures held in Rotterdam, 1939. There we find a synopsis of the sacrifice of consciousness in the ego and the three sheaths. Another fertile and revealing polarity may be found here. The cognitive path of the *Philosophy of Freedom* consists in becoming more conscious, that of being social by losing consciousness.

[11] We must point out that the process described is not an awakening on the other person but rather in the other person. See GA 54/1966/228. We only wish to mention this problem here; we shall return to it later.

[12] Disposing has two aspects. I can increasingly experience my sheaths as outside world, available to Man like all of nature, and then I may consider the sheaths of the other as important as my own. Steiner describes this as carrying the cross. (GA 99/1962/XIV). Yet I can also experiences my bad habits as mere projections in the outer world. That not I but the outer world is evil. Then I fight against myself by annihilating the other. This phenomenon accompanies other indispensable disposals like a shadow. It is impressively described by Friedrich Glas as externalization. ("Konfliktmanagment" [management of conflicts} p. 204 f)

[13] He uses the expression "antisocial." I have to differentiate between two possibilities of not being social, namely the asocial and the antisocial and, when both are meant, I use the term "unsocial."

[14] See GA 181/1967/II: "Just think about it. All social intercourse is merely cerebral communication, totally unfit as the basis of social life."

[15] If everyday practice violates this, the reason for this lies first with the doctor's and patient's immaturity, in the sense of the Basic Sociological Law. "We need to get to the point where we can allow authority to act, but also where we are able to judge their actions." (GA 168/1976/IV)

[16] In the *Fifth Gospel* Steiner presents the archetype of a correct way of answering, when he describes the reaction of the two Essenes to Jesus' words: "They sensed these words to be something like the echo of their being resounding from his being." (GA 148/1963/238)

[17] I want to offer only three quotes from Steiner: "The other, after all, is always wrong, or at least he is right only when we feel we have to agree with him." (GA 187/1979/146 f) "He is greater because he is like I am too" (Introduction to Goethe's natural scientific writings, pocket edition, p. 106). "The fact that you have recognized some truth, or that you are convinced of it, should not be a reason for you to thrust this truth on to others. You should communicate it only to those who are in a position to ask you for it in the right spirit and total freedom." GA34/1960/284)

[18] In no other area were Steiner's directions as ignored as in the case of social questions. To witness this one merely needs to

attend an anthroposophical artistic performance. Forms, colors, attire of the guests, furnishings of the room —in short the whole ambiance—all mirror the typical anthroposophical demeanor. The best seats have been reserved long before. No, not just for those who are hard of hearing.

[19] One uses the expression "social hygiene." I have not encountered it in Steiner's writings. Though he refers to "hygiene as a social question" (GA 314/ special edition 1963), yet he deals with the question by talking about the way medical achievements are able to produce improvements in hygiene in a democratic manner. In this connection we probably need to understand all health related issues. The theme addresses public hygiene in particular (p. 7). Here the expression "public" does not stand for "state'" but for "social." Next to this medical hygiene we place social hygiene in our context. In the second part of the lecture Steiner alludes to how medical hygiene relates to different members of the social organism, but he does this without using the term hygiene.

[20] In this connection see also in GA 148/1963/271 for the basic description of the Archetypal Social Phenomenon: "Jesus lived totally involved in beholding the destiny of the human beings for the very reason that the ego was absent."

[21] It is an interesting phenomenon to observe that it is much easier to be tolerant of the drives and desires of another person when one is at the edge of minimal existence rather than under well-to-do conditions. I emphasize this because I have heard many remarks about the Bochum communities to the effect that under relatively wealthy conditions such experiments are easier than when everyone has nothing. The truth of the opposite is based on the fact that we can quite easily identify with the true needs of the other because they hardly differ from our own. As the Americans say, "Below the belt we are all the same." Our common biological base allows a feeling of solidarity to rise within me, as I face an actual person and not the anonymous (developmental example) human being. It gets difficult as soon as I have to deal with the life of desires of the other person, in other words with the wishes of the consumer which arise from the soul. However generous I may be toward you when I am by myself,

as soon as you appear with somebody else, the moralist within me awakens, and the more so if he should satisfy your using "my" income.

[22] I do not know if this expression has ever been used. It appears more probably to me that the soul's path to Christ was godfather when Karl König established the Bible evenings.

[23] GA 136 reads: "That which reveals itself as being right, were wrong in my soul."

Chapter VI

The Threefold Social Order
or
The Appropriate Form for Our Time

In this chapter we will concentrate on one of the various aspects of the threefold social order, the *Threefold Order as Structuring Principle*. We can also call it "the Fundamental Structual Law"[1] if we consider the term "law" in a broader sense. The threefold idea has no specific content. What is being produced and consumed, what art form or pedagogy is being perfected, what laws, what monetary system are being developed and imposed — all this is not touched by the threefold idea. Rather, what can be said in this connection works, at best, as examples to elucidate the threefold principle. In his last public lecture on the social question, Rudolf Steiner criticized the fact that these examples had become more prominent than the law behind them.[2]

Yet nothing inferior, nor anything of a lower order or anything subordinated, is implied by the term "Threefold Structural Principle." Without order all diligence expended in the economic life, all abilities of the spiritual life, fizzle out to nothing. What would a school be in which every teacher and every pupil could show up when it pleased them? A factory where anybody could press any button? For all social life the Threefold Order is of the same existential importance as procedural law, the laws governing how one can get justice, which make justice a reality. What good would be civil law, what good the best criminal law, if there would be no legal order giving every person the possibility to "obtain justice"? Yet the most beautiful set of laws is of no use if the population lacks a feeling for justice. In the same way the Threefold Order cannot replace a lack of social commitment in the economic life or a lack of social initiative in the life of the spirit. All it can do is to make what exists fruitful.

Fundamentally, the Threefold Order outlines the task which can prevent the antisocial forces in the economic life and the asocial forces in the life of the spirit from flowing over into social areas where they have detrimental effects. They do this by interposing a separate regulating sphere between these two poles, thus changing them from a duality to a polarity, not to absolutes but to a mutually determining pair of opposites. Steiner circumscribes this in-between area in its macro social variation as "external life of rights." (GA 193/1972/II) It encompasses administrative law, state law, and the meso social variation, the statutory law. The asocial and antisocial processes are discussed in detail in Chapter I. In review, the human as a biological being must be antisocial; in other words, he must take something from his fellow men. The life of rights helps to control this antisocial drive by keeping it within its proper bounds, that of personal consumption. Therefore, the economy requires an order within which production and distribution no longer have the capacity to be used for exploit. These instruments are:

a) Private ownership of land. The different types of the earth's surface represent a gift from the past for all of mankind. It is the basis of food for all of us. The only way it comes into private hands is by occupation (taking of land) or usurpation (forceful taking). In this way artificial legalistic means were created. The injustice perpetrated by privatization of land (considered more inclusively as land and all natural riches of the earth), can be reversed if these revert to the hands of the community. The latter then can bestow rights of use under various conditions.

b) Private ownership of capital. Capital is the condensation of spiritual abilities applied to the economic process. Our present (Roman) judicial system denies the spiritual life all the excess (profit) which it has created through various means of production (machines as well as organization). But the spiritual life is the only justified owner of these excess values. Therefore, capital must be returned to the sphere of the spiritual life and the use of it granted to gifted producers.

c) The nature of labor as a commodity. The ability to work is linked to the unique personality of the human being. Selling labor, a practice of our current wage system, is selling (a part) of that human personality, or, in the final analysis, slavery. Only when work and income are separated can the question of income become a legal one. What is due to me is then expressed in relation to my fellow humans.

This approach assigns the management of land to the community, of capital to the life of the spirit, and of the distribution of income to the life of rights. This eliminates the three pillars of our economic order, namely the markets in land, capital and labor. The marketing of money will then be forced to change its character.[3] The marketing of goods then becomes the only meaningful one.

To the degree that human beings are ensouled, they must be "asocial." Not only do they have to develop in seclusion from their fellow men, but they must also convince themselves of the "truths" thus gained. As antisocial beings we have the tendency to treat other people as objects. As asocial ones we belittle their dignity in a different way, namely by wanting to resurrect ourselves in them, by wanting the other person to confirm our "truths." Freedom is particularly endangered if we use the law or the economy to accomplish this.

The life of rights exists in order to see to it that this asocial drive is allowed free reign only where it belongs - in self-development. Therefore, the life of the spirit should be ordered in such a way that the individual is protected against the asocial tendencies of his fellows. A new way of ordering the entire life of the spirit would have to grow out of what already lives in human rights, albeit as only a beginning, so far just lip service. The life of the economy must lose the rights which it has usurped, and the life of the spirit must be shielded with new rights to protect it against overreaching on the part of the state and the economy.

The different members of the complete organism, once transformed into self sufficient entities, can easily accomplish the tasks for which they are fitted by their own nature. Thus, they can create a more economic way of satisfying needs, a flowering of everyone's inherent gifts, and the creation of concrete realistic feelings for the legal system and its execution.

Beyond this the threefold order has no part to play with the content of what is created within the individual spheres. As such the content of the threefold order has nothing to say about how an emancipated but autonomous economic life develops. Even the idea of associations in "A Theory of Knowledge" (GA 23) is merely illustrative. The concept is substantiated scientifically in the book *World Economy* (GA 340). Here it is presented as the new economic principle, which the economic life *may* embrace. Threefoldness says just as little about the life of the spirit. It is everyone's own business. It is *their* business whether they choose diversity or monotony, Waldorf schools or religious schools, beatnik sessions or yoga. The Waldorf school is no more a model of free spiritual life in the macro social sphere than "Der kommende Tag" [The Dawning Day] is for the economy. Finally, the question of what should become law is the business only of persons who work within a legal system, freed from the economic life and spiritual life. Whether they retain a system of political parties or hit on different ideas, how they want to distribute income, what they consider to be worth protecting (abortion, euthanasia) is *their* business, not that of the threefold order in its role of creator of social forms. The famous/infamous ordering of money also is not part of the Threefold Order. Of course, as anthroposophists one would argue for a threefold ordering of money. But one would do this based on the discussions within the autonomous organs of the economy, all integrated with the monetary system and, hence, legitimately interested in it. It is quite possible that different solutions will emerge as a result of competition between different concepts.

This is stated with emphasis because, for the most part, taunts and quarrels between representatives of the threefold order concern these very themes. These are no business of the "threefolders." It is utopian to think in terms of dreams of a future the details of which have been filled in. It is Marxist to anticipate a development that ignores real human beings by assuming some future situation as required or called for by the structure. Both violate the threefold order as a structuring principle. "Where other systems think out an automatically functioning law, the threefolder thinks about the human beings whose thoughts, abilities and impulses he does not wish to anticipate. He knows this is where he has to stop inventing and leave the person really involved in the action to think and act.[4] Threefoldness is practiced freedom. It is a totally different matter that this ordering principle at last makes it possible for the moral impulse of the Archetypal Social Phenomenon to impact social life, that the Basic Sociological Law is really taken into account in the life of the spirit and that the Principal Social Law has real opportunities within a threefold society. Why is this?

This question brings us to the core of the societal structure. We have seen how the law of development moves forward to freeing the individual from the interests of associations. This means that the demands of individuals aim more and more toward freedom. The rights to freedom, once gained, want to be protected, and the state has to take care of this. This is what we experience today and can hardly imagine it to be otherwise. Once the time comes when it is a matter of course that others have a different view of the world because we see a welcome correction to our own narrow bias, then whose spiritual freedom is there left for the state to protect?

We have seen how the well-being of a community of people who work together depends on their social structure, that is, on the degree to which this structure prevents working for oneself. This opens the possibility for many structural levels. It is quite certain that the human inclination to exploit fellow men will make itself felt and present challenges for the state. Yet once humans feel the misery and need of their fellows, what is there left for the state to protect?

From this point of view we experience the Threefold Order as bounded by time. It is the structure appropriate to solve the social question *for our time*. Unlike in some land of utopia or in the Marxist theory, this is not followed by the perfect state. Then the social question will assume a different aspect, just as it presented a different one in our time than at the time of the Industrial Revolution. In Steiner's words,[5] then mankind will have to think of a different structural principle.

Let us attempt to sketch the forces active in the social organism.

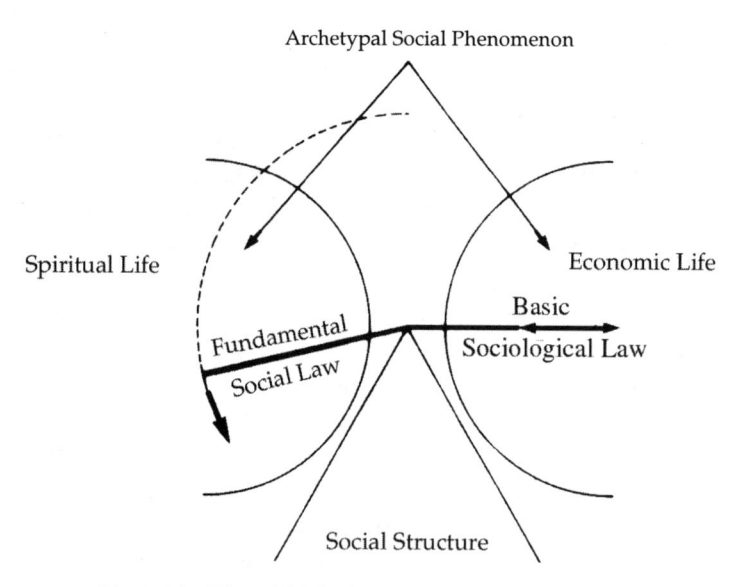

Fig.1. The Threefold Order as Regulating Principle

The Archetypal Social Phenomenon introduces a dynamism to the evolving Basic Sociological Law within the spiritual life to the degree to which the Principal Social law is being realized in the economy. This dynamism is kept in balance by the social structure.

The Basic Sociological Law gives expression to a force which works in human evolution, regardless of whether the social structure takes this evolution into account. More and more of the fetters used by the state to keep its subjects in check are broken. I would like to compare it to the hand of a (social) clock. It advances inexorably from a theocratic starting point to a situation where it appears turned upside down as the association in the service of the individual. This stands face to face with another hand, this one belonging to the Principal Social Law; this hand indicates the degree to which the human beings in the social organism work together at any one time toward its wellbeing. This shows which way the organism leans. The evolution of human capabilities affects both principles, and not merely as they are given as a potential in their development, but primarily as they are taken up by human will. If we may elaborate the analogy of the clock a little further, we may say that we deal with its escarpment. The Archetypal Social Phenomenon comes to expression in the swing of the pendulum. To what degree are the social impulses carried over to the economy? How many of the liberated forces of the individual personality which further social disintegration can be converted to growth forces within the life of the spirit?

Incidentally, the hands on this clock are very sensitive. Our society must somehow keep them in balance. The principle of structure, the last one, has this as its purpose. It must be movable enough to be able to compensate the "over-" or "under" weight of either hand, by moving the point to where it supports the structure without interfering with either. It juxtaposes the "balance wheel" of the Archetypal Social Phenomenon with the repose of the jewel (clock bearing) of the formative principle.

As previously mentioned, the Principal Social Regulating Order for our time is the Threefold Social Order. It does not exist to force those who do not want to work for others to do this, but it prevents one from keeping the fruits of one's labors for oneself. It does not exist to expel individuals from associations, but it stops the association from pushing people around. Least of all does it exist to ask people to be more social. Yet it will have to absorb social hiccups, be they progressive or regressive, and it always has to reestablish the balance.

Furthermore, we must keep in mind that, although the Basic Sociological Law is a law of development, not all associations will stay in step with it. The old continues to live and what was long ago overcome suddenly reappears. This is even more so in the meso sphere which we yet have to discuss. All this means that there needs to be leeway for all conceivable stages of development within the Threefold Order. Theocratic associations must be able to establish themselves next to anarchistic ones, hierarchical economic societies next to associative ones. This must be because it is *also* part of the present stage of development to forestall coercion toward a free social form.

This may sound contradictory, but, for the reasons given above, the social structure is the most movable part of the social clock. The Basic Sociological Law, the law of development, advances ever so slowly because it also represents the development of the human soul. The relationship between working for oneself and working for others (Principal Social Law) may have rapids in its flow. On the whole it proceeds in slow, historic waves. The Archetypal Social Phenomenon, dealing with social will, has to find its point of attack; it must take effect in both the above and in changes within the structure. Such changes can lag behind or move ahead of the development of the life of the spirit and that of the economy. The Archetypal Social Phenomenon must somehow create a balance within society. Yet this balance must *always* be unstable. The structure is constantly moving like the rhythmic system in the physical body. It has to adjust, level off, put on the brakes and stimulate. It is the present, constantly being born anew.[6]

In fact, our present time places demands on a structure that may be sketched in rough outline, yet needs to be flexible enough to be embodied in the most manifold forms.[7] Again, this structure is the Threefold Order. It allows any conceivable concrete forms within the spiritual life because it makes it stand on its own. This structure takes account of the above demand, that old theocratic formations like the Roman Church find the same right to exist as do associations who already want to be ahead of the times in the sense of the Basic Sociological Law. Although man in an autonomous spiritual life is freed from the interests of the associations, nobody stops him from subjecting himself to these interests. The life of the economy is similar. Here classical hierarchical undertakings must be just as possible as working in communes. The concrete form must see to it that coexistence with equal rights is possible everywhere. I do not mean just the outer form of equality but rather a material equality in all conditions of life. For instance, this does not exist if one can and another cannot buy information time (television) and space (newspaper ads), or if one would grant graduation privileges to one gender and not to the other. It is also not present when schools of higher learning are obligated to accept graduates from all classes of society, if one would fund all equally. And finally, even the actual juridical challenges, the distribution of income, the administration, the prison system, and so forth, would need to be amended. These are exposed to unheard of rapid changes of the consciousness of right and wrong in our time. Just think of questions concerning foreign workers (at times of boom and recession), the behavior of the police (prior and since the revolutionary army faction), the latitude given to the administration, etc. All this calls for an extremely flexible structure that makes possible a multitude of embodiments in (legal) forms.

"Thus, it is not a matter of creating a thought image of the form the social organism should take." (GA 189/1946/72) This would even exceed our powers of thought. This is why we are called on to transfer the ordering and administration of large areas to those who have their fingers on the pulse and can instantly react. The three members must be given "their own legislation and administration." [ibid] The state is merely left to control whether one remains within the threefold structure.

At this point an important distinction must be made. I will call it "structure versus form." With structure we mean the formative principle, the force that creates the concrete form. As the structure of a plant reacts to specific weather conditions in different ways (large or small leaves, deep or broad roots, short or long stems), so does the social structure react to the various social conditions with different forms. We call these laws, statutes, conventions.[8] Yet, in contrast to nature, social structures are not predetermined, but rather they are human creations. They may be the expressions of deep insights into social laws, or they can also be mere constructions. In the latter case there is always a chasm between the structure and the concrete form, for example the Marxist-Leninist model and reality in the Soviet Union. This bears the stamp of an enforced situation. It takes time for reality to prove stillbirths as such. Yet it is important that viable structures are created, pliable enough to produce the different forms as needed. In reality one can find a host of theocratic forms, all expressions of the one theocratic structural principle. These forms show us how once living structures in time grow rigid. In that case they iterate the same form, sometimes blown up to gigantic proportions (mammoth formations). Just think of the monotony of corporations in the economic realm and of the many societies in the sphere of the spirit.

The Threefold Social structure is flexible because it was gathered from the very nature of the human being. Yet this does not mean that it is an image of the threefold human being. The fact that it was gleaned from the nature of man has led to many misunderstandings. It means two things. In the first place threefoldness gives man, at his present stage of development, the opportunity for an optimal unfolding of his differentiated abilities of soul. This is the reason why threefoldness as organizing principle can be not only understood by but is quite evident to every non-prejudiced person. This is why Steiner could make the demand that the Threefold Order be hammered into the heads of men. This why the pupils in Waldorf schools were to master threefoldness like the three R's by the time they left school. This would not force anthroposophy on anybody, nor infect children anthroposophically.

To be sure, the Threefold Order is an outgrowth of anthroposophy in the same way that all social formative forces "have to be recognized by supersensible observation, then incorporated into the social life."[9] (GA 35/1965/349) Once present as a structure, it has totally emancipated itself from its source. Unlike anthroposophical pedagogy, medicine, agriculture, and so forth, it no longer requires continuous nourishment from anthroposophical substance. This circumstance makes it a questionable theme for many Anthroposophists. It waits for humans to make use of it. The Threefold Social Order is, in fact, "the organism gleaned from the human being," (GA 328/1977/95) the organism that challenges man's own social formative power, the structure of the human being who has been released to freedom. It does not wish to "shape outer arrangements so that *these* by themselves enable man to have a socially satisfying life." (GA 24/1961/70) It provides the framework "to find arrangements within which people develop really social impulses," (GA 191/1972/46) a framework within which he can "base his happiness on very different foundations." (GA 328/1977/96) The Threefold Order leads neither into God's own country nor is it a workers' paradise. Instead, it is the answer to the question: "How must humans be organized so that when they live together in this way, they find the right social impulses?" (GA 331/1963/48)

It is reasonable to conclude then that only within this system can the actual anthroposophical social impulse come into its own,[10] just like any other one. Every person wants to be free to develop; every person is interested to share the scarce earthly necessities; the feeling for justice in every person demands that, in matters of justice, every person's voice has equal weight. When reduced to basics, these three principles are really quite evident. They become questionable only when in the process of confronting a complicated problem or, perhaps more so, when under the influence of conventional points of view. Under those conditions our contemporaries start to shy away. This should not be interpreted as a sign that these principles are of dubious value, but rather as a demonstration of their necessity and of the inability to sort out complicated matters. Except for this, people's views collide when the freedom of the spiritual life, the brotherliness of the economic life, and the equality of the life of rights are to be really introduced. But at that point we have already left the domain of the Threefold Order far behind. Here ideas are to be proven in competition, and experts have to prove their expertise.

The second meaning of the Threefold Order as principle, gathered from human nature, points to the threefold mechanism of the Man's physical organization: the nervous-sense man, the rhythmic man and the metabolic man. This organization can teach us how three autonomous systems can maintain their characters and yet form a unified organism as they permeate each other. One simply must not compare their particular members. If one fails to strictly differentiate the social from the physical organism, one arrives at very mixed up analogies. Nowhere does Steiner say that the idea of the Threefold Social Order was fashioned after a human threefold organization. Steiner only states that very specific social *processes* are *comparable* to processes in the threefold human. For example, the life of the spirit is likened to the metabolic process, because in the life of society anything coming as a new idea from the spiritual life must first be "digested," before it can nourish the economic life, similar to the way in which digested food nourishes the physical nervous system. This is only a comparison, not a parallel.

Because the social life is a human creation, the forces at work within people also flow into the social life. We can recognize them most clearly in the micro social sphere, whereas they become increasingly indistinguishable in the meso and macro social spheres because they come under the influence of historical forces, forces involving the psychology of nations and other forces. With this proviso, let us make a few remarks to this theme.

Social threefoldness addresses three relationships which every person, who stands at the peak of the present time, has to perfect. As a biological being, he is forced to gain a relationship to the material world in order to feed, clothe and protect himself. Man is called upon to dominate nature (I Moses, I.28). Here he is faced with the world of the father, and he faces what is given. Then he must arrive at a relationship to himself, if you want: to God, to his higher ego, and so forth. He carries within himself the will to develop because he is an ensouled being. He gleans the Holy Spirit out of the future. And finally, there is the question of his relationship to his fellow men. He may treat them as objects (exploit them, penetrate them with ideologies), or he may acknowledge them as subjects. They demand a personal relationship only in the last case: what is due to me relative to my fellow humans? This relationship is not necessarily created because man is a biological or ensouled being. As a spiritual being he is left to his freedom to develop it. We enter the realm of the son. We have found a first "threefold order" in the micro social sphere, that of body, soul and spirit.

This clearly shows that in its striving to develop, the soul is indeed turned toward the domain of the spirit, yet that which is thus created, the spiritual life of mankind, is the domain of the soul. (GA 171/1964/212) What we take in as rights is, however, pure spiritual substance in our personal lives. "The Christ will acknowledge him as his brother who acknowledges the other person as a brother." GA 159-160/1967/318) This in no way creates a land of the spirit in society, but it is power of transformation for the earth and for mankind; it lays the foundation for an earthly kingdom. And finally the life forces which are being destroyed in the economic life (in production, in work, in consumption) create future things, starting with biologically regenerating the consumer. This revitalizing again creates the basis of the corporeal death processes which are tied to the activity of consciousness. And finally, work for the (also and precisely) anonymous fellow human creates a connection to future life: karma.

The three members of the social domain lose their uniform character as soon as the middle ground, the social principle, impacts the life of society. We need to remember that the central principle is ever in a state of instability. The moment it is about to realize itself, it seeks to connect, at least partially, to the other poles. We know this from the division of the rhythmic system into the heart and lung organization, from the dual aspect of intellectual and sentient soul, and so forth. Thus, the self-sufficient rhythm of social and unsocial may fall apart into asocial and antisocial. It is also possible that the social and both the nonsocial variations can coexist separately.

Let us look at the life of the economy. Robinson Crusoe can dominate the earth without social problems. Until Friday appears he has only technical problems. These are only the interface of his abilities (spiritual life) with the natural environment (economic life). The middle realm is missing. This is why economists love Crusoe. He could have been invented for them alone.[11] Of course, Crusoe is an abstraction. In real life scarcity of means to satisfy needs brings up the social question of who is allowed to satisfy which needs. The interhuman problem of social and unsocial is created. Do I exploit the other person (antisocial), or do I work for him (social)? The first possibility already has its legal form: capitalism. The second one is still wrestling with such a form. In the background of this stands the third demand of the French Revolution: brotherhood. By no means does this imply an equal budget for everyone, or an equal parcel of consumables. There are those men who forbid their wives to go to hairdressers because they have bald heads. This has nothing to do with brotherhood. The person who helps his or her brother or sister is the very one who helps his brother in spite of the fact that they both had the same inheritance. Recognizing the fellow human being as spiritually equal to ourselves, a characteristic of the social attitude, translates in the economic life as compassion, as help in bearing what is undeserved.

Similar thoughts apply to the life of the spirit. A hermit may strive toward an inner highflying adventure without creating a social problem. This is less of an abstraction than Robinson Crusoe, but perhaps a borderline case. True, he is free to climb up to asocial heights. Yet, in doing so, he will develop the urge for either a confirmation from others (I have described this in Chapter I as a way of obscuring one's own inadequacy) or the help of others. Here, too, asocial and social attitudes may tend to part company. Here, too, the legal form for asocial behavior has already been found. Ideological dictatorships love to practice legally supported snooping into people's convictions. See the Russian propaganda trials! The legal form for what is social is only in the beginning stages. Here the real significance of the demand for "freedom for the life of the spirit shows up in its true form. I am by no means free as I strive for knowledge. Truth is compelling because I cannot think against realized truth. At best I am free to act either with or against my convictions. Yet in so doing I am leaving the (pure) life of the spirit." Therefore, freedom of the spirit can never apply to oneself. There exists a social demand, meant to prevent forcing truths on anyone, truths which he cannot accept as such. Such truths may harm his soul life. "One should speak of the freedom of the soul insofar as humans are in the land of the soul, that is of a social condition that allows absolute reign to freedom of the soul." (GA 158/1968/ 183) In matters of social freedom of spiritual life it is, therefore, always a question of freedom of the one who thinks differently.[12] Social attitudes begin when one makes room for them, when one thinks with the other person. Recognition of the fellow human as an equal in the spirit translates in the spiritual life into sharing the other's truths, as active tolerance.[13]

Because these different qualities of the life of the soul mingle in this way in the various members of the soul life, the relationships here get very complicated. Only the life of rights provides a fixed point as structural principle, wherein the feeling human being acts. The feeling for justice is the basis wherever it is a matter of real justice, not of Roman jurisprudence. Yet this is the factor which disappears as independent entity, unless it continually replenishes itself out of the Archetypal Social Phenomenon. Justice must be reborn out of the situations of the moment.[14] If this does not happen, it becomes merely a template, an abstract means of coercion and, finally, a superstructure, an instrument of power, an instrument of interests as used routinely in today's politicking. The regulating principle is determined from without; it is destroyed as principle by itself.

If left to the nature of the asocial person, the life of the spirit represents what he brings from that life to society with his talents. Thus far this is primarily a matter of ways of thinking, if not as creator of culture, then simply as a transmission to the population, as what Alfred Weber calls the process of civilizing.[15]

Strong application of will forces is indispensable not just to enrich human culture but also, and particularly so, to impact social life, to further spontaneous creation of what moves the other person, i.e. toward an enrichment somewhat in the sense of Weber's "Kulturbewegung." One can then understand the life of the spirit either as a thinking or as a willing activity depending on the aspect involved.

Finally, in the life of the economy we apply our will forces to change the earth with our work. This is, however, only half true. Grouping economic trends without thoughts, being capable of handling them mathematically, these activities become more and more characteristic for the economy. This holds true in commerce, the manifestation of the central area, and even more so in global economy, this antisocially exploited field of social life. Therefore, depending on the point of view, the economy can be ascribed to either thinking or willing. If one has no accurate understanding of which phenomena one is looking at, this results in random correspondences, and classifications becoming indistinct.

In summary the life of the spirit is spirit coalesced as social reality. Generally speaking, we retrace it with our *thinking*. If we wish to be creatively active in the spiritual life, we must *will* the spirit, will new spirit. Additionally, economic life is human power, human *will*, coalesced as social reality. Where we have the task of working actively in the life of the economy, we need to have these forces in our thinking. Finally, in the life of rights, past feeling for justice has coalesced into laws. If a new life of rights is to arise, we need to *immerse ourselves with our feeling* into the developments of the spiritual and economic life as we follow them.

The reason why thinking lags behind the increasingly complicated economy lies in the expansion of national economy to world economy. The experiences of many different people have to be combined to arrive at insights and understanding of factual connections. It becomes obvious that it requires a collective learning process to work out socio-scientific processes. Associative living demands an increased mental ability, the transformation of thinking into the inner quality of imagination, as described by Steiner (GA 12). In the same sense the development of inner life which embraces the ideas and views of the other person provokes the inner quality of inspiration and, to crown it all, the life of rights depends on intuition.

Already in his *Philosophy of Freedom* Steiner articulates this for the realm of laws. "All state laws have sprung from intuitions of free spirits, just as did all other objective moral laws." (GA 4/1921/177) As to the general life of rights, he says, "Thus it is only possible to comprehend the life of rights by means of intuitive mental pictures, again taken from factual reality." (GA 73/1973/202) We can only do "do justice" to another individuality by becoming one with him or her.

Here again, doubts can arise. Is it not a well-established, anthroposophical spiritual concept to count thinking as belonging to imagination, feeling to inspiration and willing to intuition? Yet rights, corresponding to feeling, are assigned to intuition. To be sure questions are surfacing that have yet to be answered, questions intimately tied to the the peculiarities of social life. We shall briefly return to these in the last chapter. The problem has many levels, and the established conceptual connections do not work in many respects. Yet when it comes to our present theme, Steiner was unequivocal in his first (public) lecture where he depicted the threefold idea. He points out that the economic realm can be understood only with imagination, the life of the spirit only with inspired cognition, and the life of rights only out of intuitive concepts. (GA 73/1950/124 ff. h)

One way to approach this fact is to consider that it is the privilege of the highest intuitive spiritual forces to be effective in the lowest sheaths of the human being, right down into the physical body. Yet the *form* which man has embodied in the social organism is that which has incarnated most deeply and which can be compared to the physical part of the human being.[16] Steiner calls this the purely earthly. The life of the economy, up one layer, corresponds to the human processes of life, and the life of the spirit to those of the soul. It is man's calling to gain increasing dominance over his sheaths out of his ego. In the same way he is called upon to constantly permeate the social organism with the forces he brings to it by activities in the sense of the Archetypal Social Phenomenon.

Thomas Aquinas demonstrates the steps of the law by describing the steps of consciousness of law in an exemplary manner. *Lex humana* is that which mankind, living exclusively in the semblance of the senses, creates in its imperfection. These laws are beset with all-too-human characteristics. The person confronted with the misery of his fellow man experiences the *ius constituendum*, the law as it should be in the *lex naturalis*, the natural law.[17] The person who opens himself to the views of others experiences the "truth as compendium of all possible views of the world" (Sigismund von Gleich) by the hand of the *lex divina*, the heavenly law. Finally, we may personally experience the act of becoming one with the divine in the *lex aeterna*, the eternal law, that which for Thomas is inexpressible. We draw closer to our fellow humans from the sources of love. We respond to their biological need with mercy, we do justice to their inner striving if we are filled with justice, if we are "the being with the human countenance."[18]

So far we have dealt mainly with the macro social aspects of the Threefold Order. We have seen that the Threefold Order needs to be looked at as a purely regulating principle, a principle which enables the three areas of society to unfold in an appropriate manner. We follow this up with an attempt to come to terms with the relationships of this order to the threefold nature of the human being, as a physical, soul and spirit being. The question now arises as to whether or not social threefoldness has significance in the meso and micro levels as well. Steiner deals explicitly with only the macro level.[3] Does this say anything about the Threefold Order?

A micro social order could not have been meant, even though it was traced from the being of man, and even though for that reason the human being is referred to again and again. This is because as regulating principle it does not exist, since there is no life of rights within the individual. Only in an indirect sense can one prescribe oneself a law and obey or violate it. At least two persons are always needed for a life of rights; this is the essence of its social character. This is where we can postulate the counter pole to the Archetypal Social Phenomenon. In contrast to the Archetypal Social Phenomenon, which is exclusively an inter-human experience and can, therefore, take place *only* on the micro social level, the micro level is totally missing from the Threefold Order.

Yet it can impress its stamp fully on the meso plan, but not in the same way as in the macro sphere. This is a strongly disputed concept, and, therefore, we want to start with a simple consideration. On the macro social level, the spiritual, rights and economic life arenas are *always* all present, even if in disorder or distorted by an irrational order, because they emanate from man's very being. Man carries the needs of his biological and inner sheaths into the community life. This forces him to find some way of regulating his relationship to his fellow humans. It is inaccurate to think that he would fail to carry this need for regulation into the institutional sphere as well or have *principally* different regulating requirements in this sphere. Yet, as soon as we immerse ourselves in concrete problems we find, as mentioned at the outset, that the very basic principle of the Threefold Order, namely the total autonomy of the three areas, turns out to destroy the institutions, and the economic as well as the spiritual life. We need to look more closely at this interesting phenomenon.

Because an institution consists of human beings, it places itself into the social life, that is, into all three members. In its public activities it may be very strongly connected to these or less so, because it concentrates more on a specific aspect of human life. Even an institution such as the Anthroposophical Society, wishing to be an esoteric one, has, within the constitution given to it by Steiner, assigned a rights life to all its members in the form of members rights, and has given it parts of an economic life by making the Vorstand (and any possible additional persons) fully responsible, as well as by the obligation of paying dues. The human being also wants to unfold within the institutional life in his three relationships, namely to himself, to nature and to his fellow humans. This is the reason that he does not (or no longer will) accept spiritual authorities or bosses narrowly dictating the working conditions to his fellow workers. He does not accept it when a spiritual authority determines their benefits package or supervisors their cultural preoccupations. Just as in the macro social sphere, the conditions here are regulated only partially, ad hoc and pragmatically. In fact, only where problems have arisen or are to be expected, the threefold regulating principle is missing.

One can do without the threefold regulating principle as long as people join together in associations to help each other, in the best or worst sense. One joins if one hopes to be helped and leaves if one is disappointed. This applies from coffee klatches all the way to the Anthroposophical Society. It is only good until permanent responsibilities are taken on. As long as the student fraternity is just boozing and quarrels, no order is required. Should it, however, buy or lease a house, the situation changes. We can grasp the requirements facing institutions best if we pick typical ones of the economic and spiritual life.

Let us take a textile factory as an example. In today's economy such an institution produces certain goods based on sales either on order or "for the market." This production process is subject to the law of productivity, and the workers have to adapt themselves to this within certain regulations. These limits are mostly set from without by law. The economically optimal day and night shifts, for example, are tolerated only because of technical necessity (blast furnaces) or to social priorities (taxi service). In contrast, only reluctantly are structural organs (shared decision-making rights) tolerated alongside directions serving productivity only. Feeling its way from case to case, jurisprudence has encroached on the sole dominance of the principle of productivity. No employer nowadays would dream of forbidding his workers to partake of alcohol in the evening, because they are more productive without alcohol. Nor would they perhaps require that they return a day earlier from vacation, because they are worthless on the first day back, having raced back from Florida just the day before. No one would dare to ask a convinced vegetarian to eat meat regularly because, for example, it increases his or her presence of mind when driving. There is an intimate personal sphere that must be observed, even if it is detrimental to production. The question is whether the limits here are based on principle.

A textile factory is an economic enterprise. This means a unit with a function. Matters of rights and development must be subordinated to this function. Production of textiles that satisfy the demands of the market, therefore, acquires a constitutional character. This has two implications, firstly that a change in the function is possible only with the consent of all involved (constitutional change), and secondly, that the desires of the workers have legal or cultural significance only within what the economic constitution permits. Practically speaking, three organs can develop for this purpose: a) an economic organ, a sense organ for demands and one that responds to efficiency in production. Only experts are active in this organ; b) an organ of rights where *every* decision must obtain a majority and where all who are existentially dependent on the yield of the enterprise have a seat; and c) an organ of the spiritual life where the multiplicity of implications with the life of the spirit is being considered and in which every one can take part as long as the products of this textile factory mean something to him. The fact that this is a unit with a function is accounted for by the differentiated weight of the three organs when it comes to decision making. The spiritual organ plays only an advisory role. But the organs of economy and rights have veto power. This feature leads to the necessity of arriving at consensus by way of negotiations. For example, if the economic organ proposes to use sexist features in advertising, the rights organ, having heard what the spiritual organ has to say, may veto this. In the same way the economic organ can block a decision of the rights organ to shorten work hours with its veto. As long as the remuneration of the workers depends on the yield of the factory, there is, after all, mutual interest. In this case, one will come to an agreement, for instance, if the work force agrees to a wage cut corresponding to shorter hours. Yet if the spiritual organ is against a proposal originating with the economic organ, that the factory change from the production of cotton goods to artificial fibers, and if it cannot convince the members of the rights organ, then the spiritual organ has no right of veto.

In an institution of the spiritual life, here, too, there are three organs, but only the ones of the spiritual life and rights life have veto power. This is because the statutory goal of this organization has constitutional character. Since I have given an example, taken from life, in "Gesellschaftsstrukturen in Bewegung" [Structures of Society in Flux] (Achberg 1967), I can leave it at this. Further, certain meso social questions will be addressed in more detail in the next chapter. Then we can fill in some additional areas. Here we are only concerned about the regulating principle: let it be stated simply that the danger of the organization's falling apart is countered by the rigorous insistence on the autonomy of the three spheres of the meso level, with the primary role given to the area with the predominant role to play.

I conclude with a few words regarding meso social institutions of right, because, until now and for good reasons, they have had a shadowy existence if not encountering outright ill will. Steiner repeatedly points out that, besides polar activities (schools tend not to have farms and farms tend not to have schools), usually the independent life of rights tends to be missing. This is true if one understands the life of rights in the sense of the life of law. Yet this life of law is only one aspect of interhuman relations, even though the most important one in the macro social sphere. However, "this encompasses all conditions under which the individual human beings are brought intimately face to face..., not counting his abilities, not counting economic position. Here is the third area of the social organism," (*The Principal Question of the Economic Life*, Dornach, 1962, 25/26) In meso social connections these relationships assume great importance. Therefore, they need, apart from personal care, formal institutional nurturing.

On the other hand, we had to establish the fact that perfect threefoldness cannot exist in the meso sphere because one element always dominates the others; that is, there can be no such thing as three *totally* independent organs within an institution. This creates a serious problem. In every institution the threefold totality of the social organism is a given due to the presence of the co-workers and their human relationships. Yet the demands posed by this totality cannot be fully met with a limited threefold arrangement.

Institutions face another no less important challenge if laws contain demands and obligations that are contrary to the workers' own perceptions of rights. As far as this is concerned, a special independent life of rights is in fact missing. Specifically, their own life of rights is therefore limited. This poses the question of whether or not there exists nowadays a moral duty for individuals or institutions to bow to the law, perhaps even to act in accordance to its meaning. If one wants to avoid misunderstanding, it is hardly possible to answer that question.[20] For our present purposes it suffices if we deal with such magisterial regulations as given facts, just as one would take into account the handicap of a co-worker.

As a result, the rights organs always present two faces. On one side is the sense of justice of the co-workers, on the other, the question of whether or not the decisions they create are permissible in the sense of the law.[21] This is a very complicated subject.

It has been my experience that this fact is particularly conducive to the common, somewhat bovine, obedience to the law. Since we cannot even touch the problem here, I will simply illustrate it by way of two examples of safe (foreign), juridical conditions.

Dutch law decrees that a teacher can be dismissed only during the first year of service and later only for very specific reasons. One of those reasons is not a change of world conception. Yet what can a Waldorf school do with a teacher who was an anthroposophist when he was hired and later converted to Catholicism?[22] I know of a case where a college of teachers seriously considered closing the school because working together with a certain person appeared to be impossible. In this respect there is much to be gained if, when hired, one signs an internal agreement wherein, among other things, one agrees to leave the school should one no longer wish or be able to teach based on anthroposophical concepts. Although this obligation would have to give way to the law in case of a controversy, yet it would add a moral tone to the proceedings: if one stays on, one breaks one's word. But this is not enough, which is why I include this problem in the discussion of the structure, despite the fact that it really belongs in the area of contractual law. To be precise: it is a private matter whether someone is a Catholic, Protestant or Bible student. It concerns the school only to the degree that something of this flows into the teaching, and into the organs, responsible for it. Let me remind anyone who talks of principal incompatibility, that Karl Schubert, for example, remained a practicing Catholic all his life. Our converted person will probably invoke the fact that his belief does not hurt the teaching process, even if his reasons for staying on are not merely driven by the social security benefits. Therefore, he will not be content with the judgment of the rights organ of his own school because, from his point of view, it only represents the interests of the school and not his own private interests. As for the public judge who interprets the law, the decision is predetermined anyway, because the law is superior to the contract. The solution lies in creating one's own chosen judges who, as behooves any judge, assign the same weight to both interests.[23] The higher the moral aspects of such judges and the more they are respected by both parties, the greater the probability that the judgment will be accepted by both parties, true even if the judgment is in favor of the contract and not the law.

It is similar with institutions of the economic life. We take it as a starting point that the Netherlands has a minimum wage of about $1,000 per month. Now look at a farm where, in order to market Biodynamic products, the workers have agreed to pay a certain portion of their wages back into the farm account.[24] What should one do with a person who has subscribed to this rule to begin with, but one day asks for his minimum wage? The co-workers may be instantly biased against such a person because he has broken his word. Here the economic purpose threatens to dominate the personal one. But perhaps a mediation board would judge differently if, for example, this person could convince them that his marriage would dissolve if he failed to come home with the minimum wage.

Although we deal here with examples, taken from an incredibly complicated area, perhaps these can demonstrate that new organs in the field of rights are structurally needed in the meso sphere. Besides, this sheds light on Steiner's indication that in institutions the independent organs of rights are missing. What we have called organs of the rights life has meaning only within the institution. Yet this only inadequately meets the justifiable demands of the workers. If, however, a number of institutions is present, one can eliminate this lack by creating specific groups of judges in areas where today's law inappropriately interferes with questions of the life of the spirit and the economy, because there exists no macro social structure. In fact, by creating such groups of judges, one oversteps the boundaries of the meso sphere and enters the macro sphere, as these groups should *not* include workers from the institutions in question.

In conclusion, we return to the threefold order as regulating principle. Yet the three members have always been present. They are pulled together because *one* religion or *one* striving holds the associations together. For example, form and content were given by the priest-king in primeval times. Yet the theocratic tradition, experienced as a living force, held together even the republican peoples up to the time of World War I. Steiner reports from spiritual science that this stream was maintained by post-death, drop by drop infusions by the hierarchies. This stream has dried up and has ended. We have to resurrect it as individuals by reawakening social reality from its slumber. But now this must take place by letting ourselves be put to sleep consciously by the other person. That which earlier united the members of society as a mirroring of the divine hierarchy wants replacing by a new hierarchy as leading principle.

What is it that creates uniformity in threefoldness? Again, we need to differentiate The individual human being, earlier included in a unity, now stands in a multiplicity, autonomous in every one of its spheres. His ego, the new priest-king,[25] sends qualities of soul in threefold order into the three members of the social organism. The coordinating "Christ in me" he finds exclusively in his ego. In the meso social, where one subordinates oneself to the purpose of the institution, the ego is already further away. It makes its appearance as the guardian of the goal.[26] It appears in the circle of the founders, yet to be discussed, in the interhuman "Christ between us." In the macro social sphere the three areas are obviously independent. A unifying organ is missing. One finds its connection in the periphery, in the Representative of Man. Insofar as the single individual participates in this, unity with mankind arises within him.

Thus, we have become acquainted with the last of the principles that determines how we live together. In the form of threefoldness appropriate for our time, it has turned out to be a purely regulating principle. We could find hardly anything that really belongs to it among all that is otherwise thought of to be its content. Yet in another area we ascribe to it a significance far beyond the domain typically associated with it. Threefoldness lives in every social sphere, even if in variations, even in the meso sphere. In this area it is already possible to work with it, even in the straight jacket of the monolithic state. This means that if the regulating principle is reasonably applied, the other three principles of the Anthroposophical Social Impulse can come into their rights.

The clock as an analogy is not only valid for the social organism as a whole, but it also demonstrates to what degree concrete institutions are timely as social structures. In this respect this "clock" is the supplement to the micro social picture presented for the Archetypal Social Phenomenon in the previous chapter. When viewed this way, the threefold order becomes indeed the key concept for the Anthroposophical Social Impulse. It does not even have to wait for better times. "The threefold order is not dead; it has merely not been understood to start with, and I hope that understanding for the threefold order will grow from out of the very circles of Waldorf pupils." (GA 260 a/ 1966/647)

Endnotes:
[1] "Das Sociale Rätsel [*The Social Riddle*]" Freiburg: 1979, p. 14.
[2] GA 83/1950/203. Along with his public and macro social work, these examples are included in what he meant at the Christmas meeting: "One has remained behind by hundreds of years when someone represents things in the same manner as was the case in 1919" (GA 260/1963/204).
[3] "The healthy social organism will strip money of all its rights character, making it a mere commodity (GA 328/1477/162). Then a market in money is no longer objectionable. The commodity, money, will then become a concrete need like all other commodities."
[4] C. Lindenberg, the historical value of threefoldness, in "Acting socially as we recognize social-totality" (published by H. Giese, Rabel 1980), p. 51.
[5] GA 192/1964/388. One may perhaps anticipate a twofold social order based on the fact that a controlling life of rights may be superfluous for the sixth cultural period. This may even be understandable, because then this would mirror the dualisticPersian cultural period. I found a hint in this direction in GA 184/1968/101: "Things proceed in separate streams. On one hand, social life after socialism, on the other religious life after freedom of opinion, and scientific life after pneumatology, after recognition of the spirit." One may be permitted to guess that in the sixth cultural period religious life will take the place of the life of rights.
[6] In The *Threefold Social Order* Steiner points out that we can arrive at a feeling for the so-called Threefold Social Order if we study how the three members of human corporeality work together. In this respect GA 219/1976/XII is of importance, in particular the description of the human heart as organ of equilibrium that makes it possiblefor man to be a free human being.
[7] One may point by way of comparison to the fact that the blossoming of all possible religious confessions took place as soon as religion and state separated, that is, as soon as the ruler's religion no longer served to tie the subjects together. The principle is often found with Steiner that if one makes a force

stand out on its own, it really starts to unfold and acts positively on evolution, instead of negatively. In this connection I think of such differentiated matters, like the separation of the plant kingdom from humanity (GA 293/1932/184) as the stepping out of formative forces at the separation of the moon (GA 109-111/1965/231).

8 As early as in his introductions to Goethe's natural scientific writings Steiner rejects "a universal natural law, valid for all people and all time" as an impossibility. "Legal points of views and moral concepts come and go with nations, indeed even with individuals." "What determines a form does not flow out of what makes it into an *organic* form" (GA 30/1961/278) is valid here as it is in nature.

9 See GA 114/1923/V, GA 185/1962/228 and GA 175/1961/343: the formation of associations was, in former times, the privilege of initiates of the fourth order.

10 Incidentally, in exactly the way that threefoldness is—indirectly—a precondition for the real unfolding of spiritual science.

11 In GA 159-160/1967/195 Steiner called this novel of Defoe's an ahrimanic inspiration.

12 This is why it seems funny to me when circles who share an opinion somehow call themselves "Free Spiritual Life."

13 In GA 175/1961/1353 f. Steiner speaks about a socializing "for the physical plane" and of freedom of thought for the life of the soul, where freedom of thought is sketched as "an attitude toward the other person that recognizes the other's freedom of thought in the truest sense of the word." Yet both cannot be "carried out, unless the spirit is truly rooted in the spiritual world."

14 Morality lives only in the now. This is why Jacques Ellul speaks of theocentricity in human to human situations as the true countenance of predestination ("Le Fondement Théologique du Droit," Paris 1946).

15 "Ideen zur Staats und Kultursociologie," (ideas about state- and cultural sociology) 1927.

16 Roman Boos "Gewissensprüfungen durch Dreigliederungsfragen" [Tests of Conscience brought about by Questions of the Threefold Order] (at present 1945/2). He expresses it very graphically: "the 'law' as such is unavoidably right when it comes to the condition of the skeleton."

[17] We must stress the fact that here we do not mean something that is a given fact in the way that later Catholic literature uses the concept of natural law.
[18] GA 8/1976/138 compares this to the correspondence of inner threefoldness in GA 178/1974/202, to physical threefoldness in GA 179/1967/234, and to the theme threefoldness and the disintegration of soul forces in GA 202/1970/257. On the subject of the unity of the three social members exclusively in "der einheitlichen Menschennatur" [the unified human nature] GA 36/1961/45 and further GA 23/1919 (1st edition.)/99 and GA 305, special edition 1979/46.
[19] One finds one of the few indications of meso-threefoldness in GA 260 a/1966/435: "If you think of the free Waldorf school co-joined with the Free University, this could happen only under the auspices of the thinking underlying the threefold order. One is basically working with concrete reality when all future institutions would strive toward threefoldness." By the way, these words can also serve as an answer to those who are of the opinion that with the Christmas Gathering of 1923/24 the time for the threefold order had passed. See also on meso-threefolding GA 73/1973/196, about the head of a firm.
[20] I have dealt in somewhat more depth with this question in my article "Bürgerlicher Ungehorsam" [Civil Disobedience].
[21] See Chapter IX regarding the question of official approvals or support based on backup data.
[22] By the way, the problem would not arise if the school was organized for all teachers to be co-owners. The Dutch law would allow this form of organization, but from that moment it would withhold state support. This problem was created when the Dutch Waldorf teachers accepted their relationship to state officials for financial reasons.
[23] The "How" of this choice may also be found in the mentioned article in "Gesellschaftsstrukturen in Bewegung" (Societal structures in Flux).
[24] This problem, too, would not exist if all workers would be co-owners.
[25] In consonance with GA 57/1965/421: the ego as king, reigning over the three departed parts of the human organization. Also, GA 93 a/1976/56 the future human being will direct his threefold brain from outside.

[26] Perhaps the assumption may be permitted that the unifying force emanates from the dead, if we play the role which John the Baptist played in the circle of the disciples.

Chapter VII

An Image of the Four Elements Working Together

In the last chapter we reviewed the Threefold Social Order as a regulating principle. Threefold social reality finds adequate expression in ordering social life in a threefold manner. Taken from the true nature of man, it finds expression in the three principles of the Basic Sociological Law, the Principal Social Law, and the Archetypal Social Phenomenon. Let us explore if it is possible to provide content to this empty structural model without deteriorating to a cookbook.

As previously stated, the formal regulating principle makes it possible to realize any thought and impulse within the framework of the threefold order. To give content to threefoldness, therefore, requires a point of view. The structure is available for *anybody* and could be filled with the difficulties of daily living either pragmatically or by forced decree. However, consciously shaping it in a social manner requires insight into the development of humanity and its historical expression.

Based on our object, the determining point of view of this study can only be the Anthroposophical Social Impulse, as such. Its inner laws have already been described in the four previous chapters. Missing is the answer to the question of how we could express the connection of these four principles in the social life in a manner appropriate for our time. To do this we need to invert the way we have looked at it in the previous chapter. We have seen how the regulating principle shapes social life into three spheres. Now, given this result, let us observe how the impulse of the Archetypal Social Phenomenon permeates the threefold reality of society.

What Steiner calls the "purely earthly," the outer rights state (in more general terms, the forms which people have incorporated into the social organism), is comparable to the human physical organism, the economy to the life processes, and the spiritual life to the processes of the soul. From within his ego the human being is called upon to continually gain control over his sheaths. In the same way he must penetrate the social organism ever more with the forces he carries into it through his social thrust, that is to say, through the Archetypal Social Phenomenon.

We will begin from the micro social plane, from that which each person carries into the social organism.

The micro social plane

I refer to my discussions in "Social and Unsocial," in particular the fifth section. To work out of what is social means to give away. The extreme experience of equality with the fellow human evolves in us the sense of justice, the perception that his misery is my misery. This brings about the consciousness of one's own inadequacy. We shall try to penetrate further into this thought.

Steiner points out in various passages that spiritual life arises from a person's capabilities and talents brought from pre-birth existence and, thus, out of the past. Lucifer lives in the earthly abilities, created in this manner (GA 195/1962/76 f., see also GA 145/1957/162), as Ahriman is at work in our needs. These abilities destroy the balance which originally exists at birth. (GA 187/1979/I) Jahweh's equalizing work as we sleep (social) needs to be transformed into a conscious penetration of our thoughts with the Christ principle, so that the egocentric Luciferic force does not overwhelm us. This is an important reference to the Anthroposophical Social Impulse in the spiritual life, because we can connect this to another result of spiritual investigation, namely that the progress of one individual is always offset with retardation of another. We move forward at this expense. The social impulse from the sphere of the Archetypal Social Phenomenon counters the violation of equality that, of necessity, adheres to our developmental striving. It has the effect that our thinking, normally used to further our own development, is permeated by the Christ force from forces of will. In other words, it opens itself to the thoughts of others.[1]

The Luciferic drive toward self-perfection in our thinking poisons it with lies. When we are prepared to surrender such intelligence to him, this drive finds its opponent in the erstwhile lord of cosmic intelligence, Michael. (GA 240/1977/38 f/) The life of our spirit is being morally permeated when the truly social pours itself into it as an impulse of the will. We, and with us the life of the spirit, join Michael's stream of wisdom and find here an "inner brotherhood of thoughts of which all external ones must be the mirror image." (GA 34/1960/179)

If the Luciferic force allows us to use our talents to gain a lasting advantage, then the Ahrimanic one acts to draw an equality belonging to the future into the life of our time, and particularly so into the economic life. We shed the earthly inequalities in a slow process after death so that we are allowed to experience equality in the spirit at the midnight hour. Ahriman's striving is aimed at obliterating the consciousness of this soul journey by drawing the principle of equality into the wrong time and on to the wrong plane. This is equally true for social Darwinism as it is for socialism. Regarding the latter, Steiner says, "Mankind would love to find theories according to which one could make all of mankind live in earthly bliss."[2] (GA 172/1974/104) It makes no difference whether we elevate the animal nature that we carry within us to the only human principle — "we are all the same under the belt" — and combine this with the right to enrich ourselves in a "selection of the strongest,[3] or whether we assign to man equality in production and consumption "for the protection of mankind." Both responses miss the economic inequality we have due to the differences in our needs as well as in the means to satisfy them. In the economy, like in everything else, the driving and forward striving forces are found in inequality. Inequality forces us to deal independently with our own needs and challenges us to engage ourselves for the other person, to turn around the established inequality, to put ourselves in the shoes of the poor and, for the sake of the poverty of the other person, one thinks little of one's ownself. Both variations, the social-Darwinist as well as the socialist, are based on the forced enrichment of one party at the cost of the other. Either one enriches the strong or the have-nots. The social impulse can compel us to do just the opposite, rather to work for the other person because we are responsible.

Here, too, dangers for the future of mankind lie in wait. Working for the other person creates karmic connections, especially with people who remain unknown. Global economy and global connectedness of humans belong together. Our family tends to grow more and more. Yet it is hard to imagine the disorder created in karma because the impulse is not to work for the other person but to make money on them. Here we encounter Ahriman on many fronts. He wants to rob us of our future through his effect on social life.

The juxtaposition to this is the mercurial or, in Christian parlance, Raphaelic impulse. Raphael's being exudes goodness, well-wishing, God-wishing. (GA 727/1981/X) As precursors in antiquity to future development, we already know of Mercury as the god of commerce (then the only independent part of the economy), of physicians and ... thieves.[4] What flows into the social life is equalization, the will to heal, not will to be equal. Deeds of love are payments of debts. As we are filled with responsibility for our fellow humans, we become our brother's keepers.

The primeval home of the principle of equality is the regulating principle within the outer life of rights. Equality of spirit on the highest plane is scaled down to equality in totally mundane earthly matters. Even today, jurists call the right *ars aequi*, and not always rightly so. How do we understand this principle of equality? It is simply no more than that in equal situations, judgments are equal. There should be no privileges for the "valuable person" when we stand before a judge. The protection of rights, given to the "decent citizen," should be given equally to the maladjusted person, the thief, the robber, the murderer, the unbalanced person. Our sensibilities revolt when this principle is used arbitrarily. We carry the impulse for equality like a precious gift, as an earthly, social impulse of the life of rights into our lives through birth. (GA 187/1979/45) In the first place the law protects us from ourselves. Without it, our morals would collapse like our bodies without bones. The portals of hell would open for us. Here stands the law as protector; here stands Gabriel, the guardian of human values.[5]

When the social structure, the body of mankind, disintegrates, the human being is bereft of the place it needs as an incarnated being. This is true not only of the chaos brought about by revolution, but it applies in the same way when the universal principle of equality rules, when, in all our social actions and omissions a flood of legal regulations defines us from without. It is true when the human being no longer appears as separate from the social organism, but when we are dissolved in it in the "orderly" system of technocracy, when it has made the "human material" well ordered, equalized and subservient. The human being becomes a functionary, loses the ego.[6] Here we have to recognize the beginning of the ego-destroying work of the Asuras. Yet the will to social regulation, reaching right down to the law, allows us to experience the Christ impulse challenging us to connect with his body.[7]

The primal experience, however, the source of the Anthroposophical Social Impulse, exists in every archetypal social phenomenon. The human being experiences itself placed face to face with the Christ. We perceive our own nothingness by practicing extreme renunciation. It is a process of incineration that leaves only what is equal to the Christ. We feel the judging eye of Uriel upon us whenever we are allowed to experience this in encounters with our fellow humans.

At this point what is social appears in its real essence. What is the spiritual content we encounter "as we encounter upon the social order?" (GA 78/1952/97) If the social structure is the body of mankind, then its social content is the Christ, as man is able to experience him. The three members of the social organism are "the three lower spiritual limbs of the Christ impulse."[8] The human being placed into the threefold social order is "that which is at the same time the rightful recognition of the Christ for our time and for the immediate future." (GA 193/1972/ 54 ff.) Here we encounter the Christ in the human brother in three different ways, so that everyone who wants to be human can affirm him, independently of religious or philosophical convictions. The social impulse, as sketched above appears as the Christ impulse of our time.[9]

The *macro* social plane

As we enter the macro social plane, we face extreme difficulties, created by the question of the image of the future presented to us when the four principles work together as Anthroposophical Social Impulse. Every attempt to grasp the effect of this impulse requires an examination of the question of how real people experience it and how they carry it into social reality based on this experience. But this means that the macro image threatens to dissolve again into the micro plane. And if one wants to describe the functioning of institutional life, where, in a certain sense, the social organism makes its appearance, one reverts to the meso plane.

We can consider the question as partially resolved in at least one area, namely the economy. Steiner, in fact, deals with this in his *World Economy*, assuredly based on the Anthroposophical Social Impulse! This cannot be claimed for either the life of rights or the life of spirit. He refuses to give a course of lectures on the former. There are various interpretations as to why, and numerous remarks exist as to the latter; yet these are meant to illustrate not the function but mainly structural problems.

World Economy deals only with the forces inherent in a particular area of the economy. The laws pertaining to the life of rights and economy appear there merely on the periphery.

We must find a different point of departure for our purposes, but to follow an accurate course, one that does not contradict the description of the economic forces described in that work. From our point of view, we pose the question roughly: "What must be the content of an economic life if it is not allowed to stand in the way of individuals striving for development as appropriate for our time according to the Basic Sociological Law?" At the same time the question arises as to how the life of the spirit may be formed by closely following the Principal Social Law. From what we have discussed so far, this can mean only how the person who is, of course, unable to subdivide him or herself but stands as a whole person in the life of the economy, can maintain his autonomy as an ensouled being, and how, inversely, a person placed in the spiritual life does justice to his economic obligations. Very concrete measures are required to solve this paradox. These give content to both the spiritual life and the economic, albeit only in a very general way.

Let us start with a person who is actively working in production. His soul being may be violated in three different ways.

1. *Economic reasons* may force him to produce goods or perform services incompatible with his conscience. Even if one excludes the armament industry from such an image of the fu-

ture, enough other branches of production challenge our conscience. Should an alcohol-abstaining person work in a brandy distillery? A vegetarian in a butcher shop? Similar questions arise in workplaces producing artificial fertilizers, porno publishers, drug laboratories, and on to abortion clinics where some nurses refuse to render their services. We may remind ourselves that a threefold social structure by no means implies that demands are being satisfied based on anthroposophical accomplishments and convictions. It is not only possible but probable that goods, obnoxious from this view, are being produced.

The production aspects of this problem offer no solution. From the vantage point of our present structure, the idea of forestalling certain efforts may appear obvious to most people; it is incompatible with a threefold structure. The only reason to forbid a particular production can only be that it can harm the producer. (GA 332 a/1950/113) This brings one to the sphere of rights. Majorities have no right to decide what is needed. To prohibit production of goods exclusively for democratically defined criminal activities could perhaps be added to this list of possibilities, because in this way no *further* intervention of freedom of consumption would take place. If the application of DDT is prohibited, a prohibition of its production can serve as a control function and thus result in no restriction of the farmer's operational freedom.

Besides, prohibitions within the life of the economy not only run counter to today's status of liberation of the individual from the power of associations, but they also make no sense. They tend to create an asocial black market. The development of economic life shows that claims for damages are better protection against antisocial production. A law against nuclear power plants would, for example, be superfluous, if, as would be appropriate for the life of the economy, the operator would be liable for *all* costs and damages caused by those plants.[10] Questions of consumption are, in fact, not economic questions but questions of the spiritual life. Steiner explains this via the cinema. (GA 338/1969/148) Neither the life of rights nor the economy should get involved with the freedom to consume. Where a need exists, its satisfaction is justified. Yet in the area of production, in a production against one's personal beliefs, there is an ethical problem of collaboration.

Pointing to the Principal Social Law, "work for the needs of your fellow men," does not help if you do not agree with them. Certainly one can hold the opinion [and I share it] that "to be wicked along with wicked mankind" (GA 189/1446/50) is a social healing act of unknown power. It actually means to sacrifice one's own development for the other person. I can only have the deepest respect for the mother who takes drugs, driven not by her own desire, but so that her addicted child does not walk alone into the dark. We need not speak about the abysses and dangers of such a course of action,[11] but simply take this into account as an exception. Rather, we have to focus on those multitudes who cannot be expected to participate in the work on things they consider harmful.

We encounter the demand to separate work and income from a totally different side in this connection. Only when the income disappears with the work is it necessary to work on what one despises. As soon as my income is assured, I gain the freedom to apply my talents where I can do what is, in my opinion, socially responsible work.[12] I suppose that it is not necessary to add that a right of refusal in no way excludes mobility in one's work. Yet, if the state or the economy were allowed or mandated to force people to work, this would run counter to the Basic Sociological Law. In more general terms, this would violate human dignity.[13] "The newer life does not permit that human beings are considered mere appendages of things and of processes of production and administered along with the administration of the business." (GA 24/1961/32)

2. Do I really work for the *needs of my fellow men*? It has already been pointed out that freeing the individual from the interests of associations goes counter to the need to find one's place in the life of the economy, that it is appropriate for our time, in the sense of the Basic Sociological Law, not to submit oneself to the person of the entrepreneur but to the purpose of the company as one acknowledges it out of one's own free will. "In the end the logic dictated by the product casts a spell over the entire routine of the work."[14] One is willing to sacrifice a certain amount of one's own development for the sake of the aim of the work. The person with more ability, whom one needs to obey, is only a means to an end in this case. Put bluntly, one does not feel one's human dignity threatened as one subordinates oneself to the technical idiosyncrasies of the car one drives.

From this point of view, one readily discovers the snake amidst the flowers. No modern industrialist who asks for obedience will invoke his right of ownership in the factory. He will insist on his technical expertise. Should one perhaps employ modern inquisitors to examine his motives?

Something essentially different hides behind this question of competence. A person has every right to ask himself if he performs his work in the economy really based on the needs of his fellow humans or perhaps in order to serve the striving for profit, the drive for power, or the ideological pet idea of the employer. Of these the two last ones can remain if the ownership situation were radically changed by the disappearance of capital and the work market. The cult of clubs teaches adequately how personal ambition is part of basic human equipment, even if no financial interests are involved. Since these cannot be expunged, economic life will have to be arranged in a manner that prevents personal ambition from doing harm.

This is the case when the routine of making economic decisions based on the problem at hand has condensed into the structure of economic happenings. Here we find a connection to a principle of Steiner's which runs like a red thread throughout his definitions of the life of the economy, albeit based on very different needs, namely the association. The danger of following personal ambition is eliminated in situations where no one individual makes the decisions but where economic intelligence is based on a combination of everyone's experience and, if need be, supported by experts in the field.[15]

Association here means more than the fashionable term used for all manner of novelties in sub-economic areas. Horizontal associations force the possibilities of other producers to be voted on and, by so doing, prevent macro-economic waste caused by ignorance or ambition. Vertical associations prevent production not based on the concrete needs of potential consumers and provides a guarantee to the worker that his work is based on the needs of his fellow men in accordance with the Principal Social Law. In this case he subordinates himself to their anonymity and not to associations or individuals.[16]

3. The question of controlling the economic process is a purely economic one. In contrast, the separation of work from income represents an intrusion from the life of rights into the life of the economy. Now we encounter the life of the spirit which

wants to come to realization in the life of the economy. Or, better asked, does the life of the economy present sufficient possibilities for those active within it to unfold their capabilities?

The unfolding of the personality within economic production belongs to the domain of the entrepreneur. The need for personal development had more than enough possibilities while barter was the dominant style of economy, actually up until the large economic crisis of 1929. Even the German economic miracle would not have come to pass, in spite of the manipulations by the state, without the ambition on the part of numerous citizens to express themselves and their capabilities in the productive process. Yet, as the new world economy created its first but distorted embodiment, the entrepreneur lost more and more ground to management. Nowadays one can feel the drive toward self-realization more strongly than with entrepreneurs in what has somewhat disparagingly come to be known as small and medium companies. For that reason the feelings of oppression and anger and the tendency toward fascism are nowhere stronger than in those quarters.

In fact, a whole area, in its present form, has lost its reason to exist. Self-realization remains only acceptable in the service of the fellow human beings. Therefore, it reemerges in our time as sub-economy, as alternative projects, as self-managed workshops, and as service functions. We can ignore the large number of economic lame ducks that may only serve as work therapy. The existence of a worldwide process of education within mass production, aimed at guiding the worker from joy in his own work toward joy in serving fellow humans, does not prevent others to seek satisfaction in the creation of sound products. Both efforts are aimed at real needs. If the large concerns concentrate on justified mass production of semi-finished products and utility articles, then the sub-economy provides items which satisfy beauty, health and social requirements. In general, these activities have the import to meet only very personal wishes. Yet the sub-economy lacks, apart from trade experience, almost always one thing — capital.

As we come from the Basic Sociological Law, that is, with a background of interest in self-realization, we face the necessity of what Steiner, again coming from totally different inter-dependencies, depicts as economic necessity, namely the abolition of the capital market and administration of capital through the life of the spirit, in order to create possibilities for economic creativity for human beings with capabilities, initiative and orientation toward needs.

Whoever speaks about the life of the economy usually waxes on about production, possibly about trade as well. The consumer, the destroyer of the fruits of production, appears like death, the destroyer of life, to belong to the taboos. We wish to avoid this bad habit. Consumption as final use is a most individual matter. Here the end of the economic process immediately abuts the life of the spirit. The priorities of purchases are determined by a most intimate working together of biological needs and inner desires, both based on bodily and psychic dispositions. If we exclude the market in used goods, the economic chain ends with the sale. Anything beyond this, the physical consumption which takes place along with the actual satisfaction of wants (destruction or consuming), lies beyond the life of the economy. Yet, because purchase and consumption are woven together, criticism of buying habits is at the same time criticism of the domain of the individual. General condemnation or glorification of drug consumption belongs to the life of the spirit. Criticizing individual drug users is, therefore, not only unhygienic but, in our context, it means primarily an intervention by generalized judgments[17] into the process of free development of the individual.

If the pattern of consumption of the individual is off limits for the social domain, its influence on the life of the economy is unmistakable. In this regard I would like to reference my "Geldschleier" [*Veil of Money*],[18] in which I have discussed this domain in detail. In this chapter I will limit my remarks to showing that responsible participation in consumption is impossible without detailed information as to its consequences. Today's economic life leaves the consumer almost totally in the dark on this subject. It robs most people of their only chance to mature in accordance with the Basic Sociological Law in the life of the economy. We can observe the responsibilities of the consumer for the quality of the goods he buys (whether he uses them or not!), for the fact that they are being produced at all, for the social conditions pertaining to their production, and even for the distribution of the economic potential within the First and Third

Worlds. This examination clearly shows that the individual consumer is, as yet, totally unable to get this information. As we look at it from this side, we approach something which Steiner indicates as an institutional demand on the life of the economy, namely a movement of consumers capable of understanding the extremely many-sided and entangled economic interdependencies by using specialists, such as the agents of GA 339/1969/149. One can see the first suggestions of making these relationships in the example of producers of tobacco items being required to place informational labels on their goods, which warn that nicotine and tar may be harmful to health. The demand is growing to permit the sale of products only if labels are attached addressing physical and technical information as well as social.[19]

We have at least intimated at what demands need to be placed on an economic life, working in the sense of the Principal Social Law, to allow producers and consumers to develop in accordance with today's phase of the Basic Sociological Law. Let us now take a look at the life of the spirit to see what concrete forms are required to avoid killing the Social Impulse as it provides content to the life of the economy in the form of the Principal Social Law.

The life of the spirit is insatiable. It spans from the seeker of knowledge who wants to reach dizzying heights of cognition to the quiet, self-contained stamp collector. While such people do not utilize the life of the economy, as is the case in these two examples, their efforts remain a private matter, even if these occupations reduce their own active contributions to the product of society. One encounters this phenomena with handicapped people who are not allowed to starve even though they are unable to work for others. The striving for self-realization in the life of the spirit assumes social significance only if it takes place on an institutional level. There are always newer and better acoustic systems for use in auditoriums, always more beautiful theatrical scenery and costumes, always more sophisticated teaching resources and desirable school buildings and auditoriums, ever more expensive medical apparatus. One can constantly increase the demands placed on the student body and thus the needs for teachers and their time. The past fat years have clearly shown us how endless all this is, even if one dismisses anomalies that serve self-glorification and thinks only about demands posed by the desire for optimal satisfaction of cultural matters.

That all these things require work is, over and over, being forgotten. This is true whether the means to do it come from the state, from benefactors, or from those who benefit by the results. Behind all of these work anonymous people in support of those who work in the cultural sphere. This clearly shows the other side of the Principal Social Law.

On the individual plane the drive to expand may be limited in the transformation of all things, the Principal Social Law in view of the life of the spirit. Steiner states that, in the absence of needs, not even a truth is being created,[20] by the way, without asking for such a highly developed social talent on anyone's part. Yet on the macro level one asks oneself: What form must the life of the spirit take to avoid sucking out the economy like a leech?

The support for the needs of the life of the spirit is, for the greatest part nowadays, determined by the state establishment and by the political parties according to swings in the economy and the pleasure of the voters. All these are arbitrary (political) decisions with little or no connection to the reality of the issue.

Can we get guidance from the actual nature of matter? Certainly so! The human beings involved in the life of the economy have no desire for a spiritual life insofar as it takes more from them (costs) than it gives. Oversimplified, a community must be able to feed itself before it can afford a preacher. Even then, only if the preacher produces something that increases the wellbeing of the group, is it willing to support him from the surplus.

Here something transpires which Steiner shows in connection with the way the three members of the social organism work together, though he addresses it from a different perspective. The representatives of the economy and the spiritual life, as autonomous entities, are meant jointly to negotiate that part of the proceeds of the economic life that rightly belongs to the spiritual life. In this conception the spiritual life has a claim to the surplus which the economy has produced. The state, the work force, and capital now fight over this surplus. It belongs by its derivation to the spiritual life with its new ideas because the latter nourishes the economy and makes it more productive.[21]

Inversely, an economic life without gifts stemming from the surplus of spiritual life not only cannot take any interest in the latter, but it is not even able to carry the spiritual life, because without the manure of new ideas it dries up itself; it no longer creates any surplus. This generates the new concept of gift-money.[22] This is *right*, because the life of the spirit has a claim on the surplus, on the *rent*, without taxes getting in the way. The rent is what is left over after the work has been appropriately paid for. It is a gift because it is turned over without a clearly traceable counter service. It is turned over specifically to the institutional life of the spirit, i.e., that life of the spirit which is again in need of economic goods. This is why the Principal Social Law becomes reality all the way into the life of the economy without asking anything for itself. It satisfies its own needs from the products of the economy. The efforts flowing into it in this way limit the expansion of the impulse of the life of the spirit.

As this concept may be difficult for many to grasp, I want to touch briefly on a different type of gift-money, although this example may belong more appropriately somewhere else. Gift-money is connected with the non-institutional, specifically with the individual spiritual output of persons creatively active in the spiritual life. This gift-money does not come from the surplus of the economy but from the will to sacrifice on the part of individuals. It serves to support creativity[23] for which there is little or no interest yet. This may be particularly the case with artists (Schubert, van Gogh), sometimes with inventors as well (Robert Mayer). It requires, so to say, a prophetic confidence of the giver.

This sketchy description gives only the basic outline of the macro level. Both in mood and form a great contrast to the micro sphere is evident. If we look at how an individual person faces his fellow men, we may see him as he evolves, i.e., as a striving being (socially as well). We may ask ourselves what happens when he connects to the social impulse. In this way we can discover (and take into account) seeds which anticipate the future and redeem the past.

Yet if we look at the macro social level, we must be prepared to deal with people as they are today. Social preaching is just as great an illusion as is building up a structure with people who, in reality, are less social than needed for that structure. The human being of macro social reality needs laws. In them morality appears frozen into forms. They shout, "Stop" to the disgruntled ones, they offer support to the weak, without moralizing. They can be degraded into following a routine, as in much of our practice of the law. One can also use them for the salvation of mankind. In the same way as the human being needs the plunge into dead matter, those dead forms of the law allow for exercising freedom in the social area.

In the meso sphere we can best see the interweaving of micro social freedom and macro social fetters. The human being in his macro social embodiment is beyond good and evil. Here he lives in the form. We should throw the veil of chastity around the micro social reality of our fellow humans. We have no right to judge. (GA 103/1975/VII) In the meso social all masks are dropped. What a social work of art is created by the co-workers from the plastic form and from ever-moving life!

The *meso* social plan

Institutions have aims. Not given by nature, they are human handiwork built for a certain purpose. If one has proceeded correctly, the forms grow out of a conscious creative act. "The great principle of our time is to move exclusively within forms of society and of the state imposed on us by ourselves." (GA 181/1966/136) "In the future nothing will be done out of instinct any more." (GA 181/1967/XXI) If one has chosen a legally prescribed form of law, its purpose is usually even apparent in the bylaws or the contract. Formal (statutory) or informal regulations have this purpose. Yet, even if one composes the statutes in the organic style recommended by Steiner (GA 126 a/1966/29), a description of what one actually does, the aim will somehow find expression. Whosoever wants to join the work must submit to it. This is understood from the start. Only in a case wherein one is, for example, forced by the need to support oneself to work in a particular institution can this go counter to the potential for free development or ethical convictions. In a society where income and work are separated, one will join an institution only if one approves of its purpose. If one changes his mind or if regulations are being introduced which he prefers not to honor, one can leave. Here we already see a big difference compared to macro social life. Here we do not deal with an association with a particular purpose, nor can one simply leave, a fact demonstrated by the conscience-driven criminal.[24] This difference causes the threefold concept to diverge at the macro and meso planes at a crucial point. In the macro social realm, it is necessary to practice total separation of the three spheres because only in this way can it be guaranteed that each individual's principles of spiritual, rights and economic lives are not being randomly ravished by each other. Since the human being cannot separate from the social organism, the latter must by its nature guarantee individual development in the life of the spirit and social care in the life of the economy. But not so in the meso sphere. In a threefold macro sphere anyone can always leave the institution he is connected with, in a manner without legal or its dominant impulse economic trouble. In such a case, however, the institution may make demands to subordinate the aims, the impulses of the workers to its purposes. Depending on the institution's aims or its dominant impulse in the life of the spirit, rights or economy, it will honor the workers' impulses in the two other spheres only conditionally.

Conditional recognition does not mean exclusion. Every co-worker enters the institution as an integral personality, even if the activity is only part time. He brings with him not just his contribution, for example, as bookkeeper, but his feeling for right and wrong and his will to grow as well. It is a misunderstanding of the problem to engage a professional psychologist for his needs (or to arrange a pleasant social hour) and attempt to deal with human relations through company outings. The worker wants to have his place *in his work* as a threefold human being in the broadest sense. His work cannot be separated from the final product or service. To the degree that our economy of "division of work" splinters the work from a human point of view, still working together on a common product brings people together. The work on parts combines to create a shared manufactured product. This activity alone satisfies human requirements. It is this idea which creates the previously discussed new society, and this is why Steiner places so much emphasis on workers learning the pre- and post-production history of their product. Referring to the worker as an organ of the production process, to his part of the work, is taking only half a step toward work dividing economy and none at all toward the threefold human being.

It is just as inadequate to create an organization to which the workers can turn with their ideas or complaints. In the human organism it is not enough to cram food into the intestinal tract; there must be organs to receive, process and excrete. Nor does it suffice to have ideas and complaints somehow leach into the organization. In the same way there is a need for organs to process them, differentiated organs for the differentiated input. Hence, every healthy organization should have three groups, one for each of the three social members. Each should be configured differently, in accordance with its individual character. In the economic organ, experiences gathered in the service of a common effort should come together and can provide the basis for a decision, but never the decision itself. In the organ of the spiritual life, ideas should clash which, although presented with conviction by opposing parties, are not allowed to crystallize into decisions out of respect for all parties involved. Rather decisions belong to the third organ, the organ of rights.

The more the special character of each organ is protected, or the more strictly opinions that do not belong to it are rerouted to their appropriate organ, then the more social, the more fertile for the whole of the meso structure, will each one of the organs be. Here Beckmesser would find his place. [A figure in Wagner's "Die Meistersinger von Nürnberg," Beckmesser is an unpleasant pedantic judge of the singing of the master singers.] Nothing is more frustrating when discussing a new idea than the comment, "But there is no money for this!" This comment has its value in the organ of rights. Nothing stirs up more emotions, including aggression, than if, during a conversation in the economic organ of a school about the need of the parents for a free Saturday, a teacher interjects the opinion that this is "pedagogically irresponsible." This is what the spiritual organ is there to judge, whereas one of the functions of the economic organ is to raise consciousness of needs which the spiritual organ rejects. Nothing is more boring than to hear a recounting of another's ideas or experiences in the organ of rights. This can quickly block the ability to make decisions.[25] Yet if a question comes up in so many different areas, how can the different points of view come together?

The rights organ is the functional place where all this comes together. This is where all decisions must be made. As opposed to the macro sphere, here is where a special purpose is always given,[26] a certain preponderance of the rights organ, a specialized attitude must be granted. This does not imply, however, a prerogative nor privilege on the part of the rights! Rather, as previously noted, this is appropriate for the organ in whose domain the institution is socially active. For a school this is the teachers conference, for a nail factory the organ of the economy, and for a community the organ of rights. The prerogative indicates that no decision can come about if it goes counter to the point of view of the organ which expresses the goal of the institution.

Are the other organs then merely ornamental? By no means. Let us look at two examples, bearing in mind that in this chapter we have set out to realize the Anthroposophical Social Impulse. I want to stress this here once more, because in a threefold society, and especially so in such a society, there must be room within its framework for the greatest variety of meso structures.

Its customers propose to a meat processing plant that they add goose livers to their selection. Sales show that a sufficient demand for this is present. The additional investments, possible additions to the staff and market territory are being estimated. This package of information gives the economic organ a basis for a proposal. Moral and legal questions have no place yet. The question is whether this project serves a real need, one that includes purchasing power, in the sense of the Principal Social Law. The economic organ adds economic experiences to the proposal that may shed a different light on the subject. These may come from co-workers and from "outsiders" as well, because everyone is welcome here who feels a need for such an institution, even though there may be practical limits to this. If we now assume that economic conditions for production of goose liver pate are fulfilled, the task of this organ is complete for the time being. Next the spiritual organ has to approve before a decision can be reached. This organ contains some of the same members, but they now consider the matter from a very different angle, namely the spiritual one. If they themselves cannot manage this, they may invite experts. The issue may be raised that the raw material produced involves ghastly animal tortures. Again, no decision is made, but after the Basic Sociological Law has been fully brought to bear on the matter, an array of philosophical views will finally be presented to the organ of rights. There a decision must now be made. Again, the same co-workers may be involved, but not all of them. Only the ones who have connected themselves existentially to the institution, and thus have agreed to share the consequences of their decision, have a voice. As always, the gist of the matter is divided into two categories, an external and an internal one. Externally the question is whether the law allows production of goose liver as proposed here. It will probably be possible to arrive at a clear and decisive answer to this question. The internal aspect is mainly a matter of feeling. Will the additional need for credit make us too dependent on the bank? Are we stretching our business too far by hiring more workers? Can one inflict the smell on the workers? And so forth. The most important item will probably be to consider the report of the spiritual organ. Without directly addressing the issue of perpetrating torture of animals to satisfy human needs, the question for the spiritual organ, one has to ponder in one's heart whether one can inflict the responsibility for animal torture on one or more co-workers.[27] In more progressive times one could even imagine that the rights organ would add the question to the economic organ as to whether current customers would be lost over this issue. The result will be a collection of very personal judgments, made by every member of the rights organization based on a myriad of viewpoints, emotions and facts. No one person's judgment should be given more weight than anyone else's. Therefore, a democratic decision is arrived at. This can include a negative recommendation to the economic organ.[28] Should the recommendation be "yes," one or more co-workers may resign rather than continue and have to work against their convictions. The prerogative of the economic organ only comes into play if a proposal comes from other organs. These are not allowed to interfere with production against the will of the economic organ. This could mean for instance, that if the institution is already producing goose liver, a proposal of the organ of the spirit (or of the organ of rights, possibly because of the smell) would get no further consideration within the organ of rights if the economic one is against it.

Since the thoughts developed here are new to many, I want to mention a few other ways to look at this situation. One needs to take into account that the special position of the rights organ rests merely in the fact that decisions are made only *there*. *Which* proposals are brought before it is another question. To resume our example, a meat processing plant belongs to the life of the economy. This implies that the application of capital and work force presuppose a certain steadiness and, therefore, the operation must be spared ongoing interference from the shifting ideas of the spiritual and rights life. In fact, an emotionally-based decision to stop obtaining raw material from state X, which is guilty of some devilry, could ruin the plant, because it is dependent on a source from that region. Of course, this does not imply that the economic organ will reject dealing with new proposals. After all, it too is motivated to go with the times, so it will use its veto power as sparingly as possible.

The second example, the counterpart, an institution of the life of the spirit, will lead into a discussion of some necessary additional items to help further a harmonious structural equilibrium between self-unfolding and economic viability. We choose a therapeutic institution where doctors and therapists work together.

In our example, the patients make a request to the economic organ to have acupuncture included in the clinic's available therapies. Let us assume that there is a strong demand for this service and that one of the personnel has the necessary qualifications. The proposal comes before the organ of rights, who in turn forwards it to the spiritual organ. Now we can give full reign to our imagination. It is possible that the doctors answer with an indignant "No." Or they can report to the organ of rights that acupuncture must not be used due to lack of unanimity. In either case, the proposal would be turned down, for the conscience of the healer takes precedence over the demand. It would be interesting if the spiritual organ were to consent, and if doubts were to arise then in the organ of rights as to whether acupuncture would fit the statutory aim to provide an anthroposophical basis for therapeutic applications.

Superficially this seems to be a question of rights. Yet even a child can see that decisions should not be made by a majority vote, and less still by a judge's decision. We have uncovered a secret of the meso social area. The physician with his own practice or the butcher with his own slaughterhouse has nothing to conceal. They perform their professions according to their own consciences. But when an institution is a social formation, it has its own face. It faces its customers as well as its creditors, not simply as an individual whom one knows and trusts, but a board, possibly even a collective. And institutions have no conscience. Therefore, something else must take its place. Experience shows two viable approaches. Either one uses a personality as a cover, whose good reputation represents the institution ("the clinic of Dr. Y"), or one goes openly public with an aim or a purpose, usually a stated version of the statutory aim. Careful handling of the statute can stand in the place of the good name of an individual, in the case of our acupuncture example: "And this calls itself an anthroposophical clinic!"

The founders are forced to formulate the aim in the statute and to ban the problem of casting spiritual striving into earthly forms by the way the purpose is formulated. This is a sort of dogmatizing, a sin from a spiritual point of view,[29] a sin that can often cost dearly.[30] Interpretation of the purpose is often a point of contention. It can lead to a splintering into ever smaller sect-like groups. "A new hope awakens in Lucifer with every new foundation." (GA 130/1962/311) Yet this activity is also capable of bringing forth the highest social capabilities. This is why full approval is appropriate for the step into the institution in a general sense and the definition of the purpose in each individual case. It should only be taken well prepared.

Of course, all is clear as long as the chief defines and interprets the purpose. But this is not so in an institution of our time, driven by the Anthroposophical Social Impulse. Here it is necessary to think of ways to deal with the devil's foot. One must realize that a staff that has started to quarrel is usually not able to reach an impartial judgment, not even able to employ an impartial third party. Yet a solution has to come if the involvement of a state appointed judge (for whom the disputed points are really beyond his scope) is to be avoided. This is why a body of judges should be formed at the very founding of an institution. This body should consist exclusively of persons outside of the institution who enjoy the general trust of the members. It is wise to entrust them constitutionally only with matters which in administrative law are called "limited inquiry," for example, to determine not if acupuncture is anthroposophical therapy, but if, with a liberal interpretation, one can include it in this therapeutic setting.

Such a body is needed for another reason as well, if you will, because of another sin. As we have seen, institutions can be organized in a threefold manner only in a limited way. This is due to the purpose of the institution, whether this is based on the statutes or not. The organ of rights is corrupted in practice, depending on the purpose, because one of the three organs has to take a back seat, no longer fully autonomous. And there is a price to pay. For example, if the rights organ is rejected for this reason, something else, usually oneself, is given the power to judge. As soon as a co-worker comes into conflict with the institution, the rights organ has no choice but to side with the institution, an automatic disadvantage for the worker. No one should be the judge of his own affairs. A body of wisemen outside the framework of the institution must be available for reference.

Although this example points to borderline situations which seldom occur in an institution (even though few escape them), it has contributed much to the understanding of the laws of life of an institution. At this point, let us return to everyday situations.

We have described how the predominant organ can block proposals or desires of the other two, on one hand, and how, on the other, the organ of rights can block those of the predominant organ. This can create great tensions. However, a social formation should *not* avoid this by, for example, creating a fourth organ for the purpose of intervening in an emergency. Again and again one sees how meso structures are supposedly designed for eternity. All possible situations are taken care of, and in no case could the institution perish. But this violates the basic law of life of institutions: "One cannot found for eternity." (GA 257/ 1965/162) Human life too acquires value only through death. Just imagine the meaninglessness of a life without end! The same is true of a social structure, because of the possibility of its disintegration. It is absolutely necessary for this potential to be built in. By its essence, the threefold structure implies the inclusion of death.[31] Again and again co-workers face the road of the cross: understand each other or perish. The highest social forces are challenged *only* when the question of survival depends on them. He who knows that there is a *deus ex machina* can stubbornly insist on his point of view. The person willing to sacrifice his point of view to the common aim, takes "death" unto himself in order to allow the organization to live. Thus, the meso sphere at last leads us back to death, which we have recognized as the starting point of all creation.

One could, and should, elaborate further on the concrete problems that result in the realization of the Anthroposophical Social Impulse in the meso sphere. I have already gone to disproportionate length for the simple reason that this involves unknown territory. I wanted to show how, with the help of the structural principle, a humane and acceptable balance can be created out of this impulse, a balance between the demands of the individual to unfold and the needs of humanity, not as a final solution but as a searching which keeps in mind the miseries of mankind and the social potential of co-workers. Precisely on the meso plane we are in a position not only to *be* social (everyone can do this on the micro plane for themselves), but to model social structures which represent creative forms not only for anthroposophical institutions but for all fellow humans who are motivated by a will to create social realities. May the Anthroposophical Social Impulse itself not be reserved for only the chosen ones. By making it applicable in a practical way, we give it to all mankind. As well, the movement of the Threefold Order of 1919 was designed by Steiner not to be limited to southwestern Germany, but was rather intended to act as living example. "It is not unpractical thinking if one harbors the belief that such a small area can work as a model and that from this model a gradual healthy development of human destiny could be stimulated in a social direction."[32] It is also not at all unpractical thinking to give birth to threefold meso structures as models for the world. Where people with understanding for the Anthroposophical Social Impulse can come together, "it will be possible to form institutions with these people. But then the counter forces, too, will be able to resist more and more." (GA 196.1966/240)

Endnotes:

[1] Der Gedankenweg zum Christus [The Thinking Path to the Christ] GA 189 and GA 193/1972/63.
[2] We have to differentiate the equalizing workings of Ahriman (the future as a state of termites) and Lucifer's wishful dream, to see all man equally happy. See GA 184/1968/204 and 209.
[3] See GA 178/1974/213.

[4] Just as "the healer could at the same time be the creator of sickness"(GA93/1879/75), so the mercurial part of commerce also encompasses its antisocial face of thievery.

[5] In GA 93/1979/75 Steiner treats the form, i.e., what comes to expression in social life as "taken over from the Lemurian epoch," with which the problem of good and evil moves into mankind. The connection with Gabriel, the moon being, is obvious. The role of Gabriel in the Oberufer Paradise Plays may be thought of as an artistic expression of this.

[6] This process is being described in Chapter I, sixth paragraph.

[7] A further connection between rights and the Christ may be found in GA 93/1979/135.

[8] Paul Kipfer in "Was in der Anthroposophischen Gesellschaft vorgeht" [What takes place in the Anthroposophical Society] of February 3, 1974.

[9] There is some reason to think that the four elements, as they live in the micro social are the social aspects of the four so-called platonic virtues: wisdom, courage and thoughtfulness, all three illuminated by justice, "which is the most spiritual one" (GA 159-160/1976/I).

[10] Because this example is emotionally loaded, I would like to add that a prohibition, based on Steiner's view as described above, would be sufficiently justified because nuclear energy endangers the workers.

[11] Here we approach the mystery of Parsival. Not Galahad who fights straight through to the castle of the Grail becomes king of the Grail, but Parsival, who makes the deep detour "through the valley" of sin.

[12] It is suggested that anyone who sees this as an incentive to laziness study the ideas in "The Green Dictator" by Peter Gorf (Herbrug 1980). Additionally, the above remarks in no way exclude the fact that the damages to the soul, brought about by the work for pay economy require a less abrupt transition to keep economic continuity going. Yet these question are outside of the scope of this book.

[13] By the way, it is here that I have my main objections against Wilhelm Schmund's basic concept of economic circulation in his second picture (addendum to his "Der soziale Organismums in seiner Freiheitsgestalt" [the Social Organism in its Liberated Form] Dornach 1962). His starting point here—which turns out to be the the main pillar of his theory—

is money in the hands of the industrialist *obligates* the worker to apply his talents. Yet wherever one wishes to force people, one is forced into centralistic arrangements. It remains to be clarified to what extent Schmund's concept of obligation agrees with the conventional one.

14 Stefan Leber's "Selbstbverwicklichung - Mündlichkeit - Sozialität" [Self realization—Maturity—Social Deportment]. Stuttgart: 1978, p. 73.

15 To find out about a system of "castes" emanating from this in the future, see GA 105/1974/184.

16 Steiner pronounced a scathing judgment on the ability of individuals to judge economic conditions. To give this judgement any weight would be "harmful because the economic judgment of individuals is totally worthless. It can never be truly based on reality" GA 338/1969/144). The reader may know one of those entrepreneurs who are unable to separate their own aesthetic judgment sufficiently from that of their customers (a given fact in the economy). Bankruptcy of the undertaking is built into it in this case. Steiner looks at the common will of a works community as being just as harmful because decisions must be made based on abilities. (GA 24/1961/233). Again consideration of these abilities is a matter which can not be imposed from above, but demands "the free understanding of his (= the owners) co-workers down to the last laborer" (GA 328/1977/157).

17 An individual judgment would at best be possible based on the concrete relationship of a person to drug use, for instance, triggered by a question asked by the drug user of the physician, the priest, the friend. But then the answer is no longer a judgment but a help.

18 "Der Kommende" year 25, No. 23.

19 This example has been chosen because it represents a first step. But his motives are not what is meant here. The information should serve all of society and not utilize the fear for one's own health. This responsibility lives more strongly in the *demands,* for instance, to mark cosmetics tested on animals as such, or put a label on every kilogram of pork meat that seven kilograms of premium grain are used for feed to produce it, and that this is in part taken from countries with famines.

[20] GA 190/1971/217. One can interpret this statement in two ways, both are justified. One should not bring truths down from the spiritual world that are not needed and one should express truths only if asked. It may be a fact in our present world that the person immersed in the life of the spirit "strives for a possible field of action by freely offering his individual capabilities" without "being given a task by a demand or depending on a demand" (Lothar Vogel, "Die Verwirklichung des Menschen im socialen Organismus" [Realizing the Human Being within the Social Organism], Eckwälder 1973, pg. 339). In the sense of the threefold order such an occupation falls under the concept "game"—that is to say, as a private matter without (macro or meso) social relevance. "All experiences in the realm of the spirit which the other human beings wish to experience themselves with the particular human individuality, are justified" GA 328/1977/64 and 177). It is simply true that spiritual life without an economic aspect (need) is just as impossible as economy without spiritual life (capabilities).

[21] More to this in my, shortly appearing "Die Dreigliederung unseres Steuersystems" [Three folding our System of Taxation], in: "Aus der Arbeit mit der Dreigliederung" [from Work with the Threefold Order]

[22] More to this in my "Kaufgeld—Leihgeld—Schenkungsgeld" [Purchase Money—Loan Money—Gift Money], in "Gesellschaftsstrukturen in Bewegung" [Societal Structures in Motion].

[23] Possibly also the help for the needy. Today this is of small significance in the West. See also GA 30/1962/168: Help from person to person will then have less significance. "In its place the great adviser will appear here and there in etheric form."

[24] See my "Bürgerlicher Ungehorsam" [Civil Disobedience]

[25] This is a direct demonstration of the connection between the social and the human threefold structure. In each of the social organs *one* soul force is exercised. Our self learns to feel comfortable, even when at times it lives in only one of the three soul forces and consciously excludes the others. The process of learning takes place not by colliding with *people* but with rules which one has affirmed oneself. Those who

were given the thankless role of Beckmesser to mercilessly reject every comment not appropriate for the particular organ, do not talk as know it alls, but as representatives of a dead form, without which there is no life. In this respect the institution is a better preparation for the maturing of our soul forces than the macro organism. This latter allows us to simply switch off, because we deal with anonymous subjects. Even the most beautiful threefold organization is powerless in the face of a lack of interest. However in the institution ego-involvement is possible. This allows far stronger contact with the borders of the three other spheres. Indeed one's tie to the institution as such is not merely existential but it also involves its co-workers who are people we experience and not anonymous humans.

[26] The divine ruler was able to give a purpose to the community. Today it is appropriate to the time that the purpose is not determined by macro organisms.

[27] Of course it is part of the mission of the spiritual life to publicize animal torture on the macro plane so that, as a result, a law exists that forbids all animal torture. In this case this aspect would no longer apply to the meso plane.

[28] Interim solutions are of course possible too, e.g. a new look at whether it is possible to obtain raw material without torturing animals. Should this exist the whole process starts over again because the economic organ now must determine whether the whole thing is still feasible economically under the new conditions.

[29] "The spirit blows where it will"; he who casts it into forms excludes it. Exclusion is the original sin. The essence of being human teaches us not to avoid exclusion. The human ego "is the origin of egoism" (GA 97/1981/114), but without it there is no progress.

[30] It is therefore understandable that leading personalities of the spiritual life do not like to go this way and prefer to remain personally responsible. Yet one needs to remember that the step into the institution too is a sin but at the same time a necessary step toward social progress. The renunciation mentioned at the beginning of this chapter applies to academia as well. Steiner has made this sacrifice in an exemplary way at the Christmas gathering of 1923/24.

[31] See above all GA 125/1962/74: "In the age of the consciousness soul there needs to be developed a sense for the fact that birth and death live in the outer events and that, if one gives birth to anything, be it a children's toy or an empire, one gives birth with the consciousness that sometime it has to die ... In the age of the consciousness soul it has to be the human being who weaves death and birth into his social life."

[32] Steiner talking about Owen in GA 34/1960/209.

Chapter VIII

Anomalies of Social Life

To describe the anomalies of our social life would fill a library. There is perhaps no other area where so much good will has created so much chaos. The social architects of our time who have no inkling of social laws and, therefore, think that they can force social conditions with definitions are real experts at chaos. They have a field day because the connection between social catastrophes and ignorance of social laws is not as visible as that between the collapse of a building and the neglect of stress analysis. By now most everyone has learned the basic principles of stress analysis, even if he does not become an architect. Yet our young people are sent out into the world without any idea of social laws. Were these known, one would point fingers at our social quacks.

It suffices for our purpose to point to a few principal items in connection with the application, or rather the misapplication, of social laws. Having described the Anthroposophical Social Impulse in the previous chapters, it now remains to show how it can help us understand the social diseases of our time.

Let us look first at the micro plane. It is certainly easy to determine that the social impulse in the life of the economy has arrived at its nadir: Everyone for himself and let the state take care of those left behind! It is true that with a global economy we have reached the phase where, at least in the industrial countries, no one still works simply to satisfy his own needs in the physical sense. This would provide the technical basis for a radical emergence of the Basic Sociological Law. Yet everyone tries hard to pocket the fruits of his labor for himself. The antisocial penetrates to the most remote corners of economic social life and spawns its destructive tendencies. The size and style of the unit of support has transformed over time from the great state wherein each one used to live on what was given to him by the theocrat, as in the example of the Inca Empire in Chapter III, to the extended family which supported each member regardless of his contribution, and now the much closer unit of the small family of our century wherein the parents are removed to old folks' homes, the young children to day care centers, and the older children paid to wash or rinse the car (if they have not already secured their own private domain with a newspaper route or some similar venture). And because the state subsidizes the children's education and in some countries also their food and shelter through tax credits, only those remain as "family" who earn their pay for themselves, husband and wife. The wife looks for a paying job, not, as in the 19th century, to help support the family but to be "independent." At some point the husband and wife negotiate what minimum should or must be deposited into communal accounts, earmarked for taxation or donation. Of utmost importance is what each individual earns. Everyone lives off the fruits of their labor. Everyone lives under the illusion of their independence. Thus, each one contributes to disaster.

Years ago, so long ago that I can no longer trace the source, there appeared an autobiography of a criminal who was awaiting his execution on death row. His earliest memory was of standing on a high table in front of his father. The father stretched out his arms in invitation and yelled, "Jump!" But when the boy joyfully jumped, the father stepped back and the little one took a dreadful fall. "This should teach you never to trust anybody in your life," the pedagogical father explained, and in this manner helped to create a criminal. Such is the case of the criminal creativity we all harbor if we keep the fruits of our work to ourselves out of fear or lack of trust of our fellow humans. An economic life built not on confidence but as one that looks to individual fortunes for support — individual income, individual finances — makes life ever more expensive. Today everyone who has to take out a mortgage on his home discovers this. He also realizes this in the costs of theft insurance, because the guild of long fingers was the first to consistently apply the principle of "me first." He should also know that the substitute efforts of the state — child care, child support, cost of living subsidies, prisons, police — are far more expensive than living from the fruits of others, in fact, far more costly than meets the eye because technical innovations, brought about thanks to the life of the spirit, obscure the largest portion of the ever-rising costs.

Has "man" become much more wicked? I would hate to subscribe to this lament of doting old men. Rather, I would say we have become more helpless, because the structural backing and the social tutelage of communities (church, village, family) have atrophied. They *had to be* removed in accordance with the Basic Sociological Law and because as modern humans we no longer dare to believe in the social forces within us, the prime source of the Archetypal Social Phenomenon.

At one time Thomas Hobbs, a misanthropical state savant with a warm heart, was asked why he gave alms to beggars. "It makes me feel good; therefore it is self interest," he replied, in application true to his theory. H.J. van de Braak[1] insists that Hobbes is confusing motives, that Hobbes perhaps does not define altruism as does van de Braak, and means compassion and self interest. In the 18th century Hobbes could afford to play around with these ideas. Today they have become common conviction. Through conviction we have created a Leviathan whose purpose is to tame us in to becoming social beings.

It is true that the social impulse within us is still too weak to stand up without a structural crutch. Modern sociology has made us abundantly conversant with the problems of the "free rider," who parasitically uses social institutions without contributing himself, and the "prisoner's dilemma," one chooses a bad solution to prevent a *worst* solution which we fear out of mistrust of our fellow Men. Because they blackmail us with the worst solution, our states seduce us again and again to choose bad solutions, gagging us along the lines of Lenin's maxim that one acts rightly to gag ninety-nine innocent people in order to stop the one hundredth, the parasite.

Steiner's statement in his "Geheimwissenschaft und soziale Frage" [*Occult Science and the Social Question*] is true, that the Principal Social law can be realized only if the structure no longer allows anybody to pocket the fruits of his own labor. The striving of the states in both East and West is the exact opposite to this; rather, they use self-interest to whip and motivate their subjects to greater accomplishments. It is also true that nowadays almost every new social accomplishment of the state relieves the citizens of a social responsibility. We are given rights and deprived of moral duties; these are exchanged for tax duties. No wonder that this exact opposite of what is needed (GA 158/1968/143) keeps us in a social jungle. At best it is no more overgrown. We need structures which challenges what is social in human beings instead of choking it off.[2]

The fact remains: the release from social associations, as described in Chapter III happens as the Basic Sociological Law develops. One can hardly continue to call the state such an association. We are merely driven by our archaic national instincts. Part of this stimulation is the estrangement of the fellow human being. If we were to feel as one with the other person, we could not develop love for him or her. (GA 260 a/1966/76) Yet this form of estrangement has led to a degree of atomization that can end only in the war of all against all. If co-existence is to remain a possibility, the inexorable progress of the Basic Sociological Law will have to be linked with the Christian one to will the freedom and development of the *other* person. "*All* human beings would have been irretrievably subject to the quarrel of all against all, which will indeed come about. But it will come about only for those who have not filled themselves in the right way with the Christ impulse. ... Since one soul can no longer understand the other, they have to work against each other." (GA 112/1925/276 f.)

This brings us right to the crux of anomalies in the macro social sphere. We experience, on one hand, a rebirth of the theocratic association. The modern states from America to China increasingly demand that the ideology of the state resurrect itself in each citizen. No longer does the law appear as a last, dead, expression of the rights impulse which brings about a dignified human balance between the striving toward freedom that destroys the biological basis of existence and the striving to consume that destroys the basis of further development. It would have to be independent to accomplish that. The law appears to us rather as the great commander, Big Brother, who solves the problems we cannot handle for ourselves. Personified in the state, the law appears as the social double of a nation. It is composed of all its inadequacies, of all the things for which the population refused to assume personal responsibility. These inadequacies are by no means confined to the area of rights. Roman Boos call the laws "Equalizing formulas for contrasting economic interests."[3] And Schweppenhäuser, looking in the opposite direction, writes, "The most dangerous aspect of the totalitarian state is that it forms the human being after its own image. For it has at its disposal all means to transform humans, in contrast to the former types of absolutisms."[4] The empowerment of the antisocial and asocial forces finds clear expression in these two formulations.

Now let us take another look at our clock in Chapter VI (Fig. 1) and see what has become of it.

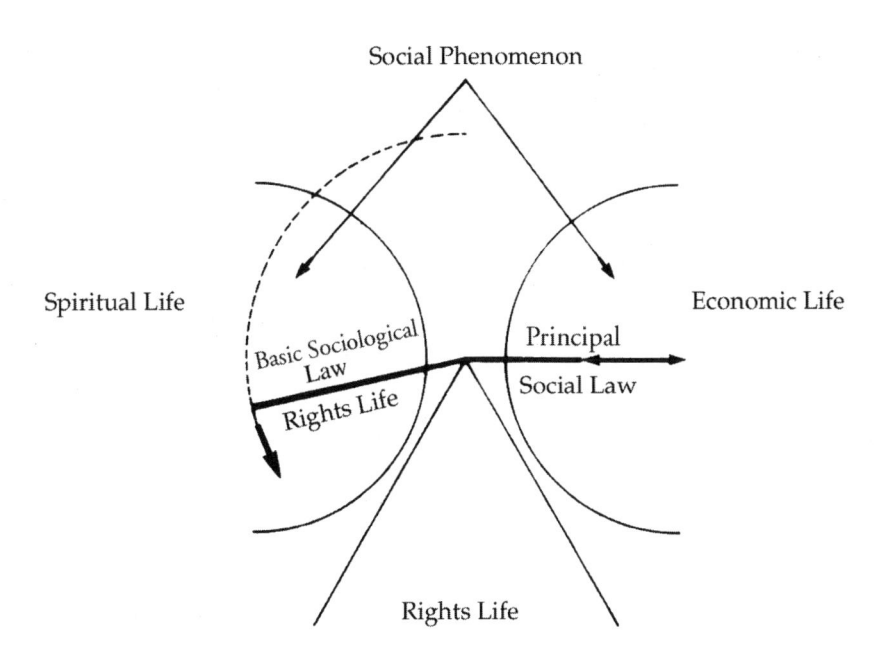

Fig. 1: The life of rights has to establish the equilibrium between the forces of the evolving the Basic Sociological Law and the Principal Social Law as it comes to bear in different ways.

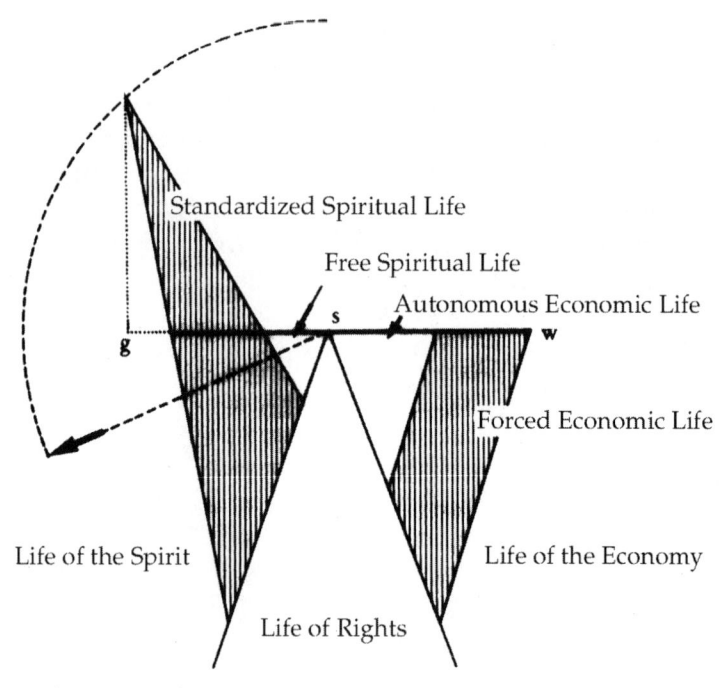

Fig. 2: The State applies prostheses. It forces back the finger of the Basic Sociological Law by supporting the life of the spirit and, in so doing, turns it into a state institution. By way of taxation it forces the economy to work for others.

The left hand, indicating the release from the associations, has moved further down. The right hand, expressing the shrunken down will to work for others in the economy, can no longer hold the balance. Therefore, the state applies a prosthesis, namely forced socialization. This, in fact, exists not merely east of the Iron Curtain. Roughly seventy percent of the Western world does not work for its own income but for that of the state (taxes), which then redistributes it under various conditions. The Principal Social Law seems to have been largely fulfilled from a purely quantitative point of view. This may be the very reason why so many young people are often, as it were, hypnotized by political economy. The pointer of the Basic Sociological Law gets a boost from the life of the state in order to stop it from pulling the organism apart. It is being pulled into and fastened to the life of rights. This is done by feeding the life of the spirit with monies taken out of the economy. Yet the conditions surrounding this action rob the life of the spirit of its freedom. Using our image of balance one can visualize this even more clearly. Only by artificially forcing back the pointer of the Basic Sociological Law can one lessen its pressure; only by forcing work done for others can one create counter pressure, thus establishing a new balance (line sg = line sw).

Understandably, one would lean to the idea that the state would have to act as substitute and take, as it were, hostages until a majority of humans would pull themselves together to bring about social impulses by creating structures and by their own actions. Yet I have already mentioned in the previous chapter, and simply reiterate here, that this thought leads in the wrong direction, because today's macro structure does anything but challenge the social will forces. The social will is, essentially, the expression of the free individual, and "the state must, by its own nature, aim at the suppression of the individual." (GA 29/1960/55) Just as it demands mediocrity in the life of the spirit, it becomes, on the other hand, one "with the conditions in the economy." It expresses "economic interests and requirements in public rights." (GA 332/a/1950/167) It makes little difference here, whether the state's controls are handled by the corporations or by the party. "The most effective principle for extending power over as many people as one needs is, in our times, the principle of economic dependency." (GA 178/1974/233)

Let us take a look at this side of today's economy. We are able to perceive three different, but interdependent forces which determine the structure.

a) Since the remaining quota of the social product over which the individual can dispose is getting smaller and smaller, each one tries to live out his passions in an increasingly small part of the economic life. This small area thus gets to be socially so obnoxious that it is no longer bearable to allow it free reign, and we encounter a self-acting force which subjugates an ever-increasing percentage of the economy to the state.

b) Because political economy cannot function economically, the real social product decreases all the time. It is increasingly less appealing for the individual to fully commit himself to his work if his work cannot appreciably increase his income. Additionally, a large part of his income comes from the state independently of his performance, if not in the form of direct support (social help, subsidies for the economy, and so forth), then through collective amenities (roads, fire-brigade, theater, and so on). In contrast, social motivation to work for the community can hardly be mustered if the result of the work no longer makes any sense. Statistics have long ago ceased to be a reliable resource. "There are liars, damned liars and statisticians" [English proverb]. Indeed, statistics include efforts merely expended to remove the harmful effects of other efforts. Everyone can see that damage caused in an automobile accident results in the *loss* of real values to the economy. But the total social product *increases* by the costs of the repairs. In this way not only the output in nuclear energy but the safety measures (whatever one understands these to be), too, are part of the social product. As an aside, I mention that the non-value of armaments (and in case of their deployment, actually negative values) are also evaluated in the same way. In reality the social products may be in a strong continuous decline, because the state is forced to repair the delayed damages of the economic wonder.[5]

c) A decrease of the social product in the presence of forced spending drives the government into spiraling taxation. Increasing resistance to taxation (see a) causes the bloodletting via taxation, be it performed formally or behind closed doors, with increasingly impertinent methods, hence, mushrooming of tax evasion, and finally totalitarian edicts. Thus, society ever more rapidly steers toward the condition when the Principal Social Law appears full-on in the official economy,[6] because *all* the social product is being distributed by the state. Under this condition egoism celebrates orgies on the black market. If you wish, you can call this a confirmation of the theory of convergence.

This is paralleled by an equally ghastly picture in the life of the spirit. The apparatus needs a state ideology as support for its economic behavior. The modern state buys the help of the most refined psychologists in order to introduce this ideology with all legal and illegal means. I cite two current symptoms, more or less at random. A student in Bavaria is given propaganda text written in favor of the deterrent theory for college entrance exams in sociology. The minister of culture advises the examiner to count only approving answers as a passing grade.[7] In the future teachers who want their pupils to pass the examinations will have to teach them state ideology. Similarly, pupils in the Netherlands are given a newsletter from the finance department which, by omitting all questionable pages dealing with tax collection, encourages an attitude friendly to the state and taxation.[8]

Through methods such as these, the state can be highly successful in manipulating and programming the social behavior of the population and reducing them to termites. With an increasing refinement of methods, this will succeed more and more often. Despite this unfolding development, the Basic Sociological Law places unequivocal limits to these efforts. The individual drive to develop rumbles just below the surface of consciousness. It finds expression in riots, lethargy, and so forth. As this duality increases in the behavior of its subjects, the state find itself forced to take recourse to the oldest of social instincts, to nationalism. For once the brainwashing of one's own population is accomplished, the murmurs for freedom are turned off, with effective steps taken to the exceptions. The *furor teutonicus*, the Roman symbol of outlived obsession with the tribe, is loosed on the ideology of another people. This goes hand in hand with a cutting down of the real social product by means of exaggerated armaments, and thus catastrophe.

On the subject of degeneration of the balancing member, the life of rights, I refer to Chapter I, paragraph six where the logical conclusion of this degeneration is presented. On one hand, the lack of a life of rights has its own significance; it can be viewed as merely an expression of situation-forced decision-making in the life of the spirit and of the economy. On the other hand, this social non-existence starts to have a life of its own. As long ago as 1919 Steiner pointed out that "in the state which administers all of society, all that is antisocial in man will come to life in the form of a chase after certain positions with the aim to capture all that can be obtained today by means of the capitalistic state." GA/330-331/1963/53) A shift in the sphere of activities takes place, even in areas that are not as yet officially run by the state. To the degree to which the state limits the grasp of unearned gains, the industrialist appears competing for extra allowances, advantages, tax rebates and subsidies. The free profession of the subsidy specialist already exists in the Netherlands to guide the industrialist through the jungle of officialdom. This development ends logically in the huge bureaucracy, in technocracy, and finally it turns the individual into a mere functionary of the (state) machine. This future already exists as a tendency in many areas. It is the state-controlled "law" which develops not merely into non-law but into anti-law, in other words, into a force that destroys every law. I have expounded on what develops at this point as anti-threefoldness through an example about tax collection (see my soon to appear "Aus der Arbeit mit der Dreigliederung" [*Out of Labor with the Threefold Order*]. The anomaly of the macro social leads to anti-threefoldness. This is the abyss.[9]

Finally, let us look at the anomalies in the meso social area. Here, too, we encounter the same symptoms as in the micro and macro social areas. Institutional life, however, adds something which usually escapes our notice on the macro plane, namely its dynamics. Macro organisms undergo a secular development, the study of which requires a deep understanding of history. Superficial observation will show the mechanism of compulsive reactions, while the development in micro organisms in individuals should be shrouded from our view. But institutions are being born, unfold and die in front of our eyes. What can this dynamic add to our previous observations?

Spiritual science shows that all evil is nothing more than the appearance of good at the wrong time. The tyrant is still engaged in theocracy and does not even notice that time has marched on. He spells the doom for the family (as domestic tyrant), for the institution (as hierophant), and for the community (as dictator). A (genuine[10]) communist lives already in future times in his life of will. He splinters the family with anti-authority oriented education, the institution with collectives with exclusively unanimous decisions, and the community with anarchy. So great is the atomization that one can really no longer talk about family, institutions or community.

The same source teaches us that, as the human being grows up, it repeats briefly the social phases of mankind. After the parents act as substitutes for the function of the infant's ego, the individual arrives at the stage of belief in authority and reaches maturity by way of respect for the experience and profound knowledge of the teacher.

It appears that for institutions no such biogenetic, but rather a sociogenetic, basic law applies. By this I do not so much mean, as described in Chapter III, that the structure of many institutions corresponds to that of outlived social forms. Should this be the case, we face symptoms of social disease. Rather, here we deal with the healthy counterpart to this: old forms are fully justified at a certain stage of development of an institution. It is the getting stuck in outlived phases (or skipping a phase here and there) that is is socially sick.

This sociogenetical developmental law has already been worked out by the Netherlands Pedagogical Institute (NPI).[11] In a way it even provides a starting point for the social activities of this organization. It encompasses the trinity of the pioneering phase, the founding phase, and the differentiating or bureaucratic phase, as well as the communicative phase. We shall characterize this developmental law briefly as a basis for further observations regarding the dynamics and anomalies in these meso social areas.

A founders circle stands at the beginning of an institution. Almost always this contains an outstanding personality whose greatness and creative willpower make the impossible possible.[12] This is the theocrat who not only knows everything and can do everything, but whose will is in no way felt by the other members of the founders circle as enslaving or even dominating. On the contrary, his will works through them and makes their wills harmonize with his. Max Weber speaks about a charismatic personality. At this initiation time each member is responsible for the whole institution, yet the bond inspired by the leader ensures that whenever a co-worker needs help, help promptly appears. Mishaps may occur, but they are not heeded, usually not even by the outer world. Later on, when one reflects on this beginning time, one experiences it like a lost paradise. The feeling is comparable to the nostalgia which drives many Germans to Italy, where one loses himself in the joy and matter-of-course atmosphere of existence in spite of its poverty, where one forgets the next moment but where nature, that which thrusts itself on one from without, already holds the solution in its lap, a world of the sentient soul.

This is followed by the paper stage. It starts with slips of paper. Instead of acting in the moment, as was done until now, we use paper to remind us to do this or that. Eventually, we have a variety of pre-printed forms. Each person has his own area which the other co-workers are to avoid unless they subordinate themselves. The backbone of the structure is no longer the theocratic principle but the bureaucratic one. In spite of the greatest diligence, mistakes happen all the time, usually because something goes wrong in communications. The mistakes are not only noticed now but resented by the co-workers and the world at large. Specialists are called in. They handle tasks in their own style, acting from their own experience, thus introducing new problems in the institution. The institution verges on becoming a structure in which human beings become objects which "fit in." The joy of working disappears, bureaucracy moves in with old age pensions and eight hour days. But at least one is acknowledged by the authorities (the world of the intellectual soul).

Institutions in the third phase, whose characteristics one can decipher, hardly exist. Yet paths toward this phase exist, as indicated by the Anthroposophical Social Impulse and described in the threefold meso structure. In its purpose-conditioned activities, the institution creates forms which do justice to the threefold structure of the co-workers' souls. This process is not complete until the three independent organs are crystallized. As in man, where impulses cannot unfold if an organ is missing, in the same way the social formative impulse remains powerless without organs. "After all, spiritual science has the additional task to really flow into the social structure." (GA 181/1967/XIV) Once this is accomplished, the theocrat and the technocrat disappear from the life of the institution. "The authority of human beings is not there to convince us but to stimulate us." (GA 97/1981/95)

Yet the fruits of specialization and renunciation must not be abandoned in this process. Rather, it is personal responsibility that must be regained, not because everyone does everything, but because everyone is present in the decision-making organs in all three areas. Each time one is present in a different role, but each time with the same mindset to carry the institution. From this point on the failure of a co-worker is experienced as one's own fault. The ego becomes conscious of its capabilities of soul (the world of consciousness soul).

This short characterization serves as a sketch of the elements needed to understand the dynamics of the three phases of development of an institution. It is not the character of institutions that allows me to find a basis for the attractive thought that the development of an institution proceeds in seven year cycles, like that of the human being. The phases of a child's development are anchored in the nature of its being, in the incarnating and unfolding of the members of its entelechy. These come to light without the individual's action. I am convinced that the time will come to speak about the members of the embodiment of a social structure as one speaks about those of a human being today. But at the present stage of our knowledge, the use of these terms is premature.[13] Although one can observe a seven-year rhythm in one or another institution, in my opinion this is either imagination or willful creation. Today's social structures are characteristically human creations on which we bestow our problems and weaknesses, at least in their infancy.

For example, we do not begin children out in the phase of authority, that is, by skipping the phase of imitation, for to try this would inflict severe inner damage on the child without accomplishing a goal. Yet it is possible and, in fact, it does happen with public schools that an institution is allowed to start with the bureaucratic phase.

We may assume that the transition for a *social* institution must be based on *social* elements and not on the course of time. Therefore, it must be the result of a deepening understanding of what is important from a social, inter-human, point of view.

During the founding phase, an institution's functioning is essentially based on the flow of the founder's will permeating the founding circle. Hence, the pioneering period should, socially, end the moment a new personality connects itself existentially with the institution.[14] I will clarify this idea from two different viewpoints.

a. Members of the founding circle need not all be present from the very beginning. There is an embryonic period during which one or another person may still join. This gestation period usually ends when the institution is presented to the outer world.

b. Not every newcomer bonds existentially with the institution, that he or she immediately becomes dependent on the institution and the institution dependent on his or her work.[15]

One neither can nor should expect it of a new co-worker to fit in with the prevailing will of the group. He arrives with his own impulses, based on his own biography, and comes with his own goals. If these are not accepted, or they are experienced as hostile during the founding phase, there are two possibilities: either the new arrival is fired or mentally maimed. It would pay to examine sometime how many there are who, having joined during the actual founding period, wind up playing a subordinate role, acting holier than the pope (in the Netherlands one calls them with the English term "his master's voice"), and always standing in the shadows, their development stunted. With time they become the horror of new arrivals and the laughingstock of the veterans. The founders circle commits a social crime toward new arrivals if, at the moment they join, it does not step back as authority and strive for true objectivity for the institution and for the human relations. Many such crimes are committed, most out of ignorance of social laws. The harm done to an individual has its effects in the meso social area, for, as of that moment, the institution assumes an unjustified structure. This is, as it were, a repeat of the fall of man. Savoring the joy of working together, the founding circle, which now often meets behind closed doors, becomes the forbidden fruit. Thus, the institution loses its invulnerability. Innocence is never regained.

Instinctually, many young institutions these days are keeping the founders circle closed in spite of a shortage of co-workers. The original circle is usually made up of karmically deeply connected individuals who, due to this connectedness, suffer life's heart-rending tests to pass over them like natural catastrophes. They postpone admission of new members. This is often impossible, for instance, when a new class is added each year in a new school. The opposite extreme occurs also, if a founding circle keeps closed up for decades. In this case no transition to the phase of sharing the work takes place, yet neither the co-workers nor outsiders feel this as inappropriate. At most, outsiders are astonished by the eternal youthful buoyancy of the group. One can see similar situations among kindergarten teachers. If they work more or less in isolation, they simply lack social contacts, the discussions with co-workers. As a result "their" kindergarten freezes in a blissful founders state. Clearly, the founders phase should not be measured in years.

The end of the next, the bureaucratic phase, does not come from without, as in the addition of co-workers in the founders phase, but from within. Two conditions must be fulfilled before the journey through the desert may be ended. First, the handling of the differentiated processes, that is, the handing out of specific tasks, must have progressed to be not merely mastered but no longer emotional. In the communicating phase this has to be accepted routine. The distribution of tasks has to run like clockwork, the unavoidable accidents no longer causing disaster or tension. Bureaucracy is put in its place, both outwardly and on an inter-personal plane. Secondly, a sufficient number of co-workers must have the burning, existential desire to introduce and fashion the communicating phase. Here nothing is simply established by the past. Each step has to be wrestled for by itself. Therefore, the transition can only come as the result of a decision, a vow. Infidelity to this vow would shake the entire institution. One can seek counsel regarding the degree of maturity of the organization, one can seek help in the technical execution of the decision, but every step of progress must be one's own achievement, based on social will.

If one looks at today's meso level, one beholds a frightful scene. The world teems with institutions that have never grown beyond the founding phase, in spite of a great increase of coworkers. One often sees the grand old man of forty years ago, now in his eighties. Death has taken most of his co-founders and, anxious, he is propped up on his throne by the very creatures he has fashioned,[16] often against his own will. Even his young wife has married the power rather than him.

Why is it so hard to say farewell to the founders' structure? Perhaps for the same reason why so many people do not want to grow up. Behind the threshold there lies the social hell of bureaucracy, the formalization of all that is human, the battle with inhumanity which, changed into a machine within an institution, is always right. And the longer one unjustifiably dallies in the founding phase, the more difficult, the more impossible, becomes the parting. Before the step can be dared, the entire generation of founders must be swept away, either by death or by their ruination of the institution.

Lucifer acts as helping spirit as long as the founding phase is justified. Without his brilliance and promise nothing would be accomplished. In the leader one experiences the father figure, carrying everyone on his wings over the abyss. "Would we have dared it, had we known what was in store for us?" One often hears this out of the mouths of founders. Yet Lucifer always tempts us to continue what was timely in the past. Do not those great ones of early days walk around "like the Gods?" And for what is all this is to be exchanged? For the soul's desert of bureaucracy. Lucifer does not lie when he points to the desert; he merely conceals the promised land.

Then the whole drama unfolds anew. One resigns oneself to the inevitable. The joy, the human feeling of belonging together is gone, but at least one has exchanged it for a decent and steady income, for security, for peace and order. One is under the protection of the masters of the world, and the stones that have replaced the former clapboards are witness to general acknowledgment. One has adapted, one is fit for good society, and the director of the institution gets a medal. All this one should give up? For what? Like lead weights Ahriman presses us into rigid forms and commands us to call this rigidity life. Measures are taken to bestow immortality on the institution down to its statutes, an immortality of *rigor mortis*.[17] A circle of fear forms around the workers in the institution and paralyses any initiative. What is behind all this?

Indeed, no paradise is behind it, but neither is it death, as the spirit of lies would lead us to believe. Rather, it is the possibility of dying and, hence, resurrection. The threefold structure, as described in Chapter VI, indeed also harbors the premise that the institution can die at any moment. It can die if sufficient social will is not brought to it to reconcile the irreconcilable, if coworkers are not ready to take death onto themselves instead of burdening the institution. No outside power will appear as a saving angel. The institution is no longer what the founder has brought down to earth as an ideal, no longer that which is anchored as a rock in the sea of statutes. It is what lives in each individual co-worker and what he has brought with him. The threefold structure includes the danger of the institution's losing its identity, and it is fearful to face this third evil power that coerces all those untimely meso organisms to lead their barren, boring existences, existences unworthy of human beings.

Endnotes:

[1] H.J. van de Braak "Belastingenweerstand." Deventer 1981, p. 86.

[2] One of the particularly beautiful aspects of Peter Gorf's "Grüner Diktator" [the Green Dictator] (Heersbruck) 1980) lies in the fact that he always prevents certain social vices and leaves those involved to solve the problems thus created to themselves. Let us remember Steiner's words as well (GA 4/1921/148) that only laws that prohibit not those that demand are fitting for the free spirit.

[3] "Der Weg zum Staat und die Grenzen des Staates" [the way to the state and the boundaries of the state], Stuttgart 1921.

[4] "Das soziale Rätsel X" [The social riddle X], Freiburg 1976, p. 118.

[5] More about this in my article in "Jonas" 1982/14-16 in "De kwitantie van der verzorgingsstaat," Den Haag 1983.

[6] One finds a reference to this similarity in GA 185a/1962/219.

[7] Anyone who can read finds confirmation of this in the answer of 16.9.1981 from Minister Mayer to questions in the Bavarian parliament, 9, election period, printed matter 9/9626.

[8] "Per saldo" since December 1979.

[9] See also GA 202/1970/257 f. One can grasp what happens when the state regulates *all* social relationships in its demonic perspective in the following words of Rudolf Steiner: "The structure of the state in relation to inter-human relations created by the state is the exact opposite of what human relations are in the spiritual world" (GA 189/1946/87). Steiner has often pointed to the significance of the dead for the social life. By its nature this relationship "is a relation to the spiritual worlds." Mankind loses its connections to its sources of social inspiration as more and more human relations are created by the state instead of by the life of the soul. By the way, this theme has many aspects beyond the scope of this work.

[10] We need to add this because communism "is the most extreme form of conservatism" (GA 199/1967/31), a " very old phenomenon" (GA 186/1963/237) and certainly does not presuppose anything that lies in the future.

[11] B.C. Lievgoed "Organizationen im Wandel" [Organizations in process of transformation], Bern/Stuttgart 1974, pg. 43 ff.

[12] If this personality is missing, or if there are more than one, the life of the institution usually starts with a crisis.
[13] I discovered a basis for such research in GA 19/1967/203 ff.
[14] And not only when one ceases to encounter each other, as Lievegoed thinks. At most one could say the the *forcing function* to enter the bureaucratic phase starts at that moment. Although the slips of paper are typical for that phase, yet its beginning should lie earlier, based on understanding the social situation.
[15] I have described the significance of this idea in chapter VI.
[16] See GA 260 a/1966/253.
[17] Perhaps one can talk here of an institutional counterpart to those magical brotherhoods which Steiner calls "Insurance companies for ahrimanic immortality" (GA/174/1966/197).

Chapter IX

Aphorisms to the Pathology of the Anthropsophical Movement

As soon as one talks about the Basic Sociological Law, the Principal Social Law and the Threefold Order, one points to something that spiritual science has made available to mankind. Man can use it or reject it without taking a stand on Anthroposophy. For example, one need not become an Anthroposophist to experience the healing power of Anthroposophical medicine. But if one wants to fully enter into the spirit of the Anthroposophical Social Impulse, it is necessary to make the force of the Archetypal Social Phenomenon, as described in Chapter V, one's own personal concern, to have the impulse to allow this force to flow into social life. Inversely, one can quite easily be an anthroposophist and totally bypass the Social Impulse, just as every anthroposophist need not become an anthroposophical doctor.

This comparison is only conditionally correct, as it is difficult to imagine that anyone who wishes to shape his life on the basis of spiritual science would not allow a therapeutic aspect to play a part in his fundamental attitude on the micro level, even if he has little to do with the medical sphere. This is also true for the Social Impulse. If one looks at the exercises Steiner gives as necessary complements to the meditative paths of development, one will find much of what has been described as the Anthroposophical Social Impulse in Chapter V. One could simply think of these exercises as the path to social development.[1]

Similar statements could be made about the macro level. In everyday life we have responsibilities toward our fellow men. This is true in the economy as consumers, in the cultural life as artists or thinkers, in the political life as citizens. It would be desirable if the Anthroposophical Social Impulse could even faintly reverberate in the antisocial and asocial drives along with the catchwords of shopping, publication, civic initiative, and so forth.

I do not underestimate the activity at the macro level. Yet it is up to the discretion of each individual. But if one works as an anthroposophist within an anthroposophical institution, that is, on the meso level, a very different significance is added. It is certainly no accident that spiritual science dared to enter the institutional world for the first time with the Waldorf school once the structural law for our time had been established with the Threefold Order. Before that, spiritual science lived within a closed circle, with occasional public lectures or performances. An exception, the Philosophical-Anthroposophical publishing house, worked under quite different conditions. (GA 24/1961/453)

Anthroposophy stepped out into the wider world only with education, medical practices, biodynamic farms, therapeutic homes, and the Christian community, thus engaging in *public* endeavors. Relationships to non-anthroposophical "clients"—parents, children, patients—were established based on the aims of anthroposophy, creating the necessity of calling on the forms that represent the anthroposophical mother impulse. In other words, the demand arose to make the Anthroposophical Social Impulse the basis of these institutional do's and don'ts. In contrast to all other Anthroposophical areas of expertise, the social aspect is a dimension of every institutional activity. One would think that an institution cannot really call itself anthroposophical without realizing the Anthroposophical Social Impulse at least in its germinal form.

In reality, the picture is somewhat different as the title of this chapter suggests. We have a full circle – a loop from total absence of any social impulse to attempts that got stuck, as well as purely formal acceptance of certain elements, all the way to serious wrestling for its realization. Today we have institutions, who call themselves anthroposophical and whose members are thoroughly convinced that the social impulse is the business of other people and that the meso sphere is not the place for it. Perhaps Steiner asked too much of his times with this idea (as is evident from the initial failure of the Threefold Movement, which he himself led). They feel that the social impulse belongs to the sixth cultural epoch. Ideas are also represented, ranging from that of thinking that Steiner tried to tempt his Anthroposophists to the one that "this was Steiner's great error." Steiner quotations are then found to support all these ideas.

In common parlance one calls a physician or a teacher social because he does something for his fellow Men. But this concept does not help us at all. The shoemaker, the shop keeper, and the factory worker, all work for their fellow men. But in the economy, is one not working for money? Does this not apply to the spiritual worker as well? Perhaps this is not always true in the first instance, and perhaps there are doctors who continue to help for no charge. (Yet somehow they must make a living; consequently, they exist at the expense of their fellow men.) Do we know if our tailor could not just as well have become a cutthroat, if his daily profession is not an act for overcoming his antisocial impulse? Just as doctors, priests and teachers *can* do their work with social dedication, so this could be the case with handymen, craftsmen and employees. The question arises: Is it socially more difficult to work for the pupil or patient in our experience or for the anonymous consumer?

The creation of "social professions" has only compounded the confusion. Interestingly, Steiner never called his work in Berlin's trade school a social activity, although he learned much from it as a social point of view. "One needs to make a sharp distinction between the improvement of outer social conditions, where this means almost nothing because very different laws hold sway there, but in fact it means a great deal for the development of individual souls, as in every real striving."[2]

From the very beginning of Rudolf Steiner's spiritual scientific activities there was resistance to the social impulse in his surroundings. In 1905 he began the essays "Theosophy and the Social Question" by pointing to the necessity of simultaneous work on the path toward cognition and practical activity in the social field. The need for this warning was fully confirmed by the fate of these essays. They were discontinued after the third edition. History repeats itself. As soon as Steiner started his work on the Threefold Order, he pointed out that anthroposophists often expressed the opinion "that the anthroposophical movement should never have burdened itself with the content of the Threefold Social Organism." (GA 191/1972/13)

To be sure, the social impulse will reach its flowering only in the sixth cultural period. But to not work on it nowadays is equivalent to being purposely immoral because the turn of the moral impulse will not occur until the seventh period. (GA 130/1962/43 f.) The saying that mankind would need to change before being ripe for the Anthroposophical Social Impulse is also inaccurate in its customary form. As early as 1919 Steiner countered this in GA 24/1961/47. He recognized this attitude as an excuse to put off making a start toward social renewal, even as a disinclination to change, because one feels comfortable in the present privileged position. Humans need not first become anthroposophists before they can do anything with the social impulse, but it is necessary that "the members of the anthroposophical movement conduct themselves socially." (GA 191/1972/14) Referring to the macro plane, if Steiner states that "it may be a long, very long time before the Threefold Order becomes reality, but we must conduct ourselves as though it may be here tomorrow,"[3] then this applies in great measure also to the meso level, where we are already in a position to give our institutions an anthroposophical social look. "One can read the degree to which the anthroposophical movement is a social factor in its manner of practicing threefoldness."[4]

It is not my intention to catalog our sins of omissions. I merely want to describe some symptomatic attitudes to facilitate the diagnosis of certain social diseases and thus lead to a better understanding of health-giving social forces, in the same way that therapeutic, pedagogical experiences can provide a great help for the future teacher. This description may be of particular help for those in the institutional life, with regard to the question of why it is impossible to master the social circumstances, despite earnest attempts. Our purpose here is not as criticism of what exists, but rather as a definitive starting point for the work toward the realization of social issues.

Probably the root symptomatic attitude is the understanding of these social issues. I think of my experience when, armed with a large portion of naiveté, I wanted to visit institutions, simply to ask how they understood their position in the social impulse. I came only as far as the first establishment. The director stared at me. "Look at our work for these emotionally challenged children!" I patiently explained my purpose. "Most certainly, all our workers work for less than the going wage." It took some courage to try again. I would have been well advised not to. "Perhaps you are referring to the Threefold Order? We have no time for such things. We are a therapeutic, pedagogical establishment and all our workers are overworked."

His annoyance showed how hopeless my attempt had been. How could I show him that working for others is in no way different from any other endeavour? That, from a social point of view, it makes no difference whether I work to meet the needs of these poor children or work for the needs of my customers as a baker? That in the former I have the added privilege of working in a profession which I can fill with heart and soul?

How could I show him that (too small) an income has a lot to do with the unsocial aspects on the macro level, *may* have something to do with the social aspect at the micro level and is far, far removed from the meso problem? That the best foreign worker is just as underpaid, but that not even the owner, for whom he works, would be willing to call his factory a social place.

And how could I help him to see that social concerns are not something on which one can work from time to time, if the business even allows it, but that social concerns are integral to every public profession? That devoting oneself to the Anthroposophical Social Impulse means that much will be done perhaps poorly in respect to a professional point of view. In fact that from time to time, or even lots of times, one will have to be bad, along with the bad ones,[5] but that even the smallest social crumb is more valuable for humanity than the most perfected technical achievement? That this is the reason why the Anthroposophical Social Impulse guards us against becoming anthroposophical Essenes?

Had I not changed the subject, perhaps the Pharisee in him would have said, "I have sacrificed my entire fortune to this enterprise." "Good works" are a great comfort to many people. This is justified provided they have been wrested from their daily bread. To give money away has nothing to do with work. This has only a remote connection to Steiner's characterization of love (GA 143/1974/206): paying off debts. Giving capital away literally means paying off debts. Private wealth *can* only be the result of unjustified enrichment. Yet it need not always be based on *one's own* guilt. Steiner is most uncharacteristically harsh when he speaks about bragging about gifts. (GA 186/1963/1689)

If only a few elements of the Anthroposophical Social Impulse are incorporated, the result will not be significantly different from totally misunderstanding it. We hear justifying statements ranging from actually standing in the middle of the social impulse ("We have done all that's possible") to the self-serving concession, to a social dream looked upon simply as a passing fad.

One example of standing in the middle is viewing self-administration as a realization of the Threefold Order. To be sure, self-administration is a precondition for being able to stand for the Anthroposophical Social Impulse in any way on the meso level. Apart from this it would have to be involved with it in the macro level: self administration as structural principle for a considerable part of the affairs of the community. One could talk about getting close to it, for example, in a case where Waldorf schools would sit down around a table with other free schools in acknowledgment of their equal status. This gesture is *not* offered as a common front against the state, but in order to overcome common problems. Yet self-administration in the macro sphere does not automatically lead to the same in the meso sphere. Why could the self-administered life of the spirit not belong to institutions governed by the state, the church, or even by some oil magnate, just as the state allows self-administered institutions in areas usually governed by it?

This is precisely the source of the misunderstanding. One makes so much fuss about self-management of schools, because this is not a matter of course (at least in Germany). In the Netherlands, where 70% of schools are not run by the state, but mostly by religious institutions, self-administration has long been a matter of course.[6] It is even true for the entire economy. Nothing in the sense of the Anthroposophical Social Impulse is manifest when Siemens, Hoesch, the Dresden Bank administer themselves! It is a question of whose will is behind the institution. A self-administered, hierarchically structured school has as little to do with the Anthroposophical Social Impulse as a classical concern, run along line/staff principles.

The almost cynical bow to the "fashion of the times," indeed, how some circles see efforts toward threefoldness, has produced peculiar structural blooms. Thus, institutions have in fact "three-folded" themselves. Three organs were created within which the employees are allowed to participate. Sometimes ignorance even goes so far as to push the female aspect into a "middle organ" to take care of "interhuman relations." This organ deals with the flower vases and quality of the coffee, an economic organ becomes the domain of the money experts, and the great ones of the spirit hold sway in the spiritual organ, with exclusion of the foot soldiers, where they make the major decisions for the entire institution. The "class society" has been resurrected. But, as one can never tell whether a revolutionary pack of scoundrels has crept in, one also finds, not by asking but rather by studying the statutes, a fourth organ. This one really "does nothing," but is only there in an emergency, in case the "existence of the institution is threatened." And because this matter is really one of public law, and thus co-workers are not qualified, it is this organ that is qualified and entitled to deal with firing a co-worker.

I have encountered experiments with the Anthroposophical Social Impulse that are not worthy to be taken seriously. These fit into the framework described above. One day an institution experiments for some reason with "something new." The label "threefold" is stuck to it but is discontinued at the first sign of conflict, often at the first difference of opinion or when the established ruler first encounters resistance. "This concept does not work. People [the co-workers] are simply not ready for it." These illusions of one's own perfection and their being threatened by the threefold order are the reasons for distaste of the Anthroposophical Social Impulse which sometimes escalate to disdain or hate.

Let me repeat that workers who represent the Anthroposophical Social Impulse in the micro social sphere can work well in institutions in which, with the best will in the world, one could not even mention as representing the first attempt toward this impulse. Yet this has nothing whatsoever to do with the institution itself. One can readily find such people as office workers in industry or even in the army. They may exemplify what anthroposophical soul exercises can bring about in a human being. Yet this behavior has no significance for the solution of the social question. This solution would have to be founded on a structural activity, capable of being carried out by non-anthroposophically schooled people. Self-sacrificing demeanor has been demonstrated in many hospital wards, in cloisters, even in households dominated by tyrants. For example, a director of a state-run institution for demented children, visiting a (hierarchically organized) therapeutic pedagogical institution, was impressed. But when one tried to tell him about anthroposophical approaches, he demurred, "I, too, can do this with saints." As previously mentioned, one does not need structures for saints, but, as the saying goes, one still needs to seek them out. Since most humans are unable to deal with their own inadequacies, the structure has to hold us up. The social lout is further strengthened in a hierarchically constructed organization. In institutions truly conducted along threefold lines, he will either change or disappear. If "personnel" is being shouted at in an institution with threefold structure, then one should take a closer look at that structure and its implementation.[7]

It is the social institutions whose workers *want* to realize the Anthroposophical Social Impulse, but who get bogged down, that are more important to our purposes. There may be three reasons this happens:

1. One fails to come to proper terms with the dynamics of the institution.
2. Insight into social laws is missing.
3. There is a lack of social abilities.

To the first reason, it is not easy for a consultant working on the Anthroposophical Social Impulse to come to a reasonable understanding of the institution he is contracted to advise. The founders circle of a social institution approaches such a person. The circle usually consists of young people who want to add the social impulse to their professional thrust. Herein lies the error: One wants less a social impulse but rather a preservative to perpetuate the miracle of meeting each other. One deliberates, and insofar as statutes are involved, paper is patient. If one hears nothing more after the founding, this is a somber sign. It often occurs that, after only one or two years, one finds the ashes of a social attempt. One or more members were thrown out or limped away in disgust. When one asks whether the structural changes were incorporated, the answer is most likely, "In the beginning we had so much to do and our human relations were so harmonious, that we thought we could wait with the structure until we were out of the woods." No, one cannot wait. Common enthusiasm and warm feelings are not sufficient once one faces common work, when one looks the other in the face and once the fight with the double starts. "On one side stand the strong egoistical forces of the consciousness soul, on the other the need to consciously found a social life, which is even greater. And one has to have a conscious position as to what it is that can further this social living together." (GA 200/1970/33) Furthering one side, the micro social exercises, is at the discretion of the individual. Hence, any help can only be tackled from the structural side, and only the hierarchy is rejected as antiquated.

The structural groundrules of the founding epoch must be present from the very beginning, if later one is able to deal with them in flexible fashion. The ideal of the communicative phase should be constantly facing the souls in vague outline. Then one knows what one stands for, then one does not forget whither one is going.

This brings us to a second objection: "We cannot afford to start off by stepping away from the usual routine; we simply start by obeying the social conventions. Yet as soon as occasions present themselves, we will take the next step." Where one proclaims this "unchristian principle of opportunism" (GA 175/1961/246), one can predict that the institution in question will never take the next step. The next step will happen to it. If a social institution does not start with its aim in mind, it won't reach that aim. The purposeful formation of a social structure may well require the same starting point as the opportunistic one. In a few years it transpires how one veers off with the latter and arrives at the desired direction with the former.

Two dangers threaten during the founders period: a too rapid or a delayed transition to differentiation. The cause of transitioning too rapidly is usually fear. Can we survive the deficit of the first years? Will the bank cancel our credit if we fail to have a "normal" business routine? What is the ministry of education going to say if we don't have a director? And then one change after another is enacted "only externally." ("Internally, of course, nothing changes.") One becomes a decent limited partnership; one has functionaries who deal with the authorities. Income is changed to salaries, one jostles co-workers to acquire official qualifications, one installs a board of directors or consultants of celebrities, one selects according to fitness for good society, and, before one knows it, the inside is like the outside: one acquires a standing. Such founders of an anthroposophical commercial enterprise did not want to have a capitalistic firm, but an association. The customers were to be represented in the leadership, and internally, too, all was to be cooperative. Then the first red ink showed. This is customary, almost unavoidable, during the first years. But to know this and to experience it are two different things. Now, cost what it may, turnover has to be increased, and the consumers have to be neutralized at the same time. Those co-workers who failed to switch to profitability have to go until the great manager alone is left at the head of the hierarchy of personnel. Now one has to cut the throat of suppliers and competitors in order to secure high profitability. All this, of course, only for the time being, until one comes out of the red ink. But one might never come out of it, because profitability demands growth, and growth furthers investment of investments. And, what would the bank say? Well, one has managed it. Today the world has another capitalistic firm and—one more disillusioned idealist. He faces the ruin of his ideal. There is no way back.

As fear drives too rapid a transition to the second phase, vanity drives a delayed one. Why on earth should one allow those still wet behind the ears to have any say? Are we not doing it well enough? And since the circle of founders does and knows everything better, other abilities are not even perceived. There is no "ill will." Quite the contrary: at least subjectively, one is firmly convinced that the anthroposophical ideal can be upheld in no other way. One feels like the "Guardian of the Grail."[8] Because, along with growth, the move toward differentiation cannot be held up, it is *seemingly* being taken. Quite simply, the situation starts with threefoldness by anticipating elements of the third phase. Organs are established so that everyone has a voice somewhere; only the decisions are made elsewhere. The founders' circle withdraws and reigns from there invisibly. Boudoir politics moves in. New co-workers are added if they pass the litmus test. Recalcitrants within the organs are fired or encouraged to leave in disgust. Beneath this pinnacle sycophants try to secure their own domain where they hold court as demigods. Thus, a caricature of the economic hierarchy is created. Usually it blows apart only when the battle of the underlings gets underway after the death of the great leaders. This is when organizational consultants are called in from outside to rescue the stuck cart. The emergency prompts their proposals to be swallowed hook, line, and sinker, regardless of how well or poorly they fit the social concept. Thus, any possibility is eliminated for a long time, if not forever, to enter the bureaucratic phase in a way to master it, to rescue the social impulse on the way through the desert, and to prepare the seeds for the third phase already in the second one. Rather, one has to wait, not just until the founding generation dies out, but until a new, closed circle can step in to breathe life into the socially empty and desolate organization. This means a new founding of sorts and at least a short repetition of the pioneering phase.

If the right *habits* can be developed in the founding phase, when everything seems to happen "on its own," then the structure can, without excessive difficulties, be tightened up in the bureaucratic phase to fit the forms which have now become necessary. These must be inexorably adhered to, however time-saving "short cuts" may appear to be. As is so often the case during development, the roundabout way is often faster. But even then, everything that happens "on its own" as development progresses is wrong.

Not much can be said about the transition to the third phase, because there are at best only beginnings of this phase taking place and no experience is available. In contrast, there are numerous institutions who eke out a life in a second phase which is no longer appropriate. The most important element needed for a transitional stage is courage. As we have seen, the very existence of the institution is held at risk during the third phase, both outwardly and internally. As an example, there was a Waldorf school where, after the founders' phase, all the founders either died or left the institution due to quarrels. A new generation had taken over, who finally succeeded in leading the institution out of chaos to recognition by the authorities. With give and take they had established friendly ties to "those up there" and had with gentle persuasion managed to obtain tenuous legal concessions. The ideal of "each teacher paid to a schedule" had almost been accomplished, the entrance tests for new children supported high average standardized test scores, and consequently tuition was, on average, high. All important decisions were made by a council of elders, and a board of respected people acted as armor. This shield discouraged attacks from possible alarmists from within and from outside. The strongman literally nearly lost his life when a wave of young teachers and parents threatened to raze the fortress with their demand for a *socially* exemplary structure. It was clearly time for the transition to the third phase. Yet the ironclad bureaucracy withstood this stress test.

There is also the question of quality of performance. The arguments of pioneers of the first phase turn into the realities of the third phase. The purity of the teaching, of the professional ideal, is endangered. The capabilities exercised in the various branches slide to second rate, the seats and thrones within the organization start to sway. The reign of experts is over. A teacher might gladly listen with attention to the therapeutic pedagogue in the pedagogical conference, but he can no longer give direction to anyone, not even therapeutic pedagogical ones. He should realize his ideas in his classroom. When it comes to commonly binding regulations, his voice counts no more than that of newer co-workers. The subsidy jugglers may describe the terrible consequences of losing financial support if this or that measure were taken. When it comes to a decision, the teacher has a voice like anyone else. He has none at all if he did not join the changeover from salary to income and, therefore, is no longer connected *existentially* with the institution. The more the status of the specialist is based on commercial or anthroposophical dogma or indeed even on tradition, the less will his voice convince the co-workers. He may perhaps reach them if he expresses his most inmost striving. In this "perhaps" lies the entire challenge of the third phase. There is no certainty that the best, whatever this may mean, will hold sway. The institution is "helplessly" exposed to the good and bad will, to the wisdom and stupidity of its members.[9] The fear of this "perhaps" reveals the same tragic situation on the meso level as it does on the micro level, as though Mister so and so is, of course, an enthusiastic supporter of the Threefold Order, as long as his fortune and his salary remain intact. The third phase is the hour of truth. The father of the lie loves us because we do not love this phase. And we hide behind the practical indications given by Rudolf Steiner in the pioneering phase of the Waldorf school.

The second reason willing co-workers get bogged down in their attempts to realize the Anthroposophical Social Impulse is a lack of insight into social laws. It is difficult to separate ignorance of the dynamics of development from ignorance of the Anthroposophical Social Impulse, and from the absence of social capabilities in co-workers. Yet all three have specific qualities. In this section we shall address certain laws, which, when ignored, make social striving impossible even when one has the best intentions. Just as the quantifier for pathologic dynamics is "too soon" or "too late," that of handling social laws is a question of "too much" or "too little." From numerous possibilities I select a few examples to illustrate here.

In the spiritual life of an institution, the freedom to unfold one's own being in the sense of the Basic Sociological Law certainly plays a large role. Yet the nature of an establishment imposes limits on this freedom. It may be possible to accede to the wish of a co-worker to start work after 9 o'clock because "his" meditation time is between 8 and 9. But it is ridiculous for a teacher to demand the same for his primary teaching time. This dichotomy appears in many permutations in practical life. For example, in an institute with a mentally ill member of the leading group, the admirable impulse to carry this person can totally erode the co-workers' powers and only increase the sick (but brilliant) person's demands. It is an old story. One should not demand freedom that limits fellow human beings. It may be a gift, but one should consider carefully whether one can "afford" a gift, even in bourgeois life. Perhaps the patient can find a circle of people who can take on the task of healing him *and* combine this task with their social mission.

This example alone shows that "too much" of one thing is "not enough" of another. Steiner describes this common law of practical life: "There is no higher development which does not cause others to be cast down into the depths." (GA 93/1979/

181) The development of one person takes place at the cost of another. One will not be allowed to escape the duties resulting from social activity, even in the presence of the greatest joyful dedication. At best one can conclude that one has chosen the wrong profession, as in the case of the teacher whose class suffered because she concentrated her attention on one or two pathological cases.

Frequently, one hides behind the welfare of the institution to interfere with the freedom of the co-workers. "It means nothing to me, but for the sake of the home, the shop, the school, the sanatorium." Then one demands of the co-worker to cease engaging in local politics, or to explain the advantages of anthroposophical medicines to the customer, or no longer to make certain comments in the classroom, or no longer to appear in public with the secretary, and so on. Unfortunately, such violations of the Basic Sociological Law are quite common. They hurt the chastised one, and at the same time, by leading to inhibitions, they hurt the health of the institution. Of utmost importance in a social structure is the observation of the healthy rule to make reproaches *only* when an agreement in the rights organ has been violated, and this reproach is made *exclusively* by the person who was given the task to do this. Regulations such as asking co-workers not to engage in party politics or to "educate" customers may be made in that organ by people with (if necessary foul) courage.[10] They must refrain from giving instructions, even in the guise of sweet sounding questions or naive wonderings, unless the person involved asks for an opinion.

This brings us to the much discussed, and, unfortunately, often misinterpreted republican principle.[11] In order to find the proper domain for this principle, let us take a look at the micro social process of an agreement. Three different elements live in this process. The agreement, as such, belongs to the life of law on earth: Two people have agreed. It starts with an assumption (the second element). The other person is acknowledged as a being with whom one *can* agree on something. This brings us to the sphere of the spiritual life of rights, where the judgment is the result of an intuition of what is right. Even if the child says, "Yes, mum" to the proposal "now we stop throwing glasses on the floor!", everyone understands that this is nothing like an agreement. Yet this case is hardly different from my agreement with an alcoholic that he will substitute for me for a week in my liquor store. To make a valid agreement, one needs to be honestly convinced that one does not demand too much of the person who accepts the obligation. The third element is the confidence one has that the other person will keep his word. If his performance is monitored constantly, he will feel like a tamed animal. He can only grow, can only truly keep the agreement, if he can count on this trust. Here we are in the sphere of the Basic Sociological Law.

These three elements also govern internal agreements in the institutional sphere. Only in this case, one human being does not confront another, but rather the rights organ agrees with a particular person. The question would likely be not if a co-worker is capable of making an agreement, but rather if this agreement places unreasonable demands on him. No matter how many experiences the circle of co-workers has, in the end the decision is a question of the legal institution. For every person with a green thumb, there is one with sure human judgment. For such a one, democracy and republicanism can only be obstacles. Such people are gifts for an institution. They can do no harm to equal rights, provided two conditions are fulfilled. First, their judgment is not a decision but a recommendation. Secondly, there is enough openness and flexibility to be able to say, "Well, if we make you do the cooking, the food will always be so salty."

Let us look at the agreement itself, the second element. "Mrs. X is responsible for the cafeteria and Mr. Y represents the college of teachers in urgent affairs." Mrs. X and Mr. Y agree between themselves, but who makes the agreement for the institution? This can only be the organ of rights. Only this organ can legitimize the representative, the delegate. This requires a democratic decision, which can rest on anything from a qualified majority to unanimity. The point of the informative process simply has to be (see Chapter VII) that everyone can make a judgment based on insight. The mark of the democratic principle is not the composition of majority but the equal weight of every voice.

How other than democratically could one decide an agreement? Those who would like to see the use of a "republican" principle at this point are usually mistaking it with the aristocratic one of "by the grace of God." There are co-workers who, due to their outstanding inner greatness (in general or in a specific area), are more entitled than others. "Well, if Mr. Z has said that....!"

Democratic voting is usually strictly rejected within the anthroposophical movement. Therefore, I make a small digression. Opponents of voting often cite GA 185/1962/69, where one finds the thought that although the personality comes to expression in parliamentary procedure, the participant destroys his personality "the moment" his will is transformed into a vote. This very death process belongs to the essence of the law. Once every member has, based on the freedom of the spiritual life, presented his understanding in the parliament or the meeting, the next step of the democratic process offers only two possibilities for proceeding to the life of rights, to the decision. One can use the Eastern method and stay together until unanimity is reached (in Indonesia this is called Muchawara). This is lovely if one has unlimited time as is often the case in the Orient. The alternative is to comply with a majority. The compliance is a dying, a sacrifice of one's own personality.

The assenting and dissenting opinions uttered on these occasions should not be erased, if for no other reason because, in any case, the choice takes place in the soul. If the opinions do not appear in public, it is almost certain that so called "after-meetings" will take place, and after the fact kindred groups will form to criticize and complain. Publicizing the choices has yet another significance. It is the only way to spare the management the unpleasant experience that, in case a decision does not work out well, "in reality" everybody was against it all along. Finally, this furthers the consciousness toward the micro social, to share in the responsibility through one's vote.

There is no third way. Taken as a legal process, to discuss problems with the colleagues and then leave the decision to the great ones or leaders is a genuine lie. To be sure, one can delegate areas of rights; let us ignore whether this is desirable in the case of typical legal questions. Let us remark that, on the meso level, this is tantamount to party politics on the macro level. In this way one does not escape voting because the decision of delegating this area must again be democratic.

Now let us return to the moment when the decision to delegate has been made. Along with the delegation, the delegate receives the expression of confidence from the rights organ. Precisely at this point, with the third element, the republican principle takes over. It states that the institution, having delegated a task to a person, gives this person the freedom to accomplish it, that it will not, unsolicited, mix into the manner and quality of his execution of the task. Steiner himself was painstakingly precise in this matter. "Once someone has been given a responsibility, the other person had to obey his orders as a matter of course, just as he has to obey his own." Steiner never interfered in a program or schedule with his own improvised wishes or moods, the way one has to allow this with other spiritual leaders.[12]

Now we need to differentiate again. Democratic decisions can either clarify a specific situation or transfer clearly defined areas of responsibility to one or more persons. This is delegation. In the first case the republican principle is applied indirectly. For instance, in the case, when the rights organ of a school decides not to allow smoking in the classrooms, and Mr. X steps into a smoke-filled room just vacated by Mr. Y, at this point Mr. X has no business to challenge Mr. Y, not even "as a friend." If he really finds it necessary Mr. X must address the person to whom enforcing the house regulations is delegated. If there is no such person, he needs to address the chairman of the rights organ. The personal reproach is avoided as a matter of course in English speaking countries but is rampant in anthroposophical institutions, based on a misplaced feeling of responsibility. If this is used in place of the functional calling to order, it can radically ruin interpersonal human relationships.[13]

The republican principle acts as an ironclad law in all three phases of delegation. In the first phase it remains slightly in the background because the common will of co-workers and the areas of responsibility are hardly differentiated. The republican principle has its most significant impact in the differentiating phase. It may undergo another transformation in the third phase. Where everyone feels responsible for the whole, one would *silently* try to help compensate for the forgetfulness or the failure of a colleague. This is possible without hurting him only if we are so deeply anchored in the Anthroposophical Social Impulse that this compensating is carried out fully in the spirit of what the higher being of the other really intended.

Here we should recognize the danger of the unfolding of the will of individuals, as it lives in the Basic Sociological Law, and can interfere with the unfolding of the institution. In numerous situations we can experience this in ourselves. We watch someone at work and immediately have the desire to find a better way. We hear someone express a thought, and right away the impulse to correct him is awakened in us. The power of the Basic Sociological Law becomes detrimental as custom and conventions restrain it less and less. Also, it gradually hides less and less behind different masks. Our asocial drives brutally strive to keep up our consciousness, even to be obliging comes from a slight unconsciousness. (GA 36/1961/298) The social component, the force emanating from the Archetypal Social Phenomenon, is too feeble. We face the social sin of the spiritual life. In the micro social sphere this sin can inflict a lifelong trauma; in the meso social sphere it robs the institution of the forces for enthusiasm, the joyful look into the future, and in this manner can destroy the institution.

Likewise, a fanatical adherence to form can also destroy the Threefold Order. It is most painful to see the participants of a meeting aimed at formulating regulations go to endless efforts to consider all sorts of possible and impossible future situations which should have been taken care of ahead of time. I have experienced this with legal colleagues who got excited about the simplest questions of law as though their professionalism was at stake. I experienced exactly the same situation during the founding of an association for the Threefold Order. Valuable hours were wasted with excessively clever talk about eventualities and more eventualities, instead of regulating the structure by the Threefold Order and subsequently strengthening the forms when actual problems do arise. Consequences arrived in the return mail, and at the very next meeting, the regulation we hammered together was shown to be impractical—it simply did not fit— and those present wanted to set it aside with theocratic conceit —*l'etat, c'est moi*. Quibbling over words is *always* nothing but a game. Although emotional, it destroys the feeling for what is right.

In fact, it is a dangerous game. The more one regulates, the more one can and must clash against one other. And, since reality is always different from what one has figured out, the temptation to ignore one's own rules increases. To disobey rules to which one has agreed, knowingly or in innocence, will bring *every* institution to the abyss. To be sure, there are people who consider the "correct" solution to be the epitome of mercurial behavior, even if every rule has to be trodden underfoot. Mercury is indeed also the god of thieves, of those who force unauthorized entrance for themselves. In practice one encounters this anomaly most frequently in superannuated founding phases, that have established rules, but only for the pedestrians. Just like the laws of our neo-theocracies, they are not meant for the rulers.

The structure also gets too much emphasis when one is *constantly* preoccupied with it. For example, I know of a sanatorium where the co-workers are, as it were, in love with their very beautiful organizational structure. And because nothing ever quite functions as one wishes, they have constant meetings, discussions, counseling sessions, and so on. The suffering patients are in the way of these considerations, and as consumers and free human beings, they often end up getting lectured in a manner out of keeping with the anthroposophical social impulse.

Is it possible to overdo the Principal Social Law, too? Yes, it is possible to work too much for one's fellow men. In the micro sphere the very social ones are those who literally work themselves to death in order to then require lifelong nursing care from others when they are burned out. Exaggeration also takes place on the meso level.

Since in the bureaucratic phase the state usually intervenes with help and direction, the excesses in this area are usually confined to the pioneering phase. One can probably count the habit in the first years of "bending over backward" as part of this phase as well, but it is probably an aspect of any founding. The matter only becomes critical once the institution has outlived its time. Indeed, these infamous places do exist wherein, even if people are being exploited "for the sake of the cause," the anthroposophical social impulse is missing. Those are the places who live only as long as they can parasitically suck the lifeblood of money and work out of their surroundings.[14] In our context these are of no interest.

To write about "not enough" of the Principal Social Law is pointless, because this can readily be seen. The primary reason is not that one is unwilling to work for one's fellow man, but that one fears the consequences of carrying out the separation between work and income. Therefore, attempts in this direction are often tentative, modest. In a remarkable inversion of social right and wrong, one considers the cash flow instead of the life of the soul toward the workers as a discreet matter. Although in many institutions one does not shy away from inquisitions into motivations and feelings, "in order to put the problems on the table," at the same time one takes scrupulous care to keep everybody's income a secret.

The manager of a firm of workers almost exclusively anthroposophical and of a purely interpersonal aim once told me, "Today one cannot support this [separation of work and income as yet." Is this fear or envy? Or fear for the personal privileged position on the scale of incomes? One day I heard one of his employees say, "I really don't mind that his salary is higher than my own. But then they should not speak of salary according to need, as it is interesting how the needs always increase with the weight of the office." One should not be surprised then that demands for higher salaries increase. "If one imposes duties on people and fails to give them rights, one has to pay them well."

To be serious about the Principal Social Law requires radical openness about money. It demands that everyone look honestly into each other's eyes, that the receiver of income accept what the community, not the business manager or the administration, is willing to give him from the communally-earned funds.

Today's macro structure places limits on work motivated in the service of anonymous fellow human beings and on the income taken from commonly-owned and fairly-distributed means. This status goes far to explain the current wage system, not payment for the work as we still find in many anthroposophical institutions, a practice which Steiner radically rejected as a remnant of slavery.

Thirdly, we shall discuss a lack of social capabilities as a reason for the failure to practice new social forms. In this regard we are all alike. It is this very lack that calls for the threefold structure, which, ironically, teaches us how to very slowly eliminate this weakness. No group of people willing to join the anthroposophical social stream can be prevented by a lack of social capability, as long as the group is ready to accept and work with the four governing laws.

This opens up a subject of major significance for the practice of the Anthroposophical Social Impulse, the question of how one can learn to be social. Steiner points out that this cannot be learned in the schoolroom, nor by meditation, but only in social practice. (See also Chapter XI.) But how?

The term "people's education" may have a negative connotation in some applications. But Steiner uses it exclusively for the art of education aimed at the children of an entire nation, not just for the elite. Today one often understands it to mean adult education. In this context it reminds one of the macro social variation; the totalitarian states who usurp the right to educate their subjects. (see GA 131/1958/46)

In his inaugural speech, C.J. Zwart said, "The concept of subsidies without influence is unthinkable. After all, adult education is undertaken for the purpose of exerting systematic influence."[15] Thus, in the sense of the social impulse, adult education is asocial because social behavior demands to help fellow humans only in areas where they ask for help, thus avoiding being mistaken as exerting influence. If I stand in front of a closed door with both hands full and my wife opens it for me, she does not influence me, not even if she has asked me, "Shall I open it for you?" As we have shown in the first chapter, the art of being social lies in working based on the need of our fellow men. In Zwart's book his colleague Glasl describes in an exemplary manner how this is possible in meso social circumstances, in other words, in situations where the well-being of the institution's needs is at stake. Even if, while serving as a resource to further development, one is asked to help, it must never be put forth to "improve" the colleagues. "The sphere of human freedom is an area where we must never interfere." (GA 120/ 1934/119) One must ask again and again what each individual *personally* wants. If the stubborn and twisted types, as described by Glasl, provoke one's emotions, understandably one is tempted to intervene. But it is very much to his credit that he can distance himself from this response.

Co-workers should renounce this inclination even more than outside consultants. Every professorial word, every "good piece of advice,"[16] works counter to what is social and, in itself, reveals social impotence. "Authority as such has no social validity. He who wants to claim the position of lord and master for himself will feel validated in his position only by the strength of his own dedication to those dependent on him."[17] Even the doctor who has our permission to operate on us has a free charter no more than a developmental consultant. "One is not allowed to offer anything that the patient fails to ask for himself, whether consciously or unconsciously."[18] Advice in the social field is always inappropriate. Either it falls on a free spirit who knows how to deal with it, in which it case it is superfluous because he does what he is able to do by himself, or it falls on one who is not yet free, and in this case it leaves him hurt and truculent or both. I interject with special emphasis since the educator lurks in every one of us and loves to find a reason to make an appearance. The prevailing choice of professions (of Waldorf pupils) are teacher and doctor, and we merchants also like to see ourselves as teachers — educators or counselors. So writes D. Heinrichs in *Social Handeln aus der Erkenntniss des Ganzen* [Social Action Based on Understanding the Whole Picture] (Rabel 1980, p. 126). We see this when the nurse sides with the doctor (instead of the patient), the social worker sides with the authorities (instead of with the oppressed one) and even the salesman, as we know, sides with the producer (instead of with the consumer); he is drawn to educate his customers. There is only one educational tool that is not asocial, namely the structure frozen to a form, severed from human associations and made objective. At the same time in its creation we re-encounter ourselves because we have affirmed it. This is why the hammer is part of decision making, as I once wrote.[19] The hammer makes us perceive in our bones that we commit ourselves with a decision (until the hammer drops again).

Steiner describes our oldest sense, the sense of touch, as the one which provides us with the inner perception of the ego. (GA 170/1978/250) Touch transmits the resistance we encounter and brings our individuality to consciousness. In the same way institutional forms create the resistance from which we awaken socially. We do not have to be better human beings in order to bring out the new meso form, but the meso forms help us to become more social.[20]

Disdain for the law hides behind the social conceit which sets itself above one's own forms and agreements. This disdain should be championed in the spiritual and economic life of the institution, where it belongs, even up to the point of civil disobedience. (See GA 31/1966/227) Instead it shows up in the institution's life of rights, in the working conditions. These conditions are too often entrusted to the "social consciousness of the institution" where they result in social backwardness (arbitrary firings, inadequate pension/retirement provisions, no free time, and so forth). These results have often prompted me to recommend that disgusted co-workers become members of unions. To show the courage to oppose the law by resistance to measures that gag schools, medical practices and farms, is a call to fight, not single individuals but the state, politicizing, if you will. Roman Boos spoke of "those timid souls who later misunderstood the principle that the Anthroposophical Society did not consider politics to be one of its tasks. They take it to mean one should constantly shut up in the face of officialdom's furrowed brows, or even kowtow to them."[21]

To conclude our discussion on impediments to the realization of the Anthroposophical Impulse, I bring up one more question which often leads to getting bogged down, namely the problem of the founder. It has long been recognized in school sociology circles that the founding phase requires quite different qualities of character than the subsequent bureaucratic phase, the buildup and stabilizing of the establishment. Tragically sometimes the great founders are displaced by doers or pushers, although this is rare in anthroposophical establishments. Somehow one senses that one cannot throw them out, not even if they get in the way of further development.

Why is one not allowed to do this? Because the founders are the ones who received the impulse for this very endeavor from the spiritual world. They continue to carry this impulse, even if they start to hold it back with their limited human personalities. The circle of founders is, in its entirety, the source of inspiration. If even a single one is forced to leave the circle, fired or forced to leave in disgust, the inspiration evaporates, and one loses the quintessence of the strength to bear and finally overcome the Ahrimanic bureaucratic epoch.[22]

There are people who live so strongly in the mood of founding that they simply leave an institution, founded as it is, in order to create another one somewhere else. This is not a problem, in this respect, as the circle of founders loses the power of its inspiration only if it falls apart. The power is not really tied to specific personalities but to continuity. One can use this knowledge and consciously allow someone new to step into the footsteps of a departing one. One can do the same when someone dies. The history of the apostles gives us the archetype for this. Someone had to take the place of Judas, not at the moment when he separated himself from the twelve, but only after his death. If every circle is an esoteric affair, the circle of founders is that in particular.

If the founders remain in the institution, it would be extremely creative and supportive for them to summon the strength to transform their area of activities. If they are not prepared to do this, then the only way to overcome the power struggles is to apply a very consequent application of the threefold structure with great severity. Yet one often fails to have the courage to do this as long as one is face to face with often deeply revered and eminent founders.

The most clear way I can describe how the tasks of the founders should change is that they should withdraw from every position in any way connected to power or the making of decisions, and that they remain silent if things go awry. If they hold silence long enough, one will approach them and ask for advice. At that point the founders assume their new and rightful place.

Here, too, insight helps in decision making. Plato was of the opinion that philosophers are capable of reigning with wisdom only after age fifty. Today we should reverse this. Because we respect the freedom of our fellow humans, we should no longer impose our gathered wisdom, as inescapable an influence as it is on us all, by continuing to make the decisions. Today wisdom should either be handed out with no strings attached or not at all. Once one accepts this, it will be easier to separate from all committees and other organs with power to make decisions when we are over fifty. Thus, we can begin again to be appropriately creative in the movement we belong to. Then the fruits of life are at the disposal of the whole movement, not just one institution.

Another "functional" task of the founders' circle in an institution is to safeguard the founding impulse, in the esoteric sense. Events will shape the vessel, wherein gratitude for success shines on the co-workers, and, at the same time, the causes of mistakes will be experienced painfully in one's own faults. Then one may hope for continuing help from the spiritual world.

Before concluding this chapter, I want to point one more conformity to law of significance for those who wish to join the Anthroposophical Social Impulse. Wherever one allows one of the four social principles too much in the foreground, the balancing social principle will suffer a setback. At Camphill, where one has made great strides in the realization of the Principal Social Law, one finds an underdeveloped Basic Sociological Law. Whoever does not subordinate himself to the interests of the association has to leave. Likewise, the constant practicing with the Archetypal Social Phenomenon is juxtaposed on the meso plane with horror in regards to the organizing principle. Inversely, where the focal point is on gaining freedom from associations, involving so-called alternative projects, we find that working for others is often very much neglected and, as a consequence, the economic side of the establishment crawls along in a sickened state. Although I unfortunately know of no example of undue emphasis on the Threefold Order, little imagination is needed to see that exaggeration of the organizing principle will shut the doors to social inspiration.

Thus, another difficult and additional task is imposed on the Anthroposophical Social Impulse. It makes little sense to work on one principle if this worsens the social aspect of the other three. The most beautiful threefold order does not help if the spiritual and economic life dries out because no new impulses flow from the source of love. The most profound social impulses can dissolve into nothing if the form that can capture them is neglected. What good is it to work for my fellow man if I fail to respect his independence? And what good is respect if I let him starve to death?

Therefore, our task is to develop the four principles in balance with each other. This is the only way to raise to a higher level the cross which they represent and which is imposed on us. We can understand the image of the cross very realistically from another perspective. A legend of the cross tells us that from

Adam's grave a seed from the Tree of Knowledge grew a new tree that yielded the wood for the cross of Golgotha. Steiner's interprets this tree to express the hardening etheric body of man. (GA 165/1981/73f) The carrier of the Christ poured himself into this hardened etheric substance. In the social area we have very much to do with this hardened etheric ether. "The community-forming force used to establish human relations is in the etheric body." (GA 123/1978/245) It is our "cross." We carry it due to the power of the Christ. With it we can redeem the life of the community.

This chapter is titled the "Pathology of the Anthroposophical Social Impulse." It has concentrated on those experiments that attempt to grasp and embody this impulse. Comments referring to symptoms of sickness were nowhere meant as personal criticism. But it is possible to highlight matters that threaten this impulse. One way to discuss disease is by detailing symptoms based on concrete experience, thus yielding possible diagnosis and, hopefully, symptomatology of social diseases. There is a danger of distorting the picture. Those who accomplish something in the social field feel pilloried, the others remain in the shade. Concentrating on the pathology of the Anthroposophical Social Impulse, namely its rejection, really does not contribute to its understanding. Up to a point only psychological interest is due to Dick's motives, whose moral intuitions are beyond any social ideas, and to those of Harry who feels that conscious mastery of the social factor belongs to a future cultural period.[23] Comments regarding common tendencies aimed in opposition to the Anthroposophical Social Impulse will be addressed in the concluding chapter of this book.

Endnotes:

[1] See for example GA 99/1962/151 ff.

[2] Quoted from Rudolph Mücke "Erinnerungen an Rudolf Steiner in der Arbeiterbildungschule" [Memories of Rudolf Steiner in the Trade School], Basel 1955, p. 29.

[3] From Herbert Hahn "Der Weg der mich führt" [the path that guides me], Stuttgart 1969, p. 684.

[4] Anton Kimpfler in "Social Handeln aus der Erkenntniss des socialen Ganzen" [Social action based on the knowledge of the overall social picture], Rabel 1980, p. 147.

[5] GA 189/1946/50: today it is necessary "that, as we stand within the social process, we develop the talent to be bad ourselves, along with our wicked human race. Not because it is good to be wicked, but because a social order that needs to be overcome simply forces each individual to live like this. We should not wish to live from the illusion how good we are and lick our chops because we are so much better than other people. We should know that we are part of the social order and live under no illusions."

Perhaps an anecdote from Steiner's life fits this sentence: His followers go to a small establishment for lunch between two sessions. There is not much available for vegetarians, and so one has fried eggs, scrambled eggs, etc. Steiner arrives and orders a good bourgeois lunch–with meat. He didn't do this to shock his pupils, but because he considered the social attitude vis à vis the landlord as more important. Then there is the saying about "the fanatical adherence to the most noble impulses" which "can have the worst effect on moral development" (GA 15/1956/54).

[6] Self administration is no unequivocal concept. The word may be used to describe that all, or a few, co-workers administer the institution, or, in a broader sense, it may refer to every non-state run administration, for instance a publishing house, administered by a church.

[7] Institutions who make false claims to threefold structures encourage expectations which, when not fulfilled, can bring about serious social difficulties.

[8] See Friedrich Glasl "Konfliktmanagement" Bern u. Stuttgart 1980 where on page 187 he deals with the "Hosts of Crusaders" with their missionary urge.

[9] See the interesting study by Albert Reps "Sociosophie" Freuburg o.j. p.3.

[10] The lack of this courage often hides behind the figure of speech "that one hates to make prohibitions" and "expects that the co-worker discovers himself . . ." The result is that from the innocent prohibition one arrives at the inappropriate, socially noxious, ordering. The age-old social control is, in fact, much worse than a bad law. One can always change the latter, the former solidifies in habits.

[11] See Ernst Lehr "Republican not Democratic," AWSNA Publications.

[12] Johanna Gräfin Kayserling "12 Tage um Rudolf Steiner" [Twelve Days around Rudolf Steiner], manuscript reprint 1949, p. 46.

[13] Just imagine that Y just had the visit of a father whom he did not wish to forbid smoking during an already delicate interview. How embarrassing for both sides to have to explain this to X. And what a redeeming laugh one can have over this with the "official." The latter even has the right to say: "Well, then all is okay." In this cockeyed situation one could hardly expect X to say much but perhaps "If I would have been in your position. . . ."

If you think that you can say everything with the right tone, imagine the difference between any citizen and a policeman reprimanding someone's speeding.

[14] GA 305/1979/9 and GA 341/1973/13. Although here Steiner talks exclusively about economic experiments, his work may apply to the entire meso sphere, because there one steps in front of the public and, therefore, has to count with an (economic) element of need. Here one finds the social effect of the asocial drive, namely to do something because one personally finds it to be correct, although the "product" fails to find sufficient public understanding. It is counterproductive because the circumstances are often likely to discredit the anthroposophical movement as a whole. See also what Steiner describes about "certain movements for reform" GA 93/1979/142.

[15] "Tussen harmonie en conflict", Assen 1975, p. 10.

[16] Even the famous "therapeutic conversation" is socially justified only if *all* participants are seriously convinced that all calamities that have hit the institution are due to their *own* mistakes.

[17] John Hemleben "John der Evangelist" Hamburg: 1972, p. 44.

[18] Rudolf Treichler "Die Entwicklung der Seele im Lebenslauf," Stuttgart: 1981, p. 164.

[19] "Lob des Hammers" [Praise of the Hammer} in "Korrespondenz der Arbeitsgemeinschaft für Dreigliederung" (Correspondence regarding the Threefold Order) 1977, No. 29.

[20] In this connection we can also learn to understand Steiner's words that becoming conscious of the life of rights puts fetters on Ahriman (GA 196/1966/76). See also GA 158/1968/145: "Lucifer is tied to insisting on one's own rights. Understanding the law redeems Ahriman."

[21] "Gewissensprüfungen durch Dreigliederungsfragen" [Test of conscience by questions of the threefold order] in "Gegenwart" 1945/1.

[22] The reason for this tragic happening may be understandable if we consider that Lucifer is involved in every founding. "A new hope arises for Lucifer whenever something new is being founded" GA 130/1962/311) even it is only because one wants to make something better than others.

> "Und wo sich Menschen von einander sondern,
> Da ist für meine Macht das Feld bereitet"
> [Wherever humans from each other part
> There there open vistas for my power]
> (Lucifer in "The Soul's Probation," GA 14)

One needs not shy away from the enthusiasm and power bestowed on one by the carrier of light—without it nothing could be accomplished, and one would fall into Ahriman's rigor mortis. Yet we have to take the consequences. Luciferic asocial aspects imprint themselves on the institution. They must not be allowed to condense on human relations. This is because all force used up in failed human relations will be lacking when the luciferic fires are again needed to oppose the rigidizing tendency when the bureaucratic phase is being entered. But then this force is no longer bestowed on us, and we must consciously cultivate it. We should not allow the luciferic force to enter the inter-human realm; we should invest it in the structure. "Lucifer hates nothing more—where people live together—than anything that reeks of the law" (GA 184/1968/169).

This requires sacrifice, either on the part of the newcomers to tolerate the asocial aspects of the founder's circle, even if these slow down the development or even retard it. Opposition would reinforce Lucifer's hopes. Or a sacrifice on the part of the founders. An institution may congratulate itself if the "Ancients" are able to make it.

[23] GA 200/1970/33: "On one hand, we have the strong egoistical forces of the consciousness soul, on the other the increased necessity to consciously create a social life. And one must take a conscious position to everything able to further living together in a social manner."

Chapter X

The Social Impulse in Rudolf Steiner's Life

Anyone who examines Rudolf Steiner's life will notice that observations regarding social questions appear intermittently. Whereas most of his themes, once introduced, are continued, expanded, enlarged and deepened, the Social Impulse retreats into obscurity after each short, or very short exposure.[1] And the last very fertile phase of writings and lectures at the time of the Threefold Order ceased abruptly on August 29, 1922.[2] Not only are the intervening periods of time long in duration, but the approach varies so much that only in very recent times has a survey of the different thrusts been compiled, due mostly to the unfaltering efforts of Georg Schweppenhäuser. Many knowledgeable anthroposophists denied any connection between the Threefold Order and the Principal Social Law until after 1977, when the very first lectures about the Threefold Order were published in a complete edition (GA 328). These thoroughly confirmed that Steiner made a direct connection between the Threefold Order and the Principal Social Law.

In each instance Steiner presents matters as they grew out of the phases of his biography. Some decisive points in time are easy to determine. The Basic Sociological Law appeared in the *Magazine for Literature* in numbers 29 and 30 of the annual set of 1898. We find the Principal Social Law in the series of essays "Theosophie und Soziale Frage" [Theosophy and the Social Question] in the journal *Luzifer Gnosis*, 1905-1906. The Archetypal Social Phenomenon is mentioned for the first and only time in the lecture of December 12, 1918 (first published under the title *Social and Antisocial Drives in Man* [Soziale und Antisozial

Triebe im Menschen], Dornach, 1942). One could assign two different birthdays to the Threefold Social Order: the so-called memoranda of July 1917 (GA 24/1961/329 ff), intended more or less as memory aids, and the Zürich lectures (GA 328), later elaborated in *The Threefold Commonwealth*.

The insistent question of what the archetypal social phenomenon is all about spurred me to conclude that both archetypal motives of the human being appear united in the latter: in the unsocial placing oneself apart the process of the entlechy becoming conscious and self-sufficient, or the (philosophically substantiated) impulse to freedom, and, in the social sphere, the impulse of love, through which the miracle of our humanity is revealed to us in every encounter with a human brother or sister. In my quest to find where Steiner expresses the essence of the love impulse, I came across the lecture of December 17, 1912, *Love and Its Significance in the World,* [Die Liebe und ihre Bedeutung in der Welt] (GA 143/1934/XII).

I will describe a personal journey of discovery, partly to avoid the suspicion of an artificial construction that would be obvious if I now state that it helped me to have a sudden revelation of a seven- year rhythm in Steiner's social work. If one acknowledges the year 1912 for the presentation of the most occult of the four conformities to law, the sequence is 1899 - 1905 - 1912 - 1919.

In spite of this revelation, I was quite startled when, a short time later, I opened the book *Rudolf Steiner Während des Weltkriegs* [Rudolf Steiner during the World War] to find his very first essay about the Social Question: "Ein freier Blick in die Gegenwart" [A look into the present time] (which appeared also in GA 31/1966/32).[3] It is not a very impressive article by itself. Viewed from a century later, anyone may even take exception to the patriotic effusions of a twenty-three-year-old. However, if one follows the development of the social impulse in Steiner's writing, this youthful exercise has a truly electrifying effect. Anyone reading it with a knowledge of the Threefold Order discovers that this article contains the germ of all the elements.

If we designate the year 1884 as the birth year of the Social Impulse in Steiner's biography, then it entered puberty in 1898 with the the Basic Sociological Law, became fully grown with the Principal Social Law, entered the seven-year sun span in 1912 with the social love impulse, was mature in 1917, being thirty-three years old and ready to be handed on to society, and finally in 1919 went entirely public. (We know that Steiner, in 1898, had already planned a breakthrough in the social area. Both this subject and the karma impulse foundered due to lack of understanding and indignation on the part of the members of the Theosophical Society.[4]) Having recognized this rhythm, the search for the missing link was unavoidable. Did Steiner contribute something to the social question in1891 as well?

The results are meager and remain conjecture. In the third article of his book *Goethe's Spiritual Nature*, [Goethe's Geistesart], originated in 1899, (GA 22) Steiner works with Goethe's fairy tale of the *Green Snake and the Beautiful Lily*. He makes connections to Schiller's *Letters on the Aesthetics Education of Mankind* and to the French Revolution. As we know, Steiner considered the *Letters on the Aesthetics Education of Mankind* and the *Green Snake and the Beautiful Lily* as the German answer to what lived, misunderstood among other things, in the three watchwords of *Liberté, Equalité*, and *Fraternité* as the social question during the chaos of the French Revolution. He later connects these same watchwords to the Threefold Order (in a footnote): "Beginning with the nineties of the 18th century, I have attempted to penetrate the spirit of the fairy tale based on the assumptions of Goethe's world of thoughts. I first expressed my results in a lecture I held on November 27, 1891 in the Goethe Society ... whatever I have either printed or expressed regarding the fairy tale is no more than a development of the thoughts expressed in this lecture." Only a synopsis of this lecture exists, by the hand of Karl Julius Schröer. Printed in *Frühwerke* [Early Works] volume 3, it in no way addresses the social question. Yet I suggest that this part of the lecture was omitted in Schröer's shortened version, because his interest resided in the literary, and not in the social, field. We know that Steiner points repeatedly to the great significance of Goethe's fairy tale for the social question.[5]

Let us use 1891 as our starting point, even if only hypothetically. Steiner treats Goethe's fairy tale as an expression of the social impulse, cleansed of political passions by the French Revolution. If this is true, it is the first time a motive appears which we will continue to encounter in connection with the Social Impulse and in the very midst of the time of the Threefold

Order.[6] It represents a very special nuance of the Social Impulse, one that moves it into the soul. In the biography of the Social Impulse one finds a fairy tale

Now to our final theme, the successive appearances of the Anthroposophical Social Impulse in the various periods of Steiner's biography. I will confine myself to a few indications, more as pointers for those who may look for a source of inspiration toward a better understanding of the four constituent forces.[7]

The year 1884 falls in the center of Steiner's years in Vienna (1879–1889). A wealth of "outer" world reveals itself to Steiner, the visitor to the belletristic circle, the political historian. He strives to penetrate this with his inner life. It is no accident that the first publications are an answer to the whole circle of civilization, namely natural science (GA 30/1961/227), psychology (ibid., p. 475) and the social question. This almost resembles the map of his entire life.[8]

In my opinion, it is during the Weimar time, when he was intensely preoccupied with Goethe and German idealism, that Steiner gives us the connection of the Social Impulse with the four kings in Goethe's fairly tale. Ninety-nine years after the ideals of the French Revolution were choked to death in a bloodbath, the first dawn of a future social culture breaks in with his interpretation of Goethe's real imagination. Not only the Threefold Order shines for the first time, but the green snake betrays the secret of the Archetypal Social Phenomenon to the golden King: "What is more refreshing than the light? The conversation."[9]

The Basic Sociological Law falls into the radical Berlin years, when Steiner threw off all conventional fetters. The Basic Sociological Law thrived on the soil he prepared as a free human being in the circle of free fellows, as a member of the atheistic Giordano-Bruno society, as a defender of Haeckel's Darwinistic natural philosophy against dogmatic concepts of the church, as a reporter of culture who directed his lightning arrows against those who stood in the way of worthy new achievements, as one professing individual anarchism together with Mackay. One might bypass this period in Steiner's life with some embarrassment had he not added the law of evolution of the human spirit to the idea of natural development of the evolutionary theory.

The Principal Social Law belongs to the period of the building up of anthroposophy and certainly bears its stamp. The series "Theosophy and Social Question" was planned as the immediate continuation of *Knowledge of Higher Worlds and Its Achievement*. With this publication, brotherliness, one of the main principles of the Theosophical Society, was assigned its proper place and, thus, was led out of the sphere of theory into practical realization. Yet the sum total results of Steiner's activity in the workers' development school also lived in the Basic Sociological Law. He reiterated the extreme importance of his experiences in working with the proletariat as the development of the Social Impulse proceeded. These were simultaneous to experiences with the leaders of the workers, and he is bitter when he talks about them as they confront him again in 1919. Their dogmatic mindset was the opposite of the tolerance which the Basic Sociological Law holds out for the future. Most importantly, the battle over wages, instead of a radical elimination of labor as a commodity, was the counterpart to what his spiritual research discovered as serving humanity's wellbeing, namely the separation of work from income. The first edition of *Theosophy and the Social Question* appears in 1905, the same year he had to abandon his teaching activities at the workers' development school on January 22.

The booklet *Love and Its Meaning in the World* is interwoven in the period of christological revelations, directly in the center of the three years commencing in October 1911 with the Karlsruhe lectures *From Jesus to Christ* (GA 131), which Steiner indicates as the ones that brought on the enmity of the church. At the end of the three years comes the Oslo cycle of October 1913, "The Fifth Gospel" (GA 148), as so very movingly reported by Bjelyi.[10] Just as the *lex aeterna* [eternal law] which, according to Thomas Aquinas, is beyond man's understanding, the social significance of the Love Impulse remains inexpressible. Expressed in words in 1918 as the Archetypal Social Phenomenon, it is merely an earthly reflection of the Christ impulse congealed from study of spiritual science and whose future effects we can only hope to fathom.

Having wrestled with both for more than thirty years (GA 21/1976/150), finally Steiner goes public with the Threefold Order,[11] and simultaneously with physiological threefoldness. He makes known a new social advance in some remarks in 1916 (see for instance GA 171/1964/IX), but the law of threefoldness receives its full, proper form in 1917 in the spiritual battle between two forces, which arise simultaneously and threaten mankind to the same degree. These are the Russian Revolution and the hopeful dream of Woodrow Wilson's Fourteen Points. Conveying memoranda through personal connections possible in a neutral country during World War I, Steiner brought the basic outline of the Threefold Order to the public initially on November 14, 1917, in a somewhat remote and almost philosophical manner (GA 73/1950/IV), and on November 23 and 24 in a much more involved and outspoken manner. ("Gegenwart" [Present Times]1950/51, Nos. 3-6) (GA 73/1950/IV).

His attempt to change the course of the war having failed, beginning in 1918 Steiner began to prepare the members for a continuation with lectures about the spiritual backgrounds of the social question. In 1919 he established a basis for the conformity to specific laws on the part of the Threefold Order. He also identified the corresponding political impulse. One can see three phenomena in these actions. First, a development over thirty-five years is completed, and the Anthroposophical Social Impulse is matured to the degree that it can now be placed at the disposal of the world at large. Second, as throughout Steiner's entire work, this impulse answers immediate needs and questions of the times. His sacrifice was great and tragic; he was reported to have said, after the failed attempt, "I knew that mankind was not yet ripe for this, but it had to be tried because I may have been mistaken." Third, as we have seen, the Threefold Impulse provided the indispensable condition for anthroposophical offshoots to arise and multiply in the world with unparalleled speed. Steiner identified 1919 as the year when "the Anthroposophical Society will go into action" (GA 257/1965/81).[12]

Endnotes:

[1] The lecture GA 56/1965/XI, "Where the germ of all four social factors can be recognized," falls into the "fallow" years—yet, as the preceding chapters have shown, it contains a wealth of aphorisitc remarks.

[2] I do not mean to say that no more statements regarding the social impulse were made in the remaining years, nor do I underestimate Rudolf Steiner's explanations regarding the constitution of the General Anthroposophical Society.

[3] Since Rudolf Steiner's first efforts have been lost, it is possible that among them there exist statements about the Social Question. This would not be surprising. A time of gestation preceded the discussion of the social law as well.

[4] Perhaps it is symptomatic that no copy exists of the lecture *Theosophy and the Social Question*, (26 October 1905). This lecture stems from the same time. Additionally, part of some lecture cycles had to be severely cut, due to lacking notes, and at the time some had to be replaced with substitute lectures. See in particular GA 135/159/65 f. in connection with the karmic impulse with, among other statements: "I see that a real basic conviction of reincarnation and karma can never thrive in a world ... where one has to earn what is necessary for life by means of one's work."

[5] In this connection see also the mysterious lines in Rudolf Steiner's letter to Richard Specht dated Nov. 30, 1890 (Briefe I. p. 124). In the same year he also speaks, almost as an aside and to my knowledge for the first time, about the separation of politics from the economic and spiritual life (GA 30/1961/299).

[6] 1899: the already named article (see also GA 28/1925/277), as well as GA 30/1961/96 f.; 1916 GA 172/1974/31/f.; and then 1919 and 1920 or GA 128/1967/146 f. and GA 200/1970/78.

[7] A geographical examination may also be worthwhile. For example, it struck me that the publication of 1884 took place in Hermanstadt, today Sibui, in Siebenbürgen. The last lecture on the Social Question took place in Oxford. This transferred the Social Impulse from roughly the most easterly to the most westerly location of Rudolf Steiner's activities.

8. See also Roman Boos' "Die Dreigliederungsidee, das Goetheanum und das Dreigliederungsideal" [The idea of the Threefold Order, the Goetheanum, and the Ideal of Threefoldness] Münchenstein, 1929). There the year 1884 is presented as the key year, whence 33 years later the Threefold Impulse was borne. In 1917 this split off into the human and social Threefold Order. The fact alone that Rudolf Steiner had stated that he only publicized the Threefold Impulse after more than thirty years of research points to the special importance that must be given to the *entire* Threefold Impulse in Rudolf Steiner's work. See also Chapter XI on this subject.
9. Rudolf Steiner himself points out a certain parallelism with the *Philosophy of Freedom*. "The latter was intended for "providing the foundation of a social and political life" (GA 185/1962/147). If one considers that, according to p. 126 the idea of this book had been ready for some years when it was published, this would point once again to the year 1891.
10. "Verwandeln des Lebens" [A Transformation of Life], Stuttgart 1975.
11. One can see that in the picture I have gained from the development of the Social Impulse there is no room for a new impulse of its own that may have been added by the *World Economy*, (GA 340). I look at this course of July 1922 in the same light as, for instance, the cycle on the theory of light (GA 320). This certainly added important things to optics but did not in essence add anything new to the natural scientific impulse. *World Economy,* also, does not do this in the social area. Incidentally, this course has an interesting precursor in GA 54/1966.IV of 1908.
12. This activity started the day after an agreement for an armistice had been reached (GA 185 a/1963/I).

Chapter XI

Questions in Lieu of a Conclusion

The preoccupation with the Anthroposophical Social Impulse has created, among others, two increasingly urgent questions. Some readers may have the same questions, and I would like to pose them at this point. The answers may be of vital importance to the continuing development of this impulse. Perhaps they may also stimulate answers or further study.

The first question may be stated simply: How is it that the Social Impulse leads such an obscure existence within the anthroposophical movement? This question has two aspects: how is it that so few within the anthroposophical movement concern themselves with the Social Impulse and why do some even reject it? Why do individuals who are strongly connected with this impulse quite abruptly turn their backs on it as soon as they join an institution as teachers, peasants, therapists, and so forth? How is it that the small group who has subscribed to this impulse is rife with quarrels and tends to scatter, all this to a degree not found in any other anthroposophically-related movement?

It would be oversimplifying to think that the answer is in the poor condition of society as a whole. One could even turn the question around. Had one taken up the Threefold Order, the Social Impulse would have been unavoidable, and contrasts may not have led to such excessive conditions. Explanations based on the biography of the individuals involved are also inadequate. Certainly in specific cases one can see the rejection of the impulse, the "collapse," the irritation caused by the way the Social Impulse is all happening, and so forth, one person being totally devoured by his institution, another unsure of social issues from a philosophical point of view, a third driven to nasty behavior by his guilty conscience over his abandonment of the social movement. Yet every teacher knows that, even if every child has a valid excuse, something is wrong if the children in a particular grade are always tardy.

One cannot find the explanation in the misunderstanding based on Steiner's sentence that, from the time of the Christmas Meeting of 1923-24, the Anthroposophical Society has nothing to do with politics. Events that lie outside of the activities of the Society, depending on what one means by politics, are, for that reason, not excluded from the activities of each individual member. "What should be particularly included are the following: the spiritual cultural aspects, theology, medicine, jurisprudence, philosophy, natural science, even technology and social life and also politics; yes indeed, this peculiar formation, too! Those who understand the times should introduce the results of spiritual science into all of this." (GA 184//1968/256) Steiner himself did not shy away from political activity. "What we call the Threefold Order is by no means merely a political program," (GA 203/1978/112) and logic tells us, after all, that, for example, the Waldorf schools are political institutions of the first order, both in their internal educational methods and in their ongoing negotiations with authorities. To hold that the Anthroposophical Society should have nothing to do with politics is, therefore, nothing more than a cloak to hide the actual dislike with which one faces the Anthroposophical Social Impulse. "There are weaklings who join this Anthroposophical Society and who say, 'Yes, spiritual science I like, but I don't want to know anything about the social activity. This does not belong.' (GA 195/1962/82) Let us concern ourselves not so much with the weaklings, but rather with the question: what is the origin of this dislike?"

The following is not offered as an answer but as considerations and thoughts evoked by this painful problem. I would like to review a few phenomena.

It is a very striking fact that Steiner gave the official weekly *Goetheanum* the subtitle "Periodical for Anthroposophy and Threefoldness."[1] Considering the accuracy with which he chose titles, the possibility occurs to me that he wanted to look at threefoldness and anthroposophy as two separate subjects. If so, it was certainly not intended in the sense of a contrast. Steiner speaks about the Threefold Order as "merely a fruit of spiritual science" (GA 202/1970/25), and he calls it a branch on the tree of Anthroposophy (GA 198/1969/213). We further note the large number of lectures to the members about the social question and the remark that the Threefold Movement had not managed to place itself on the basis of anthroposophy.[2]

Two conclusions are possible. Much more than just social thinking could have been intended with the subtitle "Threefoldness," specifically the cooperation of the three archetypal forces in the earthly sphere, such as, the threefold activities within the soul in thinking, feeling and willing. I mentioned this in the preceding chapter in connection with the essay by Roman Boos. This would suggest a difference between spiritual scientific research (anthroposophy) and the fruitful work in the physical world. One could pursue Steiner's work to look for any leads toward this concept. The other possibility is that, with the threefold order, a new element was added to the anthroposophical movement. Although the movement took this up, yet it was, in a sense, foreign to it until about 1919.

This brings us to the second phenomenon, the periodicity of the Social Impulse in Rudolf Steiner's life, as discussed in the previous chapter. The cognitive impulse was revealed to the public in 1882, with the first commentary to Goethe's natural scientific works, and it never left off, except perhaps during the neglected Berlin years of 1897 – 1899. In contrast the Social Impulse disappears under the surface after each new advance. It is as though two streams proceed next to each other: a cognitive one which logically flows into spiritual science and presents itself under the name of anthroposophy, and a social one, leading a life of its own which, to my knowledge, Steiner never explicitly connected with the cognitive stream.[3]

This brings us to Steiner's saying, "Meditating and concentrating, one can live out willing and thinking, but one cannot cultivate the life of feelings. The latter one must allow to lead and then it follows by itself." (GA 176/1922/VII-21) As shown (hopefully) in previous chapters, the Social Impulse is the impulse of the middle. It springs from what in ordinary life we call "tact of the heart," tact because it accepts the essence within itself and, in so doing finds the correct gesture. Further developed, this gesture leads to an act of taking all of mankind into oneself. This path is described as a path of cognition based on the seven stations of suffering. Steiner indicates this path as the

"Christian path of cognition," (GA 13/1925/387 and GA 99/1962/XII). Although it was not to be undertaken in 1907, it is legitimate. Yet in no way does one re-encounter the path of feeling in the Rosicrucian way of cognition with which Steiner replaced it.

Without intending to say that one should not think in the social life, it is clear, however, that the typical path of expanding one's thinking will not get us very far in this area. As Steiner repeatedly warned, neither the law (in its widest sense), nor action within the economic sphere, is to be based on thinking. The problems of human society cannot be solved by spiritual science but only by social threefold structuring.[4] Fichte and Hegel, great philosophers and theoreticians of cognition are approvingly referred to by Steiner in his philosophical work. Yet, taken in the social sphere they can lead mankind veritably to disaster. Fichte's closed commercial state is, in Steiner's words, bolshevism. Hegelianism accomplishes "nothing in the social life," (GA 322/1981/II). Following this line of thinking then leads to an abyss in the social sphere. Only too often does it result in bolshevism, as we know from social science, and as we can also sometimes observe when cognitive theoreticians lead institutions. What is social has its own way of developing in the heart and leads to a consciousness, which orients itself instantly on hand of a given situation. Of course, one depends on the act of thinking to find social laws and conformance to law as well as the basis for conformance in spiritual science. But it may well be that these differences help to explain why the philosophers in the threefold movement love to stop at the theory of the macro social and dislike to practice the meso social.

Another thought: we have learned to see the Anthroposophical Social Impulse as the Christian impulse for our time. "Whoever fails to believe in the *human being* in every person in our time, does not in truth believe in the Christ."[5] Is this not being social, as we have grown to know it? It is the Christ's expectant gaze, leading us on to do justice to the biological and inner needs of another person, or to die into him. The immediate experience comes about. "A philosophy which understands itself and has the idea of Christ does not exist. It is impossible," (GA 137/1930/45). Here we connect to the concepts covered in Chapter 2. Threefoldness is not an idea; it is an impulse. This impulse is Manichaean, as we have seen in numerous instances. What is social takes all else within itself, even in its evil embodiment. This opens up weighty questions. If, as Steiner says, all future Christianity is Manichaean, do we then encounter with the Social Impulse a phenomenon similar to that of the Christian Community? Although it was born out of anthroposophy, it nevertheless represents a separate stream.

If this is so, the following fact may appear in a very specific light. Steiner's *Knowledge of the Higher Worlds and Its Achievement* appeared first as a series of essays in the periodical *Lucifer Gnosis*. He describes the path of knowledge up to the encounter with the "Greater Guardian." Although Steiner planned to continue the series in the much larger work *Theosophy and the Social Question*, yet at this point perhaps another option is presented, a path one can tread only if the question "What ails you, brother?" burns in one's heart. This was not the case with Steiner's audience at the time, so the series was abruptly broken off. The path was reversed, leading from the encounter with the Greater Guardian down to earth and thus to the Lesser Guardian. Do we not stand facing the Greater Guardian with every encounter with another human being? Did not destiny create a symbol in the naming of the journal, bringing two streams—"Lucifer" and "Gnosis"—together, specifically the stream of knowing oneself which leads to the Christ with the indispensable help of Lucifer, the selfless egoism, and the second stream, in its Manichaean branch, starting from the Christ and wanting to redeem the entire earth down to the spirit imprisoned in the stone?

One last phenomenon needs to be added here. Following in the footsteps of Steiner's indication, Hans Peter von Manen describes the two streams of the anthroposophical movement with their source in Aristotle in his admirable book *Searchers for the Christ and Service of Michael*. In his book he also points to a third group, based on a statement from Steiner, which has not managed to break through but has somehow withered. Von Manen then refers to it in the Christian Community and in the Threefold Movement as discontented and critical personalities.

This work should give us pause for thought. Today the Threefolders kibitz everywhere, rousing anger, showing lack of respect and abundant tendencies to criticism. Frequently, they hesitate to join the Anthroposophical Society and, when they do, adjustment is difficult. From the start, constant and situational friction with the Christian Community has been experienced.[6]

We find the problem expressed for the third time as an archetype in the biography of the Camphill movement. It did not exist in Steiner's time. Although its founder Karl König came to anthroposophy by way of the cognitive stream, in founding his own therapeutic-pedagogical homes, he was focused on the social question, and not the cognitive path. Central was the conscious experience of the Archetypal Social Phenomenon in the bible evenings, work for the sake of mankind's needs in daily life, willingness to carry the destiny of all humanity in the celebration of the sacrament. Naturally, Camphill placed itself in very close proximity to the Christian Community. It was just as natural that, by increasingly favoring therapeutic pedagogy, the social task dropped to second rank, which brought the therapeutic pedagogues, as it were, automatically closer to the Anthroposophical Society.

Based on these observations of von Manen, I conclude that, in addition to the two streams he describes, a third one also exists. This is made up of groups of people who on a continual or temporary basis, either distance themselves from the other two streams or encounter personal rejection. In this stream are (most of) the representatives of the Social Impulse. The existence of a third stream explains a great deal if one can see beyond the negative side, the people who did not "make it," but can see it as a stream with its own task to fulfill. We must not be surprised if they criticize much that exists and is accepted wherein the Social Impulse is absent, or when it principally or practically appears unjustified. After all, the Anthroposophical Social Impulse is only part of the Anthroposophical Impulse. Therefore, it is understandable (but not right) when justified criticism of conditions and concepts sometimes, sadly, goes together with defamation of personalities. At such times one should recall the time after Steiner's death when the two main streams denied each other's validity to call themselves "anthroposophical," and when personal hatreds abounded, although nowadays, this is almost impossible to understand. And finally, we should remember that heretical groups have a certain attraction for unstable figures, a fact the Anthroposophical Society has experienced in its own history, and continues to do so in many countries. To be sure, one needs to look for such groups not merely in the third stream, even though they are most conspicuous there, because they fall prey to the reverse of the Social Impulse when they target individuals instead of conditions and concepts.

A more basic factor is, however, added to these more human (all too human) ones. Steiner proposed that for the actual anthroposophical societal life, one no longer (after the Christmas meeting 1923-24) had to concern oneself with adversaries. This also applies, in a somewhat narrower sense, to sister movements: a teachers conference, the board of a bank, the college of therapists can and must fulfill its task without allowing hostilities *within its circle*, regardless of whether one must wrestle with enemies *outside*. This is fundamentally different for those who represent the Anthroposophical Social Impulse. They need to follow what does not work in the world on a day-to-day basis. Therefore, they must allow reproaches regarding what does not work for themselves. This has different consequences. I would like to mention a few of those, at the risk of being viewed as "hostile" in certain circles. It is a simple fact that, if one connects to the Anthroposophical Social Impulse, helping the well-meaning vegetable man around the corner may be more valid than helping a hierarchically-designed Waldorf school. It is a simple fact that one cannot believably point to the bolshevist danger of our monolithic states and, at the same time hush up the bolshevist structure of our own institutions. It is a simple fact that one is often beset with holy wrath when defenseless against the annihilating and argument-destroying word, that one should take a good look at the behavior of one's own people, who counter with sarcastic references to the "inner mission." If today we had only one hundred institutions that realized the Anthroposophic Social Impulse in their core structure, the world would be a different place. Rudolf Lisau's challenge in the *Anthroposophical Quarterly* (XX/2, page 50) is still today the voice crying in the wilderness, "Let us consciously develop new social forms for our anthroposophical work in the Society and outside."

It is a simple fact that critical references to the "evil world outside" are common in many anthroposophical journals, while public criticism of one's own false developments is omitted. Even when it does arise from a corner of the social movement, it is often pushed aside, in its public form as hostile and in its internal form as inappropriate. It is a simple fact that he who stands inside the Social Impulse wants to encounter *every* human being, the "enemy" as well, though he risks being branded by the in-crowd as Marxist (or, more rarely, as capitalist).

Perhaps it is too limiting to say that the first two streams aim at anthroposophic cognition and its dissemination, while the third one sees in it only a means for its social work. They are, what Herbert Weinbauer calls, the abelites.[7] (It is of no importance here whether the term is accurate.) It is no wonder then that Threefolders and Christian Community members come together easily. (See also GA 93/1979/117.)

Yet one can get to the quintessence of the problem if one considers the character of the phase of development in the meso social sphere as presented in Chapter 8. In this essentially social phase one will no longer be able to hide failures behind the bulwark of a board, from whence one can defend an institution. It is only in this phase that one leaves oneself open to the world, "defenseless," clad only in the armor of one's own accomplishments. Indeed, if it does not wish to lose its integrity, any anthroposophical social movement that understands itself should have this openness from its very beginning. Every "leadership" within a social movement is a strike against its own striving. To be sure, people can join together for a common, organized action. But a movement of leaders and followers is a contradiction in itself. The founders must not intervene, they are not allowed to lead, they must not criticize. Knowing that they belong to the totality of the social stream, all they can do is to experience its fate through the pain of the errors committed, accepting them as their own, and by facilitating, through their suffering, the entry of helping forces with their suffering. The individuals who represent the Anthroposophical Social Impulse present the picture of a small quarreling group as long as the Threefolders do not understand this experience and practice it.

We have described a few phenomena about why the Social Impulse leads a relatively insignificant existence within the anthroposophical movement. They point to deeper reasons to which I have no access. I would like to add another conjecture, intended as no more than a suggestion. We have seen how the Anthroposophical Social Impulse developed in six stations in Rudolf Steiner's biography. One can wonder what the seventh, extrapolating 1926, would have produced.

Steiner expressly defined the development of the life of rights in the political, legislative, and state spheres of Middle Europe, (GA 200/1970/I and II) specifically between the task of the East in the sphere of the spiritual life and that of the West in the economic life. It is, therefore, remarkable that Steiner, who dedicated his work to such an extent to the service of the tasks of Middle Europe, said so little about the social domain of the middle, concerning the *outer* rights state, and hardly anything about the inner source of rights. Although he published much and spoke often about the life of the spirit, and he held the National Economic Course for the life of the economy, Steiner refused to give a course on rights, "although," I've been told he commented, "one could do this."

No doubt the appropriate time for this had not arrived.[8] What was he waiting for? Perhaps, although the Social Impulse existed in its elements, its bridging overview was still missing. The six sacraments, each in its own right representing a world and all together the total circumference, only become a whole in the seventh, the consecration of man, where they all reappear. In the same way, concerning the Social Impulse, one may wait for the seventh. What could this be?

What was reasonable to expect by 1926 if Steiner's life had not been shortened by illness and death? The second class of the school of spiritual science would have been established. Are we allowed to ponder that this middle one, this spiritual sunlight, would have provided the soil to afford the Anthroposophical Social Impulse full citizenship in the Anthroposophical Society?

I can be brief with my second question because I can do little more than clarify it and lay it on the table. It is: What are we really dealing with in the Social Impulse? What is the essence coming to expression in formations from marriage all the way to the mega concern? A materialistic jurist may permit himself the remark that he has never encountered a jurist when going for a walk. Yet every person with a little social sensitivity knows that an institution is worth more than the sum of its co-workers and its assets. Everyone who is ever been called upon to help in an association experiences that he chisels away on something together with his co-workers, but on what?

There are really two questions. The first one, more often asked, is: What type of beings link themselves with social formations? "What is created by an association is something quite new. But is comes about only if the individual lives in the other, when the individual derives his power not from within himself but from out of the other. This can, however not take place if he lives selflessly in the other. Thus, human associations are the mysterious places where spiritual beings come down in order to work through the individual human beings, like the soul works through the members of the body." (GA 54/1966/192) This leaves open the question about the character of the beings. Surely there are more indications regarding this question. I only want to reference how John the Baptist worked through the community of disciples and through this example, perhaps only as an intermediate link, conjectures about the workings of the dead.

The other question concerns the social formation as a whole, and not perhaps the *arrangements,* which are the work of man. (GA 34/1960/205) One is inclined to think of formations that have their own reality but escape our sense observations. We can change them with spiritual activity but only within their own conformance to laws, perhaps like geometrical figures. It is, therefore, understandable that one has thought of the etheric world. There are statements Steiner made that could be interpreted in this direction. Not only do I doubt this, I cannot believe it.[9]

If I may be allowed to state a shadowy hunch to conclude this study—one that for a long time I have been unable to dismiss—it is this. The domain of social life is not above but below the hierarchy of humanity. The Anthroposophical Social Impulse, as given by Steiner for our time, reaches deep into the subhuman, corresponding to the way the etheric world overshadows the corporeal in man.[10] What is social is the continuation of the Christianization of the earth, which started with the mystery of Golgotha. The Christ principle can only work with the social sphere (GA 139/1976/175 and GA 129/1960/220), and therefore the redemption of our earth depends on our social workings. Those who are connected to this impulse strive to prepare the kingdom of hell, whose portals Christ has opened, as the dwelling place for the spirit of our earth.

Endnotes:

[1] On October 20 1935 this subtitle was eradicated for opportunistic reasons—one tried to prevent a threatened prohibition by the Nazis. The readers were not given a reason for this. (See also the "Mitteilung" in the Nachrichtenblatt of 24 Nov. and "To subscribers of the "Goetheanum of 22 December.) Albert Steffen wanted to remove the subtitle already at the time of the Christmas Meeting (GA 260a/1966/476). Steiner's response is not recorded.

[2] GA 257/1965/67. Because this remark is often mentioned, let me quote it here verbatim: "How much opposition has been created to the anthroposophical movement by the movement for the Threefold Order because this movement had not managed to place itself on the basis of anthroposophy. Instead it based itself on all sorts of compromises with the result that in certain circles one gradually started to despise anthroposophy. Similar things happen in other areas." We see that the Threefold movement is mentioned as an *example* and this in respect of *compromises* . Certainly one can look at this as the shadow accompanying the "Anthroposophical Society as it resorts to action" GA 257/1965/95) with all its offshoots.

[3] Of course, as already mentioned this does not exclude the possibility that the part of the cognitive path, connecting to practicing, has a lot to do with the Social Impulse; perhaps it is mostly connected to the "seven preconditions", taken from *Knowledge of the Higher Worlds and its Achievement*. Strangely enough here these are not described as exercises. They simply need to be "fulfilled." Perhaps one can add another meaningful contrast. Steiner stated that his "Philosophy of Freedom" was his only book that, for the time being, was in no need of any change. He considered his "Social Commonwealth" to be totally outdated after merely three years.

[4] Bernhard Brons in his lovable book "Der Gesellschaftsgedanke Rudolf Steiners" [Rudolf Steiner's idea of Society], Basel 1965, p. 86.

[5] Sigismund von Gleich "Die Inspirationsquellen der Anthroposophie" [the Spiritual Sources of Anthroposophy], Zeist 1953, p. 15.

[6] See for instance Hagen Biesantz' article "Anthroposophy and religious renewal" (Was in der Anthroposophischen Gesellschaft vorgeht,) June 7/14 1981.

[7] "Anthroposophische Bewegung und die Christgemeinschaft" [The Anthroposophical Movement and the Christian Community], St. Ulrich 1981.

[8] In GA 257/1965/140 Steiner speaks about demands for courses "that may perhaps develop later in the appropriate speed of continuing anthroposophical life."

[9] The only reason I can offer for this is the argument that all correspondences of the etheric world, as Steiner presents it, fail in the social life. Sometimes they appear as mirror images, sometimes the middle is even displaced.

[10] One of the few indications I know of can be found in GA 193/1972/52. Steiner calls the economy the first subhuman domain which must regain human balance through brotherhood. It has been experimentally proven that the organism as such pulls man into the subhuman, even if human emotional connections are missing. Decent citizens randomly responding to advertisements were ready "in the framework of scientific investigation" to torture fellow human beings. The organization, the institution, not consciously penetrated by us with moral forces, is subhuman. It is the opposite of the etheric, which builds up. It causes disintegration.

Further let us name GA 108/1970/120 (The Building up of a New Earth for New Gods), GA 97/1981/33 ("Hell is nothing more than total involvement with the personal") and GA 97/1981/280 (What is Inside of the Earth and the Christian Path of Initiation).